FORCE AND FREEDOM

Reflections on History

JACOB BURCKHARDT

EDITED BY JAMES HASTINGS NICHOLS

Pantheon Books Inc. New York

41 Washington Square, New York, N. Y.

Manufactured in the United States of America
American Book–Stratford Press, Inc., New York

Designed by Stefan Salter

FIRST PRINTING

Contents

JACOB BURCKHARDT

by James Hastings Nichols

THE MAN AND HIS MISSION

JACOB BURCKHARDT's interpretation of history is highly original and cannot be classified under any of the usual categories. He worked with the objectivity of a Montaigne writing from his lonely tower, and spoke and wrote only of the things that interested *him,* as they appeared to him. There are strange omissions and new relationships; new vistas of implications are constantly opened for the thoughtful reader. All things are seen from a new angle, as when one first studies very familiar districts from a height with a comprehensive view, and sees the distances between objects to be quite different from what, walking on set paths, we had been accustomed to suppose.

The first and most obvious condition of Burckhardt's comprehensive perspective was his good fortune in being born a Swiss. An educated Swiss almost has to be a good European. He is in the main stream of two or three of the chief national cultures of the Continent, and yet stands aside from the politics of any of the three with all the suspicion and vigilance of centuries of sobering experience. His is a Europeanism grounded on history and fruitful for historical understanding, not a superficial intellectual cosmopolitanism. In Burckhardt's case, this peculiar Swiss vocation of the cross-fertilization of Continental cultures was prepared in his teens. Brought up in German-speaking Switzerland, he finished his secondary schooling with several months in French Switzerland, thus acquiring "a second spiritual fatherland," and began in the vacations of his late teens those Italian trips and publications which place him with Goethe and Shelley, Stendhal, Robert Browning, and the rest of the group of great interpreters of Italy to trans-Alpine Europe. Americans especially will find certain analogies and common interests between this Swiss situation and their own, and can read a Swiss like Burckhardt with more immediate profit than they can most European national historians.

In his student years in Berlin and Bonn, Burckhardt had quickly drifted away from the conventional little colony of solid Baslers in Germany, and scandalized them by finding his friendships with some very freethinking gentry. His closest student friends, in fact, for four years were mostly romantic and nationalistic German liberals of the forties, "young Germany." In the company of these enthusiastic and talented poets and artists, the reserved but passionate student from staid Basel flowered out like April foliage in the warm rains. In politics the general tone of this group was radical, even republican and socialist. Among them Burckhardt moved with his great personal tolerance and warmth of friendship, keeping his canny Swiss closeness in political views, yet evidently feeling no impossible tensions of opinion.

Yet in fact all these friendships based on a common love of humanistic German culture were destined to founder in the widening gulf between divergent political views. Burckhardt was by family tradition an Old Basler, a member of the most conservative, the most aristocratic, the most self-contained city-state of nineteenth century

Europe. A city with the sharpest of social distinctions, of strict Calvinistic orthodoxy, reserved toward outsiders, Basel could be compared in America only with Old Boston, or to save argument, with what is said of Old Boston. Fitly enough the American whose mentality is most comparable to Burckhardt's, with all their striking differences in character, is Henry Adams. And in such a background Burckhardt not only schooled his unique insight into the city-states of Greece and the Renaissance, but also enjoyed the social and political Archimedean point from which to study the nineteenth century Great Powers with anomalous distance and freedom from illusion. His liberal and nationalistic German friends, on the other hand, pressed on their deluded way toward '48 with hopes which seemed to him increasingly dangerous and crazy.

Basel was governed and owned in the first half of the century by an aristocracy composed of the wealthy patriciate on the one hand, and the scholars and clergy on the other. The Burckhardt clan, one of the most widespread, had for generations belonged to the latter class and had furnished professors to the University and pastors to the churches. That University, the oldest in Switzerland, dated from the fifteenth century when the red sandstone cathedral had been host to the Emperor, the Pope, and notables of all Europe for some years during the great oecumenical council. And now in the nineteenth century, young Jacob Burckhardt grew up beside the great cathedral where his father was the minister.

When he returned to Basel from his apprenticeship as an historian under Ranke, Burckhardt returned to the conservative circles of the cathedral and the university. His future at the university seemed rather uncertain, for in 1843 there were just twenty-eight students enrolled.

Since Basel had been severed from her rural districts in the "Troubles of the Thirties," the little town of less than thirty thousand souls had been able to maintain the university at all only by heroic efforts. In order to piece out his time and his income, consequently, the young instructor joined the staff of the *Basel Journal,* the organ of that conservative civic administration with which he had so many personal ties. As a kind of city editor and copy writer, Burckhardt sought to drive home Switzerland's proper destiny in the great German cultural community, as he did in his courses, and on immediate political questions he stood pat on the constitutional *status quo* and what Americans would call "states' rights," as against the pressure for a strong federal government.

It soon became apparent in 1845, however, that such a center position would have little weight as religious hostility embittered the opposition of the radical nationalists and the intransigent Catholic "*Sonderbund.*" Both sides used mass meetings, rioting, and private armies in the attempt to bully cantonal governments, so that Burckhardt with some justice described conditions as "South American." Such utilization of popular pressure confirmed that fear of the masses which, he had learned in the civil war in Basel in his teens, could so easily in the hands of a demagogue become a "beast," a "roaring pack."

The surprisingly short and decisive Sonderbund War broke out only after Burckhardt had expatriated himself in disgust early in 1846. Seeing nothing useful to do, he took the occasion to escape Basel, which, even apart from the political turmoil, seemed unendurably stale, provincial and colorless to him after his glorious student days in Germany, and to make that Italian trip of which he had dreamed so long. He had "given up political activity forever." "With men such as I," he wrote, "no state is built; as long as I live, however, I will be kindly and share with my neighbors, I will be a good private man . . . I can't change it, and before universal barbarism irrupts (for I see nothing else impending) I shall get a good eyeful of aristocratic cultural enjoyment, so as to be able to be active at the inevitable restoration." . . . "I should like to experience no more of these times, had I not a duty therein, for I will help rescue as much as lies within my limited power. . . . We may all go under. I will at least seek out the interest for which I shall go under, namely the culture of Old Europe."

In this second revolution within his own city, Burckhardt had thus come both to his definitive interpretation of the crisis of modern Europe, and to the determination of his own mission in it. He had passed through an experience similar to that of so many German liberals who were disillusioned by the failure of the Revolutions of '48, yet his disillusionment was a deeper one than the Kinkels and Carl Schurzes were to know, and led to a more radical resolution. He had been an old style liberal, standing for limited suffrage, and, in monarchical countries, for limited monarchy, and always for a minimum of state control of the individual. The old absolutisms were gone forever after 1789, but by judicious compromise a considerable measure of tradition and the older social structure could, it had seemed, be retained within the framework of constitutions and popular sovereignty.

But in 1846 Burckhardt became convinced that his political judgment had been wrong. He had always feared the Jacobin heritage of radical democracy bequeathed to Europe by the French Revolution. That Continental democracy was not the positive, responsible, constructive faith of Anglo-Saxon Protestantism, but the negative, individualistic, anti-clerical egalitarianism of Roman Catholic countries, which is often simply protest against all authority and all privilege, in itself irresponsible and incompetent to govern. Napoleon had shown how readily such French egalitarianism could abdicate to despotism. And that, Burckhardt now believed, was the final outcome toward which the democratic and national agitation of the Continent was driving irresistibly. He might well have said with Bachofen, and with a motive intelligible to Anglo-Saxon democrats, "I hate democracy because I love liberty."

To his German friends, in consequence, in 1846 and 1847 Burckhardt sent repeated warnings that they could never control the revolution they hoped for, that they were rather the Feuillants or the Girondists of a process which would run its course "as an event of nature, and draw to it all the hellishness in human nature." "I have no hope at all for the future," he wrote to them. "It is possible that a few half endurable decades may still be granted to us, a sort of Roman imperial time. I am of the opinion that democrats and proletarians must submit to an increasingly harsh despotism, even if they make the wildest efforts, for this fine century is designed for anything rather than true democracy."

This parallel between nineteenth century Europe and the declining Roman Empire forced itself on Burckhardt increasingly, and led him to the writing of his first full-size historical work, a panorama of fourth century Europe called *The Age of Constantine the Great.* In this volume, published in 1852, Diocletian's system of adopting as imperial successors the ablest military rulers called forth the observation that modern Europe might again provide similar experiences "for our descendants."

Joined with this conviction of the brutal tendency of European politics to militarism, however, went Burckhardt's sense of his peculiar vocation in such a crisis. He was never simply a romantic pessimist enjoying cheap melancholy over the decline of the West, or an Epicurean fugitive from a hopeless society. All his life long his predictions of military despotism were associated with a hope for a restoration, a new birth of freedom, perhaps in the twentieth century, perhaps later. And he was in dead earnest in speaking of his "duty" for the meantime, his obligation to preserve what might be preserved of the higher traditions of Europe. Here again the warm sympathy he felt for the Christian monastics of the declining Roman Empire lends living actuality to his *Age of Constantine*.

Burckhardt's German friends, however, saw in him only his social conservatism and aesthetic distaste for modern life. They did not in the forties take seriously those political analyses which corroborated his personal antipathies. How should they? Were they not on the eve of the glorious revolution to produce a unified democratic Germany? So Burckhardt now lost virtually all the friends of his student days, men the memory of whom had rendered tolerable those first years in Basel when all the people about him seemed somehow unreal. We can guess, perhaps, a part of the reason why Burckhardt's cropped head was snow-white at the age of forty. He who was "nothing without the stimulation of friends" sat in a frigid, intellectually alien city of a crumbling world, alone with his thoughts.

His first instinct, perhaps, was flight, like that of so

many of his friends who came to America after the disillusionment of 1848–9. Burckhardt, of course, passed through the same cycle three years earlier than they, and his flight was to Italy, not to America, for he could not live in a land without history and art. Thereafter he would day-dream of taking some quiet retired post as librarian or archivist with a secure income and periodic holidays in his beloved Italy. Yet he could not do it. He returned to Basel in 1848, and after all, why not? He began to sense that he would be lonely anywhere. Men who raise such questions as he did find few to understand them in any place and age.

Five years later, to be sure, he fled again over the Alps from his provincial "crows'-roost." But from this Italian journey he came back with his *Cicerone,* and then went to Zürich for the quiet and the library to write his great study of the Renaissance. Before the completion of that work, however, his loyalties to Basel and his friends there called him home. At the age of forty, he settled into his three-fold teaching office, and spent the rest of his life in bringing to Basel by the ministry of the spoken word a love and knowledge of the beauty that ennobles life, and such understanding of history as makes for humanity and responsibility. Basel bears the traces of his labors to this day.

Here few words can be spared for those two works of these years by which Burckhardt has hitherto been known in English-speaking countries, the *Cicerone, A Guide to the Works of Art of Italy,* and the *Civilization of the Renaissance in Italy,* which were written in his thirties before his final settlement at Basel. They breathe the afflatus of his most vivid experience of the spiritual comfort of art and history, an experience which had the nature of a conversion from the depths of his despair in 1846, and of which he still solemnized the anniversary full fifty years later, not long before his death.

The year before he wrote the *Cicerone*, Burckhardt exclaimed, "I would not have believed that such an old decayed historian of civilization as myself, who imagined he should accord all points of view and all epochs their own value, could at last become so one-sided as I am. It was as if scales fell from my eyes." Italy had given him "a new standard for thousands of things" in 1846. And this "new standard" is what lent the *Cicerone* an influence over the taste of generations such as has been rivalled only by Winckelmann and Ruskin. Large sections of the work are word for word the observations of Burckhardt's notebook, written on the spot or that same evening, for his first judgment usually remained his last. This was no rehash of the specialists, but rather Burckhardt's own new world of unknown or neglected works and personalities, over half of them, as was natural in Italy, from the Renaissance.

What are we to make of this conversion? We cannot, of course, expect a simple answer. If a man knows why he loves a girl or believes in his God or weeps for joy at a painting, then his love and faith are not ultimate and spontaneous. The last magic is irreducible, ineffable. But Burckhardt, at least, was able to describe his masterpieces with such tender and discriminating passion that he rescued many of them from obscurity and set them in that high place in the love of cultured Europe which they have filled ever since. His strict canons may have proved confining and unfruitful to some of the younger talents he counselled; but to many they were undoubtedly a school of beauty. Others crystallized their own tastes in opposition. He was a great teacher because of his certitude. Of all the vast array of artistic memorials he knew, these few spoke to *him* with the authentic note of beauty itself. These were unique, *his* revelation.

There is an inextricable fusion of ethics and aesthetics in Burckhardt's criticism. His gospel of humanistic idealism was a sort of Christianized form of the Greek *kalon kagathon.* The association is also the reason why Burckhardt the historian requires for adequate comprehension at least a summary knowledge of Burckhardt the historian of art. Although obviously a love of the art of the Renaissance was what first brought him to the historical study of this particular period, on a deeper level we can sense that art history for Burckhardt would always be the history of the ethos of artists and thus of the spiritual signature of past ages, of their moral and imaginative personality. Burckhardt felt a man's personality in the way in which a subject was envisioned, in the control of techniques. Because he was so much of an artist himself, he could relive the creation of a work, see the alternatives at various stages of production, and sense the *moral* choices the workman had made in the form of technical taste and dexterity. "The highest personal quality of Raphael," Burckhardt observed characteristically, "was not aesthetic but moral, namely the great honesty and the strong will with which he strove every moment for that beauty which at that time he recognized as the highest. He never rested on what he had once gained nor used it as a convenient property." Lesser critics might estimate talent in itself, and complete the personality from biographical sources. Burckhardt could make a whole judgment from the building or painting itself, by feeling what the man was who would do such a thing. This capacity explains the circumstance, at first paradoxical, that Burckhardt, the master of "history of civilization," rests much more exclusively on art in his history of art, and draws in less of social background and biography than most art historians.

Yet Burckhardt was driven on by a great necessity to write his original and, in a sense, definitive interpretation of the whole age behind this art. It haunted him as a kind of scholarly spectre. And write it he did, in seclusion at Zürich, but never to its completion. We have only fragmentary essays from it, some of them posthumous, including the *Civilization of the Renaissance in Italy, The History of Renaissance Architecture in Italy, The Sculpture of the Renaissance, The Collectors, The Altarpiece, The Portrait,* perhaps two-thirds of the concrete material which would have appeared were the work completed as first planned. No one else, however, can piece together the insights Burckhardt would have given as to the relations of these various aspects of the age to each other and the common spirit behind them all. "The Renaissance was to have been portrayed," he wrote King Maximilian of Bavaria, "in so far as she was the mother and native source of modern man, in thought and sensibility as well as in the shaping of form. It seemed possible to deal with these two great movements in a worthwhile parallel, to fuse the history of art and the history of civilization." But now, "Because of my removal to a new, rewarding, but laborious circle of activities, my available working time has been so restricted that my project is only to be discharged in limited contours and after long delay." Such a panorama of an age had never before been attempted, and when will there again be so rich and versatile a spirit as even to conceive it? Burckhardt deprived Europe of such an incomparable history to devote all his powers to the class rooms and public lecture halls of little Basel. He made, moreover, a solemn vow never to read his lectures nor to bring even a note to class. As he told a younger historian, with this method "You get other ideas and other materials, you read the sources in a different way . . . It will cost you much time all your life long, compel you to leave this and that book unwritten. But you are a *teacher,* and exercise a power completely other than those who just read off their lectures and whose courses the students attend because they have to." This process of memorization, moreover, did require carefully worked out volumes of course notes, and these are what we now value so highly, even in their unfinished clipped style as in the *Reflections on History* and the *History of Greek Civilization.* These were posthumously published, for on his own account Burckhardt never published a line after 1860.

Burckhardt had renounced all scholarly ambition, and repulsed half a dozen calls, and feelers toward calls, from distinguished German universities. For the last quarter century of his active life he was as good as dead to the scholarly world outside little Basel, so that when his death was actually announced, most people were surprised to hear that he had been alive so recently. He had even turned over his books to others for revision, so that by the time of his death they were scarcely recognizable, and he had been able to say of his own *Cicerone,* "Gentlemen, I can safely recommend it; it is no longer my book." All these things he had done deliberately and with forethought, limiting his life to a single purpose, scarcely appreciated by his contemporaries, but in which he himself felt increasingly more "courage" and "independence" and even a hint of "inner peace."

Burckhardt's teaching was by no means confined to "the little tumbledown house in the shadow of nut-trees close by the river," called the "University." All University teachers were required to give several hours a week to classes in the associated secondary school, and there Burckhardt taught gladly for years until he exchanged that assignment for the chair of history of art as well as history at the University. But beyond that, Burckhardt was almost quixotic in his dedication to civic service by public lectures, the *noblesse oblige* of the Basel intelligentsia. He refused all invitations for public lectures elsewhere as "theft from Basel." "All my nervous energy belongs solely to this soil and spot," he stated, and he spent it freely for the public, besides priding himself on never cutting a class at the University for thirty-three years. This civic patriotism reminds one of the particularism of a medieval commune, and not until 1859, in fact, did Basel begin to level down the medieval walls and bastions which tightly bound her maze of steeply climbing narrow streets.

As a speaker before the public or the students, Burckhardt was at first disappointing to those who had heard of his brilliance. He avoided all the dramatic devices of oratory, all pathos in voice or presentation. He even seemed a little distant, usually looking out over his audience or out the window as if half talking to himself. Yet there was a fine sense of form in the construction of climax and conclusion, and the material was rich and compact with that characteristic union of penetrating thought and concrete illustration which marks his writing, and all seasoned with his fine humor and irony. On the idealism of his young students especially he had a great effect, with his sharp censure of self-interest and egoism, of power for its own sake, with his admiration for moral nobility and heroism, for Christian kindliness and selflessness. When he spoke of things and men he admired, of the interior space of the Pantheon, perhaps, or of the Sistine Raphaels, sometimes his voice choked momentarily, and in the great silence the rustling of the Rhine could be heard through the open windows.

In time, also, Burckhardt began to feel a certain satisfaction in the response of the educated people of the city. Of what Burckhardt accomplished in Basel to offset the barbarizing influence of industrialism, Nietzsche later observed, "To him above all is Basel indebted for her foremost position in human culture. One can discern in every educated Basler that he belongs to Jacob Burckhardt's city." And despite the fact that politics were dead for Burckhardt, more than one of the radical politicians of his city modified his political tenets after attending Burckhardt's course on the French Revolution. And this present volume of *Reflections on History* which contains the quintessence of Burckhardt's political wisdom, grew, at least in part, from this civic function. It is not just a course for history students; it was planned and originally delivered in part for the educated public: business men, physicians, lawyers, clergymen, statesmen and citizens.

But Burckhardt was more than a brilliant lecturer to his students. They perhaps replaced for him the intellectual intercourse he had sacrificed, and reminded him again of the spontaneous delight of the comradeship of his own good days and friends in Germany. With his students, or at least some among them, the old sociable, witty, gay Burckhardt lived again as he could not with their parents, and as he would not be able to with most of them, perhaps, after their first fifteen years in a business office.

Through the sixties and seventies Burckhardt spent considerable time in this way with young friends, taking them walking, or having them in for the evening, always alone. The envied student invited in the evening would pick his way through the dusty flour sacks on the rickety stairs of the baker's house where Burckhardt roomed, about nine, when Burckhardt finished work, and would always stay after midnight, often till two or three. The bare little room, looking out over the Rhine and beyond to the city with its bridges and the mountains which might be washed by the moon, was itself lighted by wax candles. And there a student would find song and wine and conversation such that after his departure, "what he had heard might drive him about in the moon-bright night in excitement until morning was gray over the St. Alban gate."

A considerable group of authors, artists, and musicians received counsel, comfort, and even financial aid from Burckhardt in these years. To them he constantly preached his humanistic credo against the temptations of sentimentality or cynicism. Poetry was an art with quite definite duties, a discipline of the spirit as well as of language. "If you want to be a poet, you must love, 1) men, and, 2) the individual phenomenon in nature, life, and history, quite personally . . . Believe me, he alone is interesting who still loves something." Continual contemplation of the great and beautiful was one of the few things left to give a higher value to the life of modern man. One of Burckhardt's "oldest and strongest convictions" was that "character is much more decisive for man than richness of intellect," and "personality is the highest thing that there is." Indeed, if one were to give up artistic production, Burckhardt even recommended these "strict views of life and art" as "a notable substitute."

Later generations in other lands may have lost Burckhardt's confidence in the eternal absolute beauty of any works of art, and, moreover, would very likely prefer other masterworks to his holy ones. Those who sat under him, however, agree that not only did he vastly enrich, nay almost create, the vocabulary of artistic criticism, but that by the wordless communication which leaps from man to man, he could make men sense, in quite extraordinary degree, that indefinable essence, the very *beauty* of a work of art which can neither be analyzed nor expressed in any other way than in just the way and in just that medium in which the artist has here done it. There was perhaps a deep wisdom in his insistence on the spoken word, on the personal contact of teacher and hearer, as against a literary public outside Basel. As a champion of humanistic criteria in art, Burckhardt can be placed beside Matthew Arnold and Irving Babbitt, two of the most influential critics of the last half-century or so in the English-speaking world.

Because of his friends outside the academic community, Basel in time proved to be a very tolerable refuge for Burckhardt. Where else could he have found the social and political views to match his prejudices, if not his insights? The Germans who worked at Basel felt the change of air at once. When Nietzsche came there from the nomadic city-life of North Germany, he was vastly impressed by the social stability of Old Basel. Dilthey felt the contrast too, when at the age of thirty-four he came to Basel from teeming Berlin to finish his *Life of Schleiermacher*. Berlin had seemed natural and straightforward, but in Basel men were watchful, uneasy, full of foreboding for the European future, judging everything as if "from a corner." It was the very next year that from such a perspective,—Treitschke called it a "sulking-corner"—Burckhardt wrote out the first draft for these *Reflections on History*.

By its resistance to the course of Prussianization, however, Basel was able, through this very book, to become the voice of classical German culture to the new political Germany. Emil Dürr first remarked the close relationship between Burckhardt's political preferences and those of Goethe, Schiller, and especially Humboldt. Burckhardt preferred the small country, where the activities of the state were reduced to a minimum and private agencies looked after all social functions such as education, philanthropy, and health. There was vastly more individual freedom and cultural potentiality in such a state, he felt, than in a Great Power where the political and military demands and restraints on the individual were so numerous. The great age of German literature and philosophy was an age in which Germany was composed of small, undeveloped states which could nourish European as well as purely German sympathies. The whole movement toward the modern national Leviathans, by contrast, appeared to Burckhardt to be an abandonment of higher culture and its prerequisite, individual freedom, for the power deriving from mass standardization of men. His little Basel, however, could remain, from the sixties, a lone champion of German Europeanism, of the international cultural mission of the old Germany of Humboldt, Schiller, Goethe, Kant.

But the great distinction between Burckhardt and these eighteenth century anti-nationalists was that Burckhardt had none of their illusions. Humboldt and Goethe seem frivolous in their confidence that they could remain comfortably isolated from politics in their own private lives.

Burckhardt knew that it was not so, that if one shut politics out the door, it would be knocking at the window. The most important development of modern European history was always for him the Great Power, and the French Revolution and its nineteenth century continuations were the greatest impetus to the increasing centralization and militarism of the Great Power since the Reformation. And the end was not yet. In contrast to Humboldt, then, Burckhardt saw the problem of politics with a wholly realistic eye. He knew that the type of state he personally preferred lived only on sufferance in modern Europe, that the network of railroads which increasingly bound Basel to the larger economic life of the Continent was symbolic of the absorption of the small states of Europe into the orbits of the great rising military and economic juggernauts. That was why politics were "dead" for him, although he remained the keenest of political observers and thinkers. The political ideals which he would have stood for were impotent and hopeless; there remained for him only to serve as best he might the cultural mission of the small state so long as he should be able. Time and again through the sixties and later, his letters observe his satisfaction if only things will remain as they are, if nothing breaks for the worse.

Burckhardt was already living "in a state of siege," or as a cultured refugee, for whom Europe might cease to have room any day. The whole world of education, universities and scholarship especially seemed to him a house of cards. "We occupy ourselves with intellectual interests, study, music, art, as long as it lasts, since we are not as yet accustomed to anything else. But I, at least, say to myself daily, this can one day end in an hour."

Meanwhile Burckhardt considered the "existence of the

University of Basel not only desirable for earthly reasons, but metaphysically necessary." His little audience was his justification for living in a world which, despite its expressions of respect for him, really had little place for what he stood for. The prospect of Burckhardt's refusing the highest honor in his profession, Ranke's chair at Berlin, when proffered to him by the new Second Reich in the first flush of its victorious rise, reminds one irresistibly of Diogenes' reply to the world-conqueror Alexander the Great. Burckhardt too asked only his place in the sun, and what better tub than Basel?

Despite all his blindness and misunderstanding, Nietzsche, of all his contemporaries, most properly valued Burckhardt. Nietzsche grasped, as very few others did, the significance of Burckhardt's critique of bourgeois life and respected his integrity as a man who *lived* his values independent of all the blandishments of a faithless civilization. The sad story of their friendship may serve to conclude this discussion of Burckhardt's vocation and personality.

From the beginning Burckhardt and Nietzsche recognized each other's abilities and common interests. The irreconcilable divergence of their ethics became apparent only gradually. Nietzsche arrived at Basel in 1869 as professor of classics at the unheard-of age of twenty-four. Both men had classes in the boys' school at the same hour, and soon they were passing the interval before the next class together, strolling up and down in the cathedral cloisters, comparing notes on Greece. They were also bound together by a common esteem for "the philosopher," as Burckhardt referred to Schopenhauer, although we should not forget, in this regard, Joel's report that

Burckhardt's copy of Schopenhauer is annotated almost entirely with question marks.

Over the winter of 1870–71 each attended one of the other's lecture series. Burckhardt heard with admiration the inconclusive series *On the Future of our Educational Institutions.* And at the same time Nietzsche was attending the second and last public presentation of these *Reflections.* To another member of the Schopenhauer cult he wrote that the *Great Men of History* was "quite of our circle of thought and feeling." Burckhardt did seem to him inclined to tone down his opinions in public, so that, as he said, "I believe I am the only one of his sixty hearers who grasps the deep trains of thought with their strange breaks and circumlocutions where the matter approaches critical points. I am taking pleasure in a lecture series for the first time, for this is of the sort which I could have given were I older." Nietzsche never did realize that those "breaks and circumlocutions" were more than the timidity of an eccentric, and little did he think when he noted down one of the themes of this work, "Power is by nature evil," that Burckhardt would one day wholly repudiate the conclusions he would draw from that paradox. In these lectures readers may also recognize other motives familiar from Nietzsche's later works.

There was a personal barrier, however, in these years, to any closer intimacy between Burckhardt and Nietzsche. In his first spring in Basel, Nietzsche had met Wagner at Tribschen and been conquered by him. Thus were begun the most powerful personal influences in Nietzsche's life and a friendship of three or four years which was never matched again in his experience. He offered to resign his chair to become a travelling evangelist of Wagnerianism. He supervised the printing of Wagner's autobiography, the priggish Nietzsche and Wagner's tawdry true-story confessions! He rewrote his first volume on Greece to make it a Wagnerian tract, despite many "inward qualms," which only later developed into the conviction that he had "spoiled the grand problem of Hellenism."

This whole affair was of itself enough to maintain a coolness between Burckhardt and Nietzsche. For Burckhardt could not abide Richard Wagner. He had known him while he was teaching at Zürich, and had no use for the hot breath of the daimonic. He loved Gluck, Haydn, Beethoven, Mozart, and the Italians, and approved Mozart's view that melody is the essence of music. He preferred it to the abstractions of counterpoint. But Wagner was "not even a contrapuntist." He threw things together for effect only and "that is not art; those are tricks." What revolted Burckhardt more than the inferior music was the P. T. Barnum in Wagner. Wagner was the prime example of the vulgarity and commercialism which was the mortal disease of modern art, and he would be more appropriately located in Berlin than in Munich.

The circle at Tribschen, moreover, viewed the political crisis of the Franco-Prussian War and the emergence of a Prussianized Empire with far different eyes than did Burckhardt. Wagner, the liberal, almost anarchistic fugitive of 1848, had now become a violent chauvinist and anti-Semite, and at this stage of the game Nietzsche believed in everything Wagner stood for. In July 1870, when Basel was jammed with soldiers called to the colors from abroad and moving homeward across the frontiers in both directions, Nietzsche wrote the university authorities requesting leave of absence for the war. In the ambulance service he did his bit for German culture, contracted dysentery, diphtheria, and his fatal half-knowledge of drugs, and was back in Basel within three months. Shocked and sick, he could still hear the cries of wounded men on occasion, and would not talk of the war for two or three years.

Jacob Burckhardt, too, felt that German culture was involved. "You cannot hope to be a culturally significant people and politically significant at the same time," was his historical reflection. "Germany has now taken politics as her principle; she must maintain it henceforth. Oh, how wide those learned gentry who now acclaim this Prussianism will open their eyes when they see what spiritual sterility will date from the year 1870 in Germany." "Oh, how mistaken the poor German nation will be if she thinks that now she can set the musket in the corner and devote herself to the arts and happiness of peace! For now it is above all a question of further military preparation! and after a while no one will any longer be able to say what life is really for. For now the German-Russian War is coming to stand in the middle distance and then in the foreground of the picture." "I shall think of this year's end the rest of my life . . . The two great civilized peoples of the present-day Continent have fallen to flaying themselves of their whole culture, and infinitely much of what delighted and interested man before July 1870 will no longer move him in 1871." "What is most serious, however, is not the present war, but the era of wars into which we have entered, and on this the new spirit must be founded. Oh, how much that has been dear to the cultured must be thrown overboard as spiritual 'luxury'! And how strangely different from us the new generation will grow up. It may be that we shall appear to the younger generation as the French *émigrés* seemed to the people to whom they fled, prepared for nothing but a life of pleasure."

This whole vast tragedy reached its climax for Burckhardt in the report which, for the second time in his life, reduced him to tears. When the (false) news of the burning of the Louvre came in May 1871, a report Burckhardt had heard once before in 1849, he and Nietzsche hastened to each other, "filled with a passionate grief," as Nietzsche's sister reports, "each apparently moved by the thought that the other could best sympathize with his pain."

But even Nietzsche could only partly share the older man's agony, since he had but a low opinion and understanding of the plastic arts generally, and could regard this loss only as an exceptional, if terrible, accident, while to Burckhardt the Louvre was only the first of the galleries, museums, and treasures of Europe which would be carelessly offered up by the power politics of the class wars and national wars to come. "Part of me died with the Louvre," he told young Salis. "One dies gradually, in parts . . . Such events will occur again and again on this hollowed-out ground we stand upon."

Over the next winter, 1871–72, Burckhardt and Nietzsche conferred often on things Hellenic, for Nietzsche was just pulling together his essays on Greece for the final form of what was to appear about New Year's as *The Birth of Tragedy from the Spirit of Music,* while Burckhardt was driving himself as never before for his course in the *History of Greek Civilization,* which he gave in the following summer. Of some of Nietzsche's discoveries Burckhardt availed himself, but for the main Wagnerian thesis he had, of course, only partially veiled sarcasm.

Nietzsche fastened on his very specific compliments with all the eagerness of one who had written the work with "inner qualms," who had received no other scholarly acknowledgments, and who admired the older man without restraint. Burckhardt's invincible French courtesy was always a trap for Nietzsche's notorious insensitivity and social obtuseness. But even sixteen years later, Nietzsche still prided himself on these comments, for to him, and after all he was not badly qualified to judge, Burckhardt was "the deepest living connoisseur" of Greek culture.

In the remaining five or six years of Nietzsche's stay at Basel, Burckhardt exerted this same influence toward weaning him of Wagner, and in the end played the most important part in the process. The second and third of Nietzsche's *Thoughts out of Season* show this tension. *The Use and Abuse of History* seemed remote and academic to the Bayreuth circle with its attacks on the "objectivity" of bloodless professors, but in it Nietzsche sought to exorcise in himself those same inclinations to contemplative scholarship which he had been warned against in Burckhardt. There is an obvious reference to the introduction of these *Reflections* in Nietzsche's championship of the history-less barbarians, and an echo of Wagner's fear of the "cool historian" in the charge that historical knowledge cuts the nerve of action.

However in the third *Thought, Schopenhauer as Educator,* Nietzsche already set a higher value on the critical intellect which destroys illusions than on the artist who creates them. The essay has precious little to do with Schopenhauer, but rather describes the ideal teacher. Such an educator would be a liberator from conventionality, a guide to the true *man.* This ideal of personal culture Nietzsche contrasted, like Burckhardt, to the current educational ideals of patriotism and utilitarianism. He too scorned the claim that the state is the highest end of man. He attacked the school system which trained business men, officials, or scholars instead of ministering to culture, which must always be borne by individuals. Heroism should be the ideal, not bourgeois security and happiness. The circle of those who live for these duties, "to bring to light the philosopher, the artist, and the saint in themselves and in others," constitutes the vast community of European culture, and to this circle, rather than to church or state, Nietzsche, like Burckhardt, pledged his loyalty. One cannot escape the conclusion that the program is Burckhardt's, and that the idealized portrait in fact fits Jacob Burckhardt more aptly than either Schopenhauer or Wagner. This essay prepares us for the later statement in the *Twilight of the Idols* that the one man in the educational system serving the cause of culture, the one liberator from cant, the one most rare exception in the educational system, an *educator,* was Jacob Burckhardt.

This transition from Nietzsche's romantic Wagnerian phase to Burckhardtian scepticism reached its culmination with *Human, All Too Human,* which was originally dedicated to Burckhardt. When Nietzsche left Basel, he had his publisher send back to the old "educator" a copy of each of his further works as soon as they were printed. What he had come to esteem in Basel and especially in Burckhardt was "the value and attractiveness of an original and essentially monastic tendency in life and in understanding." To Burckhardt himself, in his letter presenting the *Genealogy of Morals,* Nietzsche wrote, "The largely intellectual and painfully involved life I have hitherto lived . . . has gradually brought with it a loneliness against which there is no more help. My dearest comfort is always to think of the few who have suffered it under similar conditions without going to pieces, and have been able to preserve a kindly and lofty spirit. No one can think of you more gratefully, respected sir, than I do." Zarathustra himself, in his self-chosen loneliness, in fact became Nietzsche's great literary memorial to Jacob Burckhardt, the laughing stoic, a memorial erected by a man who likewise attempted solitude but was broken by it.

For Jacob Burckhardt outlasted Nietzsche. On five of the works Nietzsche sent him after leaving Basel, Burckhardt returned comments, all but one interesting only for the variety of graceful and amusing ways he found to evade the main issues by protesting his philosophical incompetence, and complimenting Nietzsche on his wit and style and on his specific incidental historical insights into Greece and modern Europe. Once, however, Burckhardt challenged him directly: was not the injunction "Be hard!" an invitation to eventual despotism? And at last, despite Nietzsche's personal and pressing appeals, Burckhardt could no longer bring himself to maintain even a guarded relationship. Nietzsche's last works aroused in him feelings which were not far from horror. And what was more, Nietzsche and C. F. Meyer had acclaimed him as the prophet of a Renaissance cult to which he was definitely hostile. The creative, life-giving personalities Burckhardt admired in the Renaissance were very different men from Frederick II and the Borgias whom Nietzsche had at last fastened on. "I have never been a worshipper of the men of power and the outlaws of history," Burckhardt protested, but "have rather considered them even as *flagella Dei.*" When Nietzsche gave the signal of his final descent into madness by the terrible letters he wrote the old man from Italy in 1890, claiming Burckhardt as well as himself to be a criminal, it was only a shocking exaggeration of what had been going on for some time.

For Burckhardt's epitaph on his most gifted and unhappy student, we can perhaps do no better than to quote his comment on another Dionysiac genius, written nearly fifty years before. When, after a brief and violent career, Ackermann, one of the German friends of his youth, had committed suicide in 1846, Burckhardt reflected, "This comet which swept, so infinitely strange and interesting, through our circle, has burnt out thus before our eyes. But what a man! . . . He was of truly divine race . . . I can't say that I really loved him; he was too violent for me from the beginning for that, too unrestrained by far." Moreover, it is "the misfortune of genius to make him lonely in whom it dwells all too mightily.—And *this* nature had to be at the same time so unevenly composed that it lacked the crown of all existence, quiet form!—and in life, indeed, as well as poetry . . . Taking it all in all, I say,—God forgive me—it is better not to be a genius and to have, instead, good strong nerves and a strong conscience, that, when one has sinned, is cured and refreshed in hearty benevolence to others. That, you see, would be *my* ideal."

Jacob Burckhardt had by his way of living earned the right to preach, even past the careers of Bismarck and Nietzsche, that ideal of self-disciplined personal culture learned in his boyhood from the humanistic idealism of Goethe, Schiller, and Humboldt, and to commend it as his spiritual heritage to that age of totalitarianism he foresaw so distinctly.

BURCKHARDT AS PROPHET

Jacob Burckhardt was somewhat given to prophesying, and, what is more, held confidently to most of his predictions. Before the days of Freud and Jung he felt the close relationship of dreams, clairvoyance, and premonition, and had enough personal knowledge of the meanings of these dark phenomena not to brush aside the respect other ages and civilizations had had for them. His own previsions of the Europe to come, in their cumulative weight, have an aptness that is uncanny. Time and again one hears amid the crises of the twentieth century the exclamation from those who know his thought, and particularly his *Letters to Preen*, "He saw everything that has happened."

Burckhardt's predictions were not just random shots in the dark. The general outlines of his twentieth century landscape were blocked out as early as 1848 (see above, pp. 7 f.), and for fifty years he was filling in the figures and the faces, the colors and the highlights of that one same panorama. He worked, of course, with the tentative pragmatism of the historian, rather than the dogmatic "laws" of some sociological positivism. He knew that both wishing and fearing "can make fools of us all," and that there are creative and wholly unpredictable powers which can spring up overnight to transform a situation. And yet as a man he did not try to avoid that calculation of future probabilities from present powers which is in fact necessary for day to day living. As a penetrating and objective critic of the nineteenth century, he was in a position to make better guesses about the twentieth than the majority of men who wrote the newspaper editorials and the histories, delivered the sermons, the campaign speeches, or otherwise carried on their activities chiefly within the domain of the idols of theatre, market-place and tribe. To this must be added the essential health and poise of Burckhardt's personality, which saved him from the extremes of wishing and fearing, from hopeless bitterness and from simple-minded confidence, from ready assumptions of either univeral progress or total decline. Instead he projected the existing tendencies as he saw them into the unknown with the constant aid of analogies from history, in which he was one of the nicest, and most critical assessors, as this volume will show. The general success of his augury is thus not entirely accidental, or mystically psychic, if you will, but rests on at least three or four quite tangible and definite advantages of his situation and personal equipment.

We should begin with his analysis of the nineteenth century, with the lines of force which he mentally projected into the twentieth. It is perhaps surprising at first to find him characterizing its basic political danger in spiritual terms, indeed, in theological language. In speaking of the reported destruction of the Louvre and the further vandalisms he expected, Burckhardt explained, "The reasons lie deeper than you think; they belong with that giddiness about liberty, with Rousseau's ideas of the native goodness of man. Christianity has made its doctrine of the corruption of the human heart distasteful, to be sure, with all sorts of additions, but it rests on a much deeper insight into human nature." Thus Burckhardt, the "honest heretic," reduced the origins of the European crisis to the religious inanities of the optimistic Enlightenment, a development which in many respects began with his own Renaissance. Surprisingly, too, he rested his hope of ultimate reconstruction in a revival of other-worldly religion out of the age of despotism. Nicholas Berdyaev, the contemporary Eastern Orthodox thinker, has given general currency to these fundamental Burckhardtian notions of "Renaissance" and "new middle ages" in theological language. And in many respects the closest analogies to Burckhardt's political views in his own day were to be found in the attitude of the Roman Catholics. Rome at least set other goals than those of power and comfort, steadily opposed the increasingly totalitarian claims of the national states, and maintained that intelligently realistic view of human nature which Burckhardt considered essential to political responsibility.

It was this political consequence of a religious attitude, rather than psychological or philosophical implications, that Burckhardt developed most fully, and this it is which concerns us here. What Rousseau and the other theoreticians of equality and human perfectibility had done was to remove all the bonds of inner political discipline. They had taught the mass of people to think that all things were possible in human society, and that everyone has an equal right to them. And since the mass of people seeks chiefly material things, these conceptions were translated into terms of material comfort and power. They did not teach, on the other hand, that sense of responsibility, that respect, that inner acceptance of authority, that readiness to renounce for the good of the whole which give Anglo-Saxon Protestant democracy its substantiality. That is why "liberalism," as in Burckhardt's case, was often found opposing "democracy" in Europe.

Burckhardt returned again and again to this "terrible intellectual nullity" of radicalism. It could only level, destroy, or dissolve, it could not build. Its only program was greater material comforts for the masses, but it had no services or responsibilities or respect to demand of the citizen. The democrats even lacked respect for their own laws or constitutions, and would toss them aside as soon as some new demagogue or journalist thought up a new public service for the people to claim as a "right of man." The result was the "chief political phenomenon" of the nineteenth century, that all political and social and even religious institutions and relationships were now become "provisional." All things now depended on the whims—or manipulation—of public opinion. With the new popular suffrage, public opinion had now taken the place of divine right and tradition as the sanction and authority for all political arrangements.

But that was as much as to say that no political arrangements could again be stable. There was always some group or some interest which could profit by a change, and the reign of public opinion in the style of French egalitarianism meant that everyone was now licensed to demand anything because someone else had it. Such demands could be, and were, pressed with no reference to like or contrary desires of other groups or classes, or to the interests of the community as a whole. Let everyone get what he could, and the devil take the hindmost. Only the tiniest fraction could succeed in rising in the world; the vast majority would only become soured with the lot in which they must still remain and ripe for a political "saviour."

One aspect of this process was the gradual lowering of the quality of political leadership. Men of education, tradition, and character were suspected and hated by the traditionless, rootless masses, even if not actually ostracized in Athenian fashion. Burckhardt felt that he was watching in Europe the same degeneration that occurred in Greek democracy where the worse coinage in political leaders quickly drove the better out of circulation. The man of scruples in this kind of politics only has so many weapons the less and his very distinction and abilities can be used to make him unpopular with the masses who understand only mediocrities or men of their own type. By virtue of impossible promises an intelligent and scrupulous man would not make, the journalist and the demagogue ruled in his place, and the trend, Burckhardt felt, was toward the more corrupt types. In the end would come the generals.

All these demands of popular democracy were made of the state, and no one seemed to observe that as the state took over these things, individuals became more dependent on it. If the state ran schools for everyone, then everyone's children would learn what the state wanted to teach them. If the state provided free public baths, free hospitals, old age pensions, and the like, then the state in turn would demand supervision and control of all related matters in the lives of its individual citizens. Burckhardt, in fact, saw a century ago what many liberals are now discovering, that all progress toward a "social service" state was at the same time loss of individual liberties and initiative, and that the democrats were sacrificing liberalism for—at best—paternalistic control.

And back in the days when there was scarcely a socialist

party of note in Europe, Burckhardt foresaw economic socialism as the end of this democratic tendency. When all the other "rights of the people" had been exploited, and "envy and greed" encouraged by their success, then would come the turn of personal and family property and wealth. "I don't fear the evil will come from sudden attacks so much as from gradually increasingly socialistic legislation."

Socialism and all the rest of the democratic program, however, would certainly some day bow to ruthless military authority. Here was Burckhardt's second great insight into the program of the progressives. He saw that while in their program they were postulating an ever increasingly despotic state to do their errands for them, in fact they were offering this over-developed state machine to any political adventurer bold and ruthless enough to seize and exploit it by force. More or less pacifistic in intention, the democrats were building European military despotism brick by brick.

This whole process seemed to Burckhardt to be summed up in the paradigm of the French Revolution. It was the logical sequence Rousseau-Napoleon, which in a symbol presented his whole prophecy for the democratic movement of the Continent. Those two personalities represented the two claws of the pincers in which Europe was caught, and their pernicious influence dominated the whole century. The revolt of the masses against authority, and militarism as the only remaining possibility of order—that was the history of the people's revolution on the Continent. We should remember that *The Age of the Revolution* was Burckhardt's fullest and most influential course, and that it summed up in essence all subsequent history. In 1870 Burckhardt saw himself in the eighty-third year of the Revolution, and "the worst is yet to come." In 1884, only five years short of the centenary of the Revolution, he must make a strenuous effort to suppress the sense of present actuality he felt in treating of that period. For at this fag-end of the century, Burckhardt looked abroad on a Europe which had lost tradition and respect and would yield to no authority save a Napoleonic one. All Europe, like the France of the Revolution, was busy arguing theories of liberty and equality and national fraternity, and was in actuality the destined prey of military despotism. Burckhardt's analysis of the Revolution was thus akin to that of Tocqueville and Taine, the two French historians with whom he is in general most comparable. The Revolution was in essence a process of centralization and augmentation of state control, continuing and sharpening the despotism of the *ancien regime,* save that now the tyrant was no longer called "Louis" but "Republic." Except for certain limited areas, as in the case of peasant serfdom, the Revolution meant the sacrifice of liberty for standardization. Then came Napoleon to demonstrate how readily the egalitarian program could be fitted to that of despotism, which is all the stronger for the leveling of all privileges and liberties which might have limited its omnipotence.

And yet the doctrinaire Rousseauists with their crazy and heartless optimism as to human nature could never understand how the Goddess of Reason had been replaced on the throne by the iron Satan of military dictatorship. In their folly and their theory, they had no comprehension of the type of mind which cares only for power and thinks only in terms of the means of power. And they let a dictatorship arm itself under their noses. "Anything is possible in Europe since the Paris Commune," Burckhardt wrote, "chiefly because there are everywhere good, splendid, liberal people who do not quite know the boundaries of right and wrong and where the duty of resistance and defense begins. It is *these* men who open the doors and level the paths for the terrible masses everywhere." But from his teens Burckhardt knew the "hellishness in human nature" which comes to light when once the order of society is made a public question. He knew the criminal types who utilize revolutionary programs simply as the means to power or wealth. He knew what would happen to quite respectable men once social constraints were down and temptation beckoned. He never needed the schooling in Marx and Freud which has at last brought modern liberals back to the fundamental truths of Christianity's "original sin," that universal lust in man to use and exploit his fellows for self-aggrandizement and then to rationalize his justifications. Burckhardt knew that all the heights of his civilization left man still with all the potentialities of a "beast of prey," and in his regular reading of the press of four countries he followed carefully the fluctuations of "real worldly power," military power. And he would contrast with troop maneuvers the mass meetings of the "plebs" and their orators who flattered themselves that they were disposing of the course of nations.

Not only had these radical democrats rendered the states of Europe increasingly liable to *putsches* by undermining their authority, and at the same time increased the area of state control of the individual, but they had also called into question all the established international relations. The Revolution had bequeathed Europe egalitarianism, and also nationalism. And there was scarcely a frontier on the map of the Continent which was not challenged by the new popular nationalism. The "national will" was the new ideal, and one which might well threaten both a people's rulers and the peace with neighboring states, for neither the established boundaries nor the actual governments of Europe were based on such a principle. Revolutionary nationalism, seeking to include all of one race and tongue, and perhaps a little more, had thus been a major factor in every great war of Burckhardt's lifetime and promised more bedevilment for the future. Since from the point of view of the nationalists one's neighbors almost always had minorities to be liberated and "redeemed," every country must arm to the limit of its powers for offense and defense. And since any number of these national hopes could be realized only at the expense of others, the possibilities of conflict were infinite, and a settlement satisfactory to all impossible.

One result of this nationalistic program in Europe, which Burckhardt observed especially as a symptom of "Bismarckophobia" after the Seven Weeks' War, was that "complete lack of confidence in all small states which is spreading. Whoever does not belong to an empire of thirty millions cries out, 'Help, Lord, we sink!' " "The Philistine feels pale and empty unless he belongs to a great power which affords him security and comfort. It may very well be, of course, that his sons will die in field hospitals." Nationalism meant militarism, and militarism meant the end of independent small states with their cultural advantages.

The existing regimes of the Continent, mostly monarchies, had, of course, little real belief in either the democratic demands of the lower classes or the new goals of popular nationalism. They had no intention of conceding their own power, however, and would rather ride with the stream than try to fight it and go under. The postulates of national unity, in fact, current since Napoleon, opened to them imperialistic vistas which some could not resist. Nationalism, moreover, could be *used* by rulers to hold their people in line, and thus a certain international unrest was the safest condition for a dynasty at home. Militarism and truculence were heightened generally as the regimes flirted with world war to suppress or distract domestic disaffection. "As soon as it is a matter of cutting off a threatening revolution, they themselves effect something which passes as the equivalent and concentrates all weapons in their hands. How long can that continue? The result is the series of wars into which Europe has passed. The nations of Europe, oppressed by militarism, are setting about visiting infinite affliction on each other, chiefly because of *internal* ferment."

In 1870, Burckhardt wrote to his friend Preen of the "terrible completeness" of Bismarck's revenge on France: "Do they want to send troops on as far as Bordeaux and Bayonne? For to proceed logically, all France would have to be occupied, perhaps for many years, by a million Germans. I know very well that it won't happen, but it would be the logical consequence of what has gone before." "A new element has entered politics, a thoroughness that former conquerors knew nothing of, or at least made no conscious use of. They try to humiliate the conquered as deeply as possible in his own eyes, so that in the future he shall not rise again to any self-confidence."

The immediate change in the German situation brought about by Prussia's defeat of Germany and France, was that for the new Germany "the military has become the model of all public life." An unreconciled France and a jealous Russia left but one hope for the continued existence of the new Empire: armaments. And in consequence, "The Prussian dynasty," Burckhardt said, "is now so placed that it and its staff can never again be sufficiently powerful in general. There is nothing more to be said of restraint on this path. The very salvation of Germany drives them on." "Isn't it true that all our activity has become dilettantish, precious, fantastic, in increasingly ridiculous contrast to the high efficiency of the military machine, elaborated in every detail?" "For you, friend," he wrote the government official Preen, "it is now most interesting to observe how the state and administrative machine is reformed militaristically; for me, how the schools and the educational system are taken in hand, etc. When it comes to the working people, the change will be most remarkable of all. I have a premonition which sounds like utter folly, and yet which positively will not leave me: the military state must become one great factory. Those hordes of men in the great industrial centers may not be left indefinitely to their greed and want. What must logically come is a definite and supervised stint of misery, with promotions and in uniform, daily begun and ended to the sound of drums. (To be sure, I know enough history to know that matters are not always brought to logical conclusions.)" Thus, seventy years ago there hovered before this man the vision of the absorption of the economic and industrial life of the nation into the military machine, with conscript labor battalions marching off to duty, in the uniforms and with the inducements of quasi-military organizations.

All this militarism was necessary, however, for Europe was now entering upon an "era of wars" in which Germany would soon have to contend with Russia. She had embarked upon that adventure in conquest from which there could be no turning back. And Burckhardt promised her the same end to her military glory which Napoleon and Philip II had come to, so that a patriotic German could scarcely contain himself while hearing him. Burckhardt was thenceforth only surprised that the "mighty national conflicts" delayed so long after 1871.

Burckhardt gave the dynasty one generation more in Germany, which was not far wrong. In 1871 he saw the royal family and felt a profound sympathy with the attractive Crown Prince, for "He will pay the price!" "The Hohenzollerns are digging their graves," he told young Salis. "The tremendous movement they have started will go on over their bodies. They are undermining royalty in general. For if princes themselves no longer respect monarchy, then who is to care about it?—When the Hohenzollerns in 1866 deposed princes with whom they had so often lunched, then who was to respect princes? . . . Belief in invisible immemorial foundations of existence, political-religious mysticism is gone. The dynasties will cease to exist because only extraordinary capacities will be wanted." Burckhardt speculated on the possibilities of the dynasties maintaining themselves by employing these "extraordinary capacities" as condottieri, or adopting them into the succession as in the Roman Empire. However it be organized, "long voluntary subjection under individual *Führers* and usurpers is in prospect. People no longer believe in principles, but will, periodically, probably, in saviours." "For this reason authority will again raise its head in the pleasant twentieth century, and a terrible head."

Burckhardt's beloved "land of frescoes and chestnuts" he now found scarcely endurable in its similar degeneration to militant nationalism. "The enormous falsity which lies in Italy's desire to be a great power and a military and centralized state, must revenge itself." Italy in the late seventies was being run by a "clique of lawyers" and the continued existence of the dynasty depended on just a few factors, for the air was "thick with revolutionary miasmas." With "this imposing people, these first-born of Europe," things were going as with France: "all sorts of business and material developments with a sharp falling-off in the political security which should accompany such business and its pleasures." The liberal industrialists might well "fall on their knees" before the popular leaders and beg moderation of them, but the latter were forced to show continual change to the voters to persuade them that "progress" was being made. "One thing after another must be sacrificed, position, property, religion, distinguished manners, higher scholarship," for the power to stop the process "(as I have for a long time complained to you) can scarcely proceed from any but the worst elements and will have hair-raising effects."

The two new states in the European constellation, Germany and Italy, now set the tone for the rest. The ancient house of Austria was measuring out its last years. In the eighties, again, Burckhardt was waiting for Russia to give the cue, whether the break would come from the wanton recklessness of the aristocracy, pan-Slav imperialism, or the nihilist revolutionists. And France, "poor France," corrupt and mercenary and menaced by royalists, Bonapartists, Boulangists, how long could she last? And how ominous, in 1942, sounds Burckhardt's observation that the army was no longer, as in Prussia, a career in France.

The "extra persons," whom Burckhardt awaited, especially in Germany and Italy, could not simply be individual dictators. It is too easy to eliminate any one man. With startling clarity he looked forward to the twentieth century politico-military "party" movements. "The sudden change from democracy will no longer result in the rule of an individual,—for he would be put out of the world with dynamite, etc.—but in the rule of a military corporation. And by it, methods will perhaps be used for which even the most terrible despot would not have the heart." He recognized in the more formidable criminals of the daily press the political possibilities of the ruthless egotism, the colossal will to power out of which in fact the higher ranks of the criminal cliques directing the twentieth century fascists and communists would be built. "My mental picture of the *terribles simplificateurs* who will overrun our old Europe is not a pleasant one," he wrote a friend. "Now and then, in imagination I already see such fellows bodily before me and I will describe them to you." What faces *did* the man see?

The shock would be considerable for the optimistic liberals, both in business and in political institutions. It would be a revelation to many to discover that the state was really entertaining quite independent aims and could even become quite careless of commerce and industry and those business interests that supposed they were directing it. "People may not yet like to imagine a world whose rulers completely ignore law, prosperity, profitable labor and industry, credit, etc. and are then in a position to rule with absolute brutality." But "somewhere, finally, after more unmeasured violence, a real power will be formed, which will make desperately few concessions to the right to vote, popular sovereignty, material prosperity, industry, etc. For this is the inevitable end of the constitutional state when it has fallen a prey to majorities."

Such political and economic revolution would, of course, have a disastrous effect on the creative arts, on scholarship and education, on the world of higher culture in general. But even before that, all these would suffer from the brutalization of life caused by industrialism. Burckhardt quite distinctly saw this happening as early as 1870, as more and more of his talented students, who a decade earlier would have gone into the professions, turned instead to business. And in business, due to its all-absorbing requirements, they would have to hire other men to be cultured for them, much as the wild medieval nobility had had other men to pray for them. The whole sociological basis for higher culture was being disintegrated, "all the little circles in which the German mind and spirit nested cosily beside German Philistinism are being shattered," and the uprooted artist or writer must make his way to the metropolitan centers and in that hothouse atmosphere compete for the attention of journalists. Both the theatre, for example, and the novel, had already become simply part of the amusement business, catering to the taste of tired business men and their bored wives. The only serious purpose still conceded to them was that of political propaganda, and writers must submit to party imprimaturs. Books of poetry seemed to Burckhardt to be selling chiefly by virtue of their bindings, as Christmas presents for bedside table decoration. Poetry was no longer a serious concern of life. The clergy and the aristocracy, again, who had set the great themes and placed the commissions for the plastic arts at the heights of the great styles, would no longer do so. To suit the taste of the new patron and Maecenas, a painter would treat primarily of cats, children, and cherished furniture, on which no great style was likely to be formed. The natural capacities and talents for art and literature, as Burckhardt frequently observed, were as great as ever, but society was such that the artist or writer who worked out of inner necessity and with strict conscience would be swamped by all the clever little talents who could adapt themselves to a vulgar taste and make a good business of it. These folk would at any rate drop by the wayside when the storms came, for they had no real compulsion or right to artistic expression anyway. Under great difficulties and with great sacrifices, the genuine artists alone might then continue to work. Burckhardt's "humble hope" was in these ascetic artists of the twentieth century. But what would their employment be? The commercial and industrial baronage was addressing itself to art, to be sure, as an appointed luxury, a form of conspicuous consumption, but the loot gathered in its galleries and museums, as Burckhardt saw them in England, was all the great art of the past. What was to happen to living art in the meantime? What was to happen, in fact, to these collections? For Burckhardt expected many of the galleries and churches of Europe to go up in the holocaust, partly because of the resentment of the masses against all higher culture as an appurtenance of their former masters, and partly from the passion for criminal notoriety such as led Herostratus to fire the temple of Diana of Ephesus. Those who have seen the Russian Revolution and the Nazis over Europe know.

In the world of schools and education, likewise, Burckhardt read the signs of the times. He steadily opposed the demand for free public education and the construction of new schools, for, he said bluntly, all this arose not from any concern for culture but simply as an expression of the desire to rise in the world socially and economically. All those persons who would burn the Louvre, he observed, were "educated." People moved into the cities to raise their children among such advantages, hoping to find them posts in business or the professions. The quantity of "educated" youth turned out by the schools, in consequence, was out of all proportion to the number of such positions available. At his retirement from teaching art, Burckhardt watched for the race for his chair among the "hundred well-crammed art historians," for whom there was no place "either on earth or in heaven." The schools and universities, in fact, were pouring out "those endless generations of the discontented," who would turn in their unemployment and disillusion to the promises of any demagogue, as Germany was actually to discover about 1930. And in the schools themselves, this utilitarian and vocational intention of the mass of the students could not be met much longer, Burckhardt feared, by the classical education which assumed a love of culture. In his own lectures on Greek civilization he looked forward with foreboding to the future of the liberal arts. In economic depression and political revolution, finally, even the most practical sciences would become luxuries, and the over-expansion in education would be thoroughly remedied. "Bare existence" would then be problem enough.

One particular aspect of the Central European crisis which also promised ill for the future was the Jewish problem. Anti-Semitism, Burckhardt prophesied, was a popular trump which liberalism could not afford to let Catholics and conservatives hold indefinitely. Of the Jewish-Catholic hostility, which reached a climax in the early eighties, Burckhardt expected an enduring aftermath. He would advise slick manipulators like Rothschild to be careful. And for the professions: "I won't guarantee the Jewish legal gentlemen their careers for much longer," he wrote in 1880. "The Jews, in brief, will have to do penance for their completely unjustifiable intervention in everything possible, and newspapers will have to dismiss their Jewish editors and correspondents if they wish to continue publication. Something of this sort can happen suddenly and contagiously overnight."

As to the future of Christianity, Burckhardt predicted two phenomena which have come as a surprise to many people in the twentieth century: the evaporation of liberal Protestantism on the Continent and the unique resistance offered to totalitarianism by the conservative churches. "In the twentieth century," he prophesied, "those amazing caricatures of so-called 'reformed' pastors and professors will no longer endure," for "all this agitation will scatter like dust as soon as people fall into real distress." As in the Roman Empire of the fourth and fifth centuries, optimistic this-worldly religion would give way to pessimism as to man's nature and earthly fate. From such "genuine Christianity," moreover, in contrast to the "optimistically inverted variety," no "enlightened" state would be able to restrain serious people in their trouble, for they would not fear even martyrdom. "The Catholics do not fear it even now," he wrote, and persecuting governments "might meet with a resistance of the strangest sort from such minorities." For the sake of the churches themselves, however, Burckhardt continually advocated disestablishment to avoid the attempts the Great Powers would assuredly make to use them for secular ends.

It is indeed curious to see how Burckhardt, nurtured in the essentially pantheistic mood of modern art and literature, and resolutely heterodox in renouncing the asceticism of true Christianity as he conceived it, nevertheless estimated the Church so highly as a factor in the modern world. At the first impact of the Franco-Prussian War his hopes took the direction of a revival of the old Germany from a religious core. "The great new liberation," he wrote, "must come from the German spirit, and of course, in opposition to power, wealth, and business. It must have its martyrs. It must be something which by nature can keep its head above water in all catastrophes, political, economic, or otherwise . . . If the German spirit reacts once again, out of its deepest and most original source of power, against this great violation, if it is able to oppose to it a new art, literature, and religion, then we are saved, if not, we are not—I say religion, for without a transcendent urge which outweighs all the clamor for power and money nothing will be any use."

The clamor for power and money, meanwhile, could of itself have but one result. In his own day Burckhardt perceived that certain social classes were already quite willing to relinquish all cultural individuality in Europe for the economic advantages of standardization and "through night trains." The American General Grant proposed such a simplification. And hand in hand with this tendency of economic development would go the logic of military conquest and consolidation among the "nominally republican military commandos" who should rule the states of twentieth century Europe. This might not come all at once; more likely there would be a series of wars and consolidations until at last Europe should settle down into one military and economic area. "The ultimate consummation could once more be an *imperium romanum* (only after we are dead, of course), after there have first been several Assyrias, Medias, Persias. Such an *imperium,* as we know, has no dynasty, but only a central administration, and (thanks to the soldiers) a *beata tranquillitas.*" "What I am writing probably sounds strange now, and yet it is fundamentally true."

Still, as Burckhardt watched the generations of university men come and go, he could draw hope from the certainty that the "human material is as good as ever." They would learn how to live in the new Europe which he would never see, and he made it a principle to keep his fears for the future from them entirely. "Those in their forties, to be sure, are already noticing some things themselves." For himself, also, since he did not "believe people are made better and wiser by continually staring into chaos," he thought as little as possible of these things, but tried to "preserve good humor and sleep at night." Day after day, meanwhile, he gave his strength to what *could* make men better and wiser, the guidance and consolation of history, much as Boethius had in an earlier day commended to a brutalized Europe the *Consolations of Philosophy.*

THE MEANING OF HISTORY

It was in the crucial years from the Prusso-Austrian War of 1866 to the establishment of the German and Italian states in the early seventies, that Burckhardt voiced most of the prophecies we have mentioned, prophecies rising out of his interpretation of the deeper meaning of the crisis. In the same half decade or so, he developed his most profound insights as to the meaning of history, both with regard to Greece as a grand paradigm, and more generally but in much briefer fashion in the work now before us. The first draft of these *Reflections on History* was written out during the Summer of 1868. In the Fall, Burckhardt revised his manuscript, and once again in the Winter semester, when he delivered it as a lecture course at the University. That course constitutes about two-thirds of the present volume. The present chapters five and six were not part of the original course. In November 1870 Burckhardt gave a series of three public lectures on the *Great Men of History,* and a year later another on *Fortune and Misfortune in History*. During that war winter of 1870–71 when it seemed as though the Almighty were shaking the earth to discover what could and what could not be shaken, the lecture course had, fittingly, been given a second time. Burckhardt never offered it again and it has really come into its own only in posthumous publication with the associated lectures and under the impact of the world wars and revolutions of the twentieth century.

Between the first publication of these *Reflections* and this first translation offered to the English-speaking world, a long generation has passed. Such a publication is extremely unusual, for histories are normally out of date in twenty or thirty years. Of this work, by contrast, one might venture to say that its understanding is now really possible for the first time, that only after seventy years are we in a position to comprehend the Continent of 1871 as Burckhardt interpreted it. Indeed in 1871 Burckhardt understood 1941 better than most of us did in that year itself.

Burckhardt's interpretation of history, in most compact form here, has in the interim been much read and commented on. It has been almost perversely misunderstood by two of the most discerning and solid historians of historical writing, Eduard Fueter and Benedetto Croce. Neither has been able to forgive Burckhardt for his opposition to liberal politics and, in consequence, both damn him with patronizing praise of his style and aesthetic sensitivity. Thus is repeated the legend of Burckhardt the irresponsible but delightful Epicurean. Almost the exact contrary is the case, as a thoughtful reading of these *Reflections on History* will show. Burckhardt, far from evading the problems of historical thought, was perhaps the most consciously selective and critical of all the great nineteenth century historians, and his history might be described as the "history of the values of Western civilization." Such a description, indeed, would be much more helpful than the highly misleading term, "history of civilization," which he often used himself. And these *Reflections,* while they contain little advice on how to win an election or a war, form a great political book. There is something here of the depth and scope with which Plato and Machiavelli searched the past of the two greatest democratic city-states of all time, Athens and Florence, when their freedom was forever lost. As Augustine surveyed all time and existence under the shocking impact of the report of looting Goths in the halls whence once the world had been ruled, so Burckhardt, reading the ominous signals of a rising among the barbarians already within the gates, mounted to a higher altitude and told of many things the busier politicians could not or would not see. The years just around the Franco-Prussian War brought to final articulation that highly critical type of historical thought which Burckhardt had claimed for his own since the early forties. "A quite remarkable phenomenon has become clear to me as a teacher of history," he wrote at the end of 1870, "the sudden devaluation of all mere 'events' of the past." Henceforth his courses would retain only the most indispensable framework of "lumber" on which to convey not the antiquarian fads or novelistic fantasies of what is often called "history of civilization," but what, for any cultured citizen, was really worth knowing of the history of the West.

In the latter half of the nineteenth century, when Burckhardt was writing, the vast majority of historians had, in fact if not in theory, quite abandoned such scope for more limited areas of study, particularly national histories. This was due partly to the increasing demands of the critical method in conjunction with increasing accumulations of material, so that one could hope to winnow thoroughly only a very restricted field. And then the great political conflicts from the forties to the seventies turned the attention of both students and public to political and national problems. The easiest solution was for an historian to become a specialist in the history of his own country.

Against this prevailing trend of the middle of the century, Burckhardt's book stands out in sharp contrast. He was neither a specialist nor a national historian and had no desire to be. The *Introduction* of this volume reveals something of Burckhardt's attitude toward the specialists, the "*viri eruditissimi,*" or "*capricorn-beetles,*" as he called them in private. The conception of history as an art of evaluation, which underlies this book, stands in complete contrast to the notion of history as the "science" of establishing "what actually happened," however trivial, with its further illusion, that as soon as enough "facts" are accumulated, enough "contributions to knowledge" turned out in the factories of scholarship, the world of man and history will be "covered," and, presumably, understood. But to Burckhardt such men seemed rather like deluded folk trying to dig up a mountain. "They begin, dig a deep hole, which, however, is nothing in comparison to the mountain. Death comes meanwhile, and what do they leave us?—The rubbish lying beside the hole they dug." Burckhardt was well aware that the history of humanity in its infinite variety and individuality was too utterly vast ever to be "covered," and that what was important was rather selection, the discovery and appreciation of those findings of human experience which were worth preserving. And perhaps he was the first of all the great historians to recognize the inescapable subjectivity of viewpoint. "History," he once said, "is on every occasion the record of that which one age finds worthy of note in another." And every historian, indeed, the same historian at different ages, will find different interests. The sources too are inexhaustible, so that there may be a fact of first importance in Thucydides which will only be recognized a hundred years from now.

One result of Burckhardt's own inadequate respect for philology was that he was not always abreast of the special research in the fields in which he worked, as details in this volume will show, and sometimes, especially in his *History of Greek Civilization,* made use of sources which had been proven unreliable. The specialists, in consequence, resenting his sovereign unconcern for their life labor, at first tended more or less to share in the boycott pronounced by Wilamowitz, "This work does not exist for science." As the years have passed, however, the work of the specialists has been rendered obsolete by more specialists, whereas Burckhardt has himself demonstrated Mommsen's prediction that his works would still be read and still be true though every sentence in them should stand in need of correction by advancing research. Every one of Burckhardt's half dozen major works was a new discovery, but in interpretation, not in documentation. He cared less about accumulating new facts than about reassessing the significance of what everyone supposedly knew already. His reinterpretation of the Renaissance, for example, still stands in all its essential features, despite eighty years of debate and new research.

With equal decisiveness Burckhardt opposed the second great trend of historical scholarship after 1850, nationalism. If one must write national history it should be "in its parallels and relations to universal history," as a chapter in the history of man, and "historical judgment really ought always to be of such a nature that all nations at least, if not all parties, could subscribe to it." "In the realm of the mind and spirit, one must simply reach for the higher and highest attainable." Anything else, however patriotic, is a putting on of blinders, and three-fourths of the histories written in his generation Burckhardt would probably have described as "political journalism, or material for it." History, on the contrary, along with philosophy and "some other fine things," should be raised above the strife of parties and nations and directed toward the attaining of a deeper wisdom. "If history is to help us in any way to solve the great and difficult riddle of life in even the slightest degree, then we must look back from the areas of individual and social anxieties to a land where our vision is not immediately clouded with egoism. Perhaps from quieter contemplation at greater distance there will arise an intimation of the true character of our earthly pilgrimage."

Granting the value of universal history, it will still come as something of a surprise to Anglo-American readers to discover how Burckhardt conceives of it. It may take a second reading to penetrate beyond admiration for this and that incidental insight and for the versatility and command of the work to a grasp of the implications of its argument. The Anglo-American reader, more than the professional historians, is still accustomed to think of world history in terms of an evolutionary progression toward ever higher levels of civilization. Mr. Wells' *Outline of History* is an example of this popular pattern of thought, which is constantly fed by the successes of modern technology, and—in peace time—of humanitarian advances.

Burckhardt, however, rejected this theory from beginning to end. He would have refused to classify historical periods by any such technological criteria as produce "Stone Ages," "Bronze Ages," and if he might have accepted the "Machine Age" for the nineteenth century, in his mouth it would not have been an accolade to progress.

Fortune and Misfortune in History, it will be discovered, denies both intellectual and moral progress in history; "Neither man's spirit nor his intellect has demonstrably improved in the period known to history."

The theory of evolution in history as "Progress" appeared to Burckhardt as simply the arrogant complacency of the modern bourgeoisie in the face of all other types of historical life. The real persuasion of this theory lay, he would say, in the implication that money-making was now easier than ever before. Thorough policing, an established property and commercial law, modern insurance, all these protect modern man against the violence of past ages—except in war, when all the most primitive horrors reappear, systematized. But even while such security exists, said Burckhardt, it should not be esteemed as a *moral* advance. The very Lake-Dwellers certainly knew sacrifice of life for others, and what moral "progress" is there beyond that? Most of the great ages of civilization, such as the Homeric Age, the Age of Pericles, the Middle Ages, the Renaissance, have played for high stakes, for victory or death, which is "wildly foreign" to sensible moderns with their shrewd little compromises, but not for that reason less elevated in moral achievement. "The greatness of an epoch or a cause depends on the quota of those capable of sacrifice, on whatever side it may be . . . on devotion to something, whatever it be, with complete extinction of personal vanity." From such a viewpoint Burckhardt repudiated Gibbon's treatment of Christianity, and championed the Middle Ages against Voltaire, "the impudently ignorant mocker." What the "Progress" theorists really meant when they said "morality" was *happiness.* But as Burckhardt watched his neighbors, he observed less *content-*

ment than in earlier centuries with lower living standards and less material comfort.

Equally decisive was his denial of intellectual evolution. The nineteenth century had technological advances to bear witness to its intellectual capacities, but that preoccupation had cost it much in the realm of higher culture, which Burckhardt personally valued above railroads, telegraphs, and electrical appliances. The material complexity of its civilization, moreover, was not only stealing time and energy from better things, but was itself outrunning human capacity to control. Man's intellectual and moral capacities remained the same, while the social problems they must cope with grew ever more intricate. The division of labor which made all this possible bore the danger that there were ever fewer minds capable of understanding and directing the whole. In consequence, "civilization could easily trip over its own feet."

The final twist to the mechanistic theory of progress which was given by the Darwinian "survival of the fittest" seemed to Burckhardt a good epitaph for the theory. There was only too much truth, he conceded, in this portrayal of human life as continual conflict either by war or economic competition and exploitation. But if one is to argue any change in the human species from this struggle, as Hartmann sought to do in his *Philosophy of the Unconscious,* then, said Burckhardt, the prospect is a horrible one. "Men would gradually become veritable devils," and finally deformed by overdevelopment of the brain along with bodily atrophy.

In thus rejecting the roughly unilateral pattern of history which Anglo-French thought has largely retained from the eighteenth century "Enlightenment," Burckhardt might seem to awaken the expectation that his own pattern would be the relativistic pluralism characteristic of German views of history since the beginning of his century. In reaction to the enlightened rationalism of the French Revolution and Napoleon's democratic Terror, the "romantic school" of German historians had risen up to champion the proper variety of history, its infinity of unique historical traditions in law, constitutions, religions, literatures as against French *Gleichschaltung.* In this sense for the incommensurable communities of concrete historical life, in contrast to the standardized "mankind" of the *philosophes,* was born not only that unequalled talent of the modern German for concrete historical understanding and writing, but also that contrast of intellectual climate between Germany and the Anglo-French West which had never existed in any such degree before, but which has persisted ever since.

With regard to our specific problem of the conception of universal history, the difference has been that when the Anglo-French historian has tried to reduce all history to "laws," he has turned to physical mechanics as a pattern, while the German inclination is rather to apply biological analogies to these separate cultures whose individuality he senses so keenly. Perhaps the most generally familiar example to be set up as counterpart to Mr. Wells' *Outline* is Oswald Spengler's *Decline of the West,* even though it shows some marked elements of Anglo-French positivism. But it becomes clear very quickly that the arguments of *Fortune and Misfortune in History* undermine the cycle theory of the waxing and waning of civilizations as much as they do the theory of progress. It is thus legitimate to interpret this work largely as a reply to the *Decline of the West.*

The cycle theory was represented in Burckhardt's day by the man who serves almost as a silent partner of the dialogue in these *Reflections,* Ernst von Lasaulx. He is cited many times, and his ideas are alluded to more often still without acknowledgment. This is something of a puzzle, for Lasaulx himself, a follower of Schelling and Görres, and son-in-law of Baader, was a speculative, uncritical historian who scarcely seems to merit any such attention, and whose work is largely forgotten. Why did Burckhardt refer to him so frequently? It is hard to say, except that it is clear that Burckhardt takes the opportunity of courteously differing from Lasaulx on matters which would be far better represented by more well-known men. Perhaps in this way he thought to avoid the scholarly debates he so detested.

It is the ideas which concern us, in any case. Lasaulx was perhaps the first historian to apply the classic Greek theory of historical cycles, as found in Plato, Aristotle, Polybios, and resumed again in modern times by Vico and Schelling before him, to the demonstration of the decline of the contemporary West. Every people, he wrote, was allotted a certain quota of vital energy which they then lived out just as a plant would, passing through stages of childhood, youth, maturity and old age to death. The period of political expression was normally about two thousand years, and always followed the sequence of types of government from monarchy to aristocracy, and through democracy to final military despotism, "Caesarism," as Aristotle described it.

The development of culture also followed a regular pattern in every case, the various arts and sciences emancipating themselves in the same order from the religious cult which in every case gave them birth. That religious core of the civilization was the key to the cycle, for after itself creating a secular culture, the religion was always attacked in turn by rationalism and scepticism until its naïve creative vigor was lost and the whole civilization became a mighty frame without the lifeblood of conviction and the sense of duty which alone could maintain it. Then any barbarian invader would find conquest easy. And in that cycle, wrote Ernst von Lasaulx in 1856, nineteenth century Europe was far advanced into "old age." His hopes went forth to the next culture in Europe, a Christian Slav civilization, or one from European elements "beyond the Atlantic ocean."

It is possible, as one reads through these *Reflections* of Burckhardt, to reassemble his observations on the rise and decline of various historical factors into the pattern of a cycle very similar to that of the romanticists. But although the cycle scheme is much more subtle and complex than the pattern of unilateral progress characteristic of Anglo-American thought, and can absorb successfully far more of the concrete phenomena of history, it is obvious at once that Burckhardt has broken the back of the theory, simply from his observation that he had dallied with the thought of a systematic sociological arrangement of his materials, rather than the roughly chronological one finally adopted in the chapter on *Reciprocal Actions*. He denied the cogency of historical divisions according to biologically conceived cultures just as he did that of divisions according to stages of "progress."

The systematic criticism here appears in analysis of the value judgments implicit in such divisions of history. A theory of either cycles or progress assumes a certain type of civilization as a standard and ideal and from that ideal pronounces other periods to be "primitive," "decadent," and the like. But, Burckhardt observed, so various are the ideals of historians that there is scarcely a major period of history which has not been regarded as a grand climax by someone and as a lamentable "middle age" by someone else. The several aspects of civilization, state life, religion, art, literature, economic activity, have rarely flourished equally in any one period of history. And even supposing a consensus could be reached among historians as to those periods of civilization which exhibited the happiest development of the greatest number of aspects, even then no one could count the end of that age a disaster. Such a "happy" state of affairs could only be perpetuated by petrifaction, for all creation and life demand change. Were some Utopian program ever uniformly accepted in Europe, said Burckhardt, then men would raise an opposition simply out of boredom. And as a matter of fact, Burckhardt also pointed out, the "golden ages" were not times of happy adjustment, but were epochs in which the magnificent achievements of man in one regard were paid for by terrible costs in another. Burckhardt's accounts of the prices paid for the Age of Pericles, the *pax Romana,* the beauty of the Renaissance have become famous. He is the great destroyer of historical illusions, both in regard to the great ages of cultural creativity and to the triumphs of modern "Progress."

Instead of dividing history up into periods in the conventional way, in consequence, Burckhardt analyzed each epoch in terms of its peculiar equilibrium of the several typical interests of humanity. Like Dilthey, he looked in each epoch for the structure of its life-interests, its characteristic "hierarchy of values" among religious, political, and cultural concerns. He could thus achieve a far truer picture of a period than could conventional political history or church history, since there is no such thing in fact as an abstract "state" or "religion" or "culture," but each can only be understood in a specific historical situation where its nature is always largely determined by its relation to other institutions. Political history in the Middle Ages, for example, is largely a chapter of church history, while in the Age of Pericles, or in the Renaissance, religion lives, if at all, as a state function or as an aspect of individual culture. "One side is never exclusively active in man," Burckhardt wrote, "but always the whole man, although individual sides may be weaker and unconscious." Human society cannot be divided up into functions for abstract analysis any more than human personality can. In every developed civilization, state, religion and culture continually affect and modify each other so that in these mutual interactions one can only point out the temporarily dominant factor. Instead of marching onward and upward from one noble synthesis of civilization to another, history presents rather a continual shifting of the values in tension in all societies. Progress in one regard is made at the expense of retrogression in another. And Burckhardt recommended that an historian should be well acquainted with typical cases of each equilibrium, the life of a religious despotism like Byzantium's perhaps, and of a free society like Athens. He would have his own preferences, no doubt, but as an historian he should seek to understand all the metempsychoses of eternal *man.*

It may help the Anglo-American reader to comprehend this type of analysis if he contrasts the mental climate of his own society with that from which Burckhardt interrogated history. Burckhardt's *Reciprocal Actions* and *Fortune and Misfortune in History* betray the sense of conflicting values characteristic of the generation of '48. Between 1830 and 1848, when that generation was growing up, Metternich's international balance and the social hierarchy was more and more evidently doomed, the compromise of Christianity and modern culture represented in various ways by Hegel and Ranke and Schleiermacher was disintegrating, the challenge of industrialism and militarism to religion and higher culture was becoming more serious. That generation included a Treitschke but also a Karl Marx, a Kierkegaard, a Burckhardt, men for whom neither liberalism nor nationalism provided an adequate answer to the crisis of European civilization. Ranke, to be sure, had organized his history around a conflict of values, the tension of Church and state, but from the calm viewpoint of one who knew the final compromise in which the interests of both were best served. Both he and Hegel could trace the succession of political communities down through the ages with the general assumption that the interests of religion and culture followed the same fortunes. The great eighteenth century and Restoration states, benevolently protecting culture and religion, were models for their theories. But now Burckhardt and Overbeck, like Kierkegaard, could no longer hold their peace about this Christianity domesticated by state and culture, and established a Basel tradition to be made famous in the twentieth century by Karl Barth. Genuine Christianity, these men all proclaimed, was in complete and irreducible opposition to modern political, economic, and cultural life. Marx, similarly, called down apocalyptic doom on the caricature of justice in capitalist democracy like an old Hebrew prophet. Burckhardt, and after him Nietzsche, pointed out the incompatibility of political and cultural greatness. The great ages of culture, said Burckhardt, were not those protected by the mighty states of the past, as

Hegel and Ranke seemed to assume, but were the work of communities whose political significance was infinitesimal.

Curiously enough, on the other hand, these very peculiarities of Burckhardt, his anti-militarism, his individualism, his moralism, make him congenial to Anglo-American readers in the same degree that German thought finds him eccentric. For us he builds a bridge to an earlier Germany of Kant and Schiller, reminding us that the cult of tribalism of recent Germany is not, in fact, a matter of either German blood or German soil. And the World Wars of the twentieth century have for the first time given Englishmen and Americans a vivid picture of the background of Burckhardt's hopes and fears, the kind of situation against which he struck off these conclusions. Now, as never before, Anglo-Americans can understand "the State" in Burckhardt's sense, and even "the Church."

This suggestion may be worth a little elaboration. If we think of the chapter on *Reciprocal Actions* as an essay on three great problems: Church and State, State and Society, Church and Society, little of it would have had direct relevance for nineteenth century America. The relation of the Church to secular culture, to be sure, has produced many problems—those of the historical analysis of the Bible and church history, the issues of censorship of literature, stage and screen, religious education, divorce, birth control, ethical criticisms of industrial relations, e.g., although in many or most of these areas, as Burckhardt prophesied, the state has extended its all-inclusive regulatory and controlling influence. The second relation, however, that of Church and state, has not been a live issue for several reasons. In the first place, America alone of the great Western nations has for a century or so practised that separation of Church and state which Burckhardt advocated for Europe, but which has never been generally adopted there. This circumstance itself has prevented conflict and thought about this issue. And then in the second place, it is only in the twentieth century that either the fact or the concept of "Church" and of "State" have come home to the American people. Until recently the American did not think in these terms. For a variety of historical reasons American Christianity did not think of "the Church" but of "churches." The sectarian traditions of much of American Christianity joined the humanistic voluntaryism of the dominant Lockian theory of the Church to form the typically American conception of the Church on the analogy of a "lodge." The frontier further decentralized religious life and encouraged local independence, lay control, denominationalism. It is only the twentieth century movements toward unification of Protestant denominations, and closer international fellowship, that have again awakened the live sense of "the Church."

Americans have not had much occasion in the past to think of the "State," either, at least not in the European sense. For a long time political power was decentralized among "the states" and local communities, and throughout the nineteenth century the will to power, which Burckhardt made the prime political motive, expressed itself in America chiefly in industrial imperialism. Then too, so long as there was no danger of military attack from without, the government did not need the military machine all European states required, with its attendant controls of civilian life and demands of universal military service. The frontier, finally, was until the end of the century a refuge and a protection from state control of the individual. But in the twentieth century the protecting oceans have suddenly shrunk and the United States, like Germany after 1871, faces a future of militarization. The individual, moreover, can no longer flee over the mountains to the frontier; he has but a few none too secure constitutional rights against a vast bureaucratic federal state which is increasingly absorbing into itself the political powers local agencies can no longer administer successfully. The United States, in short, has become a Great Power, with most of the characteristics, problems, and dangers of the Continental state at the end of Burckhardt's life. Henceforth Americans will think much more of both "Church" and "State," and perhaps of their relationship, than they have had occasion to in the past.

As to the problem of state and secular culture, the ever increasing claims of the state have made that too a more difficult issue than ever before for Americans. Hitherto America has known the problem almost exclusively in the sphere of economic and industrial relations, where the liberal program of free enterprise long maintained itself with a vengeance. The twentieth century, however, has brought a change.

As to the relations of the state to higher culture, and the social groups which produce it, questions are beginning to arise concerning education, radio and movie productions, state commissions in the plastic arts. As Burckhardt said in this connection, there are some branches of culture which really exist only by state patronage. And since Burckhardt's individualism is not primarily that of the business man as against state control, as is ours in the tradition of Locke, Adam Smith, and the utilitarians, but is rather derived from the idealism of German humanistic culture, he can serve as a helpful corrective to a nation just becoming culturally articulate as a whole and still disposed to take too seriously, perhaps, its assembly lines and its plumbing.

With Burckhardt's situation as compared to that of his present readers in mind, we may return to his method of portraying conflicts of values in history. The name "history of civilization," as he saw, was really "too narrow" for what he was trying to do, since it was primarily defined by the efforts of the *philosophes* of the Enlightenment. For them it had meant chiefly institutional history rather than political and military narrative. But Burckhardt did not share their opposition to political history; his books usually interpret a society first of all by its political conditions. So far as political interest goes, he belongs with Ranke, Droysen, Treitschke, rather than with the "historians of civilization." The difference is that he sought political *conditions* and *attitudes* rather than narrative. Nor did he trace the development of institutions, legal, economic, religious, cultural, as does most history of civilization, although he studied all these things; he sought in institutions, as in events, the "spirit" which they revealed. In all the libraries of historical records, he sought only that which documented "in quite extraordinary degree" the fundamental conceptions of peoples.

Burckhardt agreed with Ranke that every historical power, however brutally political or economic, always had some values of civilization interwoven with the purely material motives of power and physical satisfactions. Art and literature, consequently, as much or more than official documents and statistics, were primary sources for Burckhardt in learning how men in the past had really *felt* and *thought* and *believed,* their forms of sensibility and expression. These, he thought, must remain interesting and valuable so long as men are men, whatever happens to outward civilization. And this is the most profound and delicate type of history, not to be mastered by brute determination and effort, but only by the most sensitive and sympathetic perceptivity attuned to catch the sensibilities, the hopes and loves of other men between the lines of their writing and often in their significant silences. Such an approach, moreover, has more certitude than narrative history, since the evidence for any one specific event is often questionable, but Burckhardt's history "lives in greater part on that which sources and monuments betray unintentionally, indeed unconsciously, and even through their falsifications . . . to say nothing of those matters which they deliberately set forth, defend and glorify."

The results of such research are types, generalized characteristics. Even if specific deeds were not done as described, the fact of describing them reveals certain assumptions and ideals in the narrator and his period, and such a characteristic was more instructive to Burckhardt than any specific overt act. These general types, Burckhardt suggests, are the truest "real content" of any given period, rather than the specific institutions and events accumulated by ordinary history. By his method he felt that in a brief lecture course he could better "assemble the spiritually significant content of a period embracing many centuries, than narrative presentation" could. In his courses on modern European history, for example, he would speak of "leaving aside the mere lumber of external historical facts" so as to refine history to "historical psychology." His method of constructing concrete types, "the man of the Renaissance," "the Greek of the heroic age," for example, might also have been called "historical sociology." In this method as well as in the peculiar tension between his ethics and the materials he presented, he resembles Max Weber.

This conception of history as a succession of "styles" of life, of what in a more restricted intellectualized area are called "climates of opinion," points up at once the differences between Burckhardt's conception of "great men" and the romantic conception of Carlyle, Lasaulx, Nietzsche. At first sight it would seem that individuals as such would be quite eliminated, that Burckhardt's "history of civilization would be a history without great men." "We must, of course, sacrifice their life histories," he admitted, but their fame would be undiminished when they were mentioned only as illustrations of individual aspects of an age, since they would be the chief expression and "highest witnesses of the things of the mind and spirit." Great men, in fact, are the creators of these styles of life; that is their claim to greatness. Burckhardt's studies of Greece and the Renaissance, then, are highly colored by allusions to notable individuals, like Ranke's history, but the individual as such is never allowed to distract thought from the main concern: the forces and physiognomy of the epoch. Though paying all honor to the mysterious creative achievements of great men and their incommensurability by common standards, Burckhardt always maintained enough intellectual and ethical independence to preserve his sense of their mere humanity and to save himself from any such dangerous *cult* as brought Carlyle and Nietzsche to idolatry.

In Burckhardt's history, in fact, great men played more of a role than in Ranke or Hegel. For them the protagonist of history was a Providence using men as pawns; great men could be no more than decoration on a vast process moving onward with or without them. For Burckhardt, on the contrary, great men were great only in their freedom. For him history was closest to being the history of the *free* human spirit just when and because it displayed the greatest number of original and great individuals. Such periods were fifth century Greece and the turn of the fifteenth century in modern Europe. To point up the importance of great men Burckhardt was fond of speculating on the "ifs" of history. What would have been the course of the Reformation without Luther? Of the English Revolution without Cromwell? Of the Thirty Years' War without Wallenstein? Without Richelieu? How "inevitable" the collapse of the Frankish kingdom without Charles Martel! Of these speculations one that fascinated Nietzsche was, what if Cesare Borgia had succeeded in making himself pope? Burckhardt, in short, did not grant to Ranke and Hegel the "inevitabilities" of history. History had been made by men, and it might have been otherwise.

On all the chief schemes of historical periodization, the naturalistic views either of theology, or biology, or mechanics, Burckhardt, "the anti-fanatic," always opened a sceptical barrage of questions. He was sure there were necessities in history, and that individuals are borne along on great movements beyond their control, but he doubted the adequacy of any of the explanations of these necessities and causalities which he had seen. For him, then, there was no sure growth or decline within the historical oecumene. States might come and go as the human lust to rule expressed itself under varying degrees of moral restraint and direction; man's eternal "metaphysical need," said Burckhardt, using Schopenhauer's term, man's sense of dependence, his dissatisfaction with mere empirical experience, would find various expressions in institutional religion; and the free play of human intellect and imagination in every situation, either in full liberty or in constricted areas, could shape the life of culture. But it was always the same *man,* faced with similar problems, enduring, suffering, creating under the same stars, whom Burckhardt sought and questioned. And in his history Burckhardt always looked at life from the point of view of the generation he was writing about, with its blind surmise of the power of fate and hidden causalities, its inability to learn of them except by trying them. Thus Burckhardt rescued the ethical integrity of past generations, and saw them as men, not as pawns in the hands of some general principle. He gave them more *freedom,* not metaphysically, for he too believed in destiny, but empirically, in the way in which men know it in life. Burckhardt loved the "ifs" of history, the possibilities of future development as they might have seemed to past generations, the alternatives among which men chose or which were chosen for them. His history derives more of its actuality and extraordinary vividness from this perspective *in medias res* than from the brilliance and color of his language. And by this very scepticism of teleological developments in history, Burckhardt was freer to use absolute norms in ethics and aesthetics. He tried to see every generation in its immediate relation to God, or whatever it held holy, and not measure it by some contribution to a later development which might be fortuitous. The kind of ethical relativism that justified everything that had happened as a "necessary" stage, he called "shallow and unsatisfactory." "To begin with, not all things are necessary, not by a long way, but much is accident and personal guilt, and second, the worst verdict, namely the approval of the *fait accompli,* of success, is easily substituted for what was intended to be a suspended judgment."

Burckhardt thus throws us back on faith. The faiths by which we must live are illumined by history and their implications suggested, but they are never "confirmed" by history. Unlike most of the historians of his generation, to say nothing of those who called themselves philosophers of history, Burckhardt was certain of no "developments" in the larger sense; no one could demonstrate to him that history was "going" anywhere. The past was no more "dead" to him than the present; he did not believe that we can now see "what was really happening" in Rome any more than the Romans could. We can see how it finally came out, but as to just why, or whether it was a good thing that it did come out so, we can have only hunches or fragmentary knowledge. He took far more seriously than their authors Ranke's saying that each age has its immediate meaning in the sight of eternity, and Hegel's that history is the record of freedom. He really extended to the past that observation which he made about the present, that it is *undesirable* to know the future, that men should take their positions, for example, because they are *right*, not because history argues their success. All theories of historical progress or development are simply more or less sophisticated versions of the old Christian idea of "Special Providences;" they always assume that the universe has assigned a djinn to give aid and comfort to this or that group or institution or movement. Even the supposedly atheistic mechanisms adopted by the Marxian and Anglo-French versions of Progress from classical economics and Darwinian biology prove upon analysis to be concealing such theism. Burckhardt himself had a theistic logic; he believed in a moral order, but one in which goodness is displayed as much in suffering as in success, and which carries with it an irreducible amount of apparently meaningless suffering and undeniable positive evil. He was thus more profoundly Christian than the good churchmen Hegel and Ranke.

It is true that he loved variety and contrast and color, like the artist he was, and also that he did his best as an historian to portray sympathetically views of life repugnant to himself. Joel suggests that only Kierkegaard exhibits a comparable tension of ethical and aesthetic standards, and that like Beethoven, Burckhardt might have written an *Eroica* as a paean to power and then repudiated the actuality when confronted with it. But Burckhardt's motive in all this had more dignity than a savoring of the flowers of evil; that notion is a Nietzschean caricature of him. His was the ethical demand to see life honestly and to see it whole. He permitted himself no sentimentalities, no such diplomatic euphemisms as Ranke, he looked at a thing for what it was and called it by its name.

We have already noted what Burckhardt's ethical and aesthetic standards were. The severity of his judgments on the great men of politics and the nature of the state in this volume require no further elaboration. Every great state or political structure, he declared, was built on violence and crime. "It is a general mistake to suppose that a dominion built on egoism, lies, and violence cannot be solid, as if the powers of this earth were, as a rule, built on anything else." "Satan is prince of this world," he would declare, and "evil is certainly a part of the great economy of history." Like all thinkers with a strong ethical strain, Burckhardt refused to let positive evil be dissolved in any idealistic gnosticism like Hegel's. Nietzsche thought, "Satan prince of this world—then be Satanic!" But Burckhardt drew the opposite conclusion. "Do not value this world more highly than it deserves." No earthly goals, not even patriotism, could outweigh in Burckhardt the conscience schooled by generations of Calvinistic otherworldliness. He refused in any state the claim to absolute loyalty, and held the moral imperatives supreme. He had no trace of the stupidity and hypocrisy so frequent in Anglo-Saxon moralizings in this sphere, but saw the problem of "moral man and immoral society" from the point of view of a realistic liberal, and knew all its tragedy. Alone of all German historians of the liberal epoch, he recognized the demonic element in the modern state.

Burckhardt always regarded politics from a certain distance, not the distance of the analyst of the sport of war and diplomacy, but the further distance of the moralist, or even theologian. He would have understood those sombre reflections of the statesman Max Weber that the essence and appeal of politics is the exercise of rule over other men, and that perhaps more often than not in politics one brings about just what he fears by his efforts to prevent it, as much recent history would illustrate. Burckhardt's observations on the political activities of his contemporaries revert to this theme again and again. To the tender-minded, however, such cool objectivity as this is intolerable, almost immoral. One values Montaigne in history, but not in one's own neighborhood. And yet once the shock is absorbed, we can be grateful for a humane wisdom which can make us better *men* whether in victory or defeat.

In fact when Burckhardt speaks of the value of historical insight to personal culture, his tone becomes very nearly religious. The significance of history is for him not the undeniable rise and fall of civilizations, but the enduring and permanent tradition of those values created by men in a thousand situations and carried onward in the collective memory of the race as a guide and inspiration. No one knew better than this author of the *Renaissance* that cultural values can be carried from one civilization to another, and live on in adapted form. The "soul" of the Greeks, for example, lives in *us*. And historical tradition to him meant especially the body of the aspirations of men, a summation of the intrusions of the eternal into time, as delineated in art and literature in every generation. And here, he would say, in this strange land, half reality and half the intimation of an ideal world, is our true home. Through historical knowledge we become members of this fellowship of mankind and can perhaps draw on this treasury of merits against our own imperfections. The greatest works of art and literature had a veritably sacramental character for Burckhardt, and the maintenance of this continuing tradition in general was his religion. Like Schopenhauer, he felt that historical consciousness is what distinguishes the civilized man from the barbarian, and that the race has a sacred duty to preserve the memory of its greatest trials and triumphs. It is not *all* the race, literally, but nevertheless "the continuum is extremely magnificent. The peoples around the Mediterranean and over to the Persian Gulf are really *one* animate being, active humanity, *par excellence*." Here alone common memories hold a continuous tradition, and here alone there is real change in contrast to the almost static spiritual history of the East. The continuum had been created primarily by three great formations, the Hellenization of the East after Alexander, the political and cultural unification of the whole territory under Rome, and lastly, the preservation of the whole complex of ancient culture by the Christian Church through the Middle Ages. It is because of these, Burckhardt would say, that "we know so much more and *are* so much more than all the peoples who have not known the living historical breath of the Mediterranean." Only in these events which created and established the continuum of tradition does Burckhardt retain an element of teleological interpretation. And he summoned all civilized men to the responsibility of this tradition. We do not live, he said, for ourselves alone, but for past and future as well. From this treasury of beauty and courage and idealism Burckhardt drew much of his strength for "staring into chaos" without Dilthey's despair, Nietzsche's hysteria, Ranke's callousness, or Hegel's gnosticism. He presented a view of history without forced or illusory reconciliations and called upon men in the face of this mystery to live cheerfully and responsibly on faith, in the continued consciousness of tragedy.

I

Introduction

OUR work will consist in linking up a number of historical observations and enquiries to a series of half-random trains of thought.

After a general introduction defining what we shall take as falling within the scope of our enquiry, we shall speak of the three great powers, State, Religion and Culture, dealing first with their continuous and gradual interaction, and in particular with the influence of the one variable, Culture, on the two constants. We shall then discuss the accelerated movements of the whole process of history, the theory of crises and revolutions, as also of the occasional abrupt absorption of all other movements, the general ferment of all the rest of life, the ruptures and reactions—in short, everything that might be called the theory of storms. We shall then pass on to the condensations of the historical process, the concentration of movements in those great individuals, their prime movers and chief expression, in whom the old and the new meet for a moment and take on personal form. Finally, in a section on fortune and misfortune in world history, we shall seek to safeguard our impartiality against the invasion of history by wishful thinking.

It is not our purpose to give directions for the study of

history in the scholar's sense, but merely hints for the study of the historical aspect of the various domains of the intellectual world.

We shall, further, make no attempt at system, nor lay any claim to "historical principles." On the contrary, we shall confine ourselves to observation, taking transverse sections of history in as many directions as possible. Above all, we have nothing to do with the philosophy of history.

The philosophy of history is a centaur, a contradiction in terms, for history co-ordinates, and hence is unphilosophical, while philosophy subordinates, and hence is unhistorical.

To deal first with philosophy: if it grapples direct with the great riddle of life, it stands high above history, which at best pursues that goal imperfectly and indirectly.

But then it must be a genuine philosophy, that is, a philosophy without bias, working by its own methods.

For the religious solution of the riddle belongs to a special domain and to a special inner faculty of man.

As regards the characteristics of the philosophy of history current hitherto, it followed *in the wake of history*, taking longitudinal sections. It proceeded chronologically.

In this way it sought to elicit a general scheme of world development, generally in a highly optimistic sense.

Hegel, in the introduction to his *Philosophy of History*, tells us that the only idea which is "given" in philosophy is the simple idea of reason, the idea that the world is rationally ordered: hence the history of the world is a rational process, and the conclusion yielded by world history *must* (*sic!*) be that it was the rational, inevitable march of the world spirit—all of which, far from being "given," should first have been proved. He speaks also of the "purpose of eternal wisdom," and calls his study a theodicy by virtue of its recognition of the affirmative in which the negative (in popular parlance, evil) vanishes, subjected and overcome. He develops the fundamental idea that history is the record of the process by which mind becomes aware of its own significance; according to him, there is progress towards freedom. In the East, only one man was free, in classical antiquity, only a few, while modern times have set all men free. We even find him cautiously putting forward the doctrine of perfectibility, that is, our old familiar friend called progress.

We are not, however, privy to the purposes of eternal wisdom: they are beyond our ken. This bold assumption of a world plan leads to fallacies because it starts out from false premises.

The danger which lies in wait for all chronologically arranged philosophies of history is that they must, at best, degenerate into histories of civilizations (in which improper sense the term philosophy of history may be allowed to stand); otherwise, though claiming to pursue a world plan, they are colored by preconceived ideas which the philosophers have imbibed since their infancy.

There is, however, one error which we must not impute to the philosophers alone, namely, that our time is the consummation of all time, or very nearly so, that the whole past may be regarded as fulfilled in us, while it, with us, existed for its own sake, for us, and for the future.

History from the religious standpoint has its special rights. Its great model is St. Augustine's *City of God.*

There are also other world forces which may interpret and exploit history for their own ends; socialism, for instance, with its history of the masses. We, however, shall start out from the one point accessible to us, the one eternal centre of all things—man, suffering, striving, doing, as he is and was and ever shall be. Hence our study will, in a certain sense, be pathological in kind.

The philosophers of history regard the past as a contrast to and preliminary stage of our own time as the full development. We shall study the *recurrent, constant* and *typical* as echoing in us and intelligible through us.

The philosophers, encumbered with speculations on origins, ought by rights to speak of the future. We can dispense with theories of origins, and no one can expect from us a theory of the end.

All the same, we are deeply indebted to the centaur, and it is a pleasure to come across him now and then on the fringe of the forest of historical study. Whatever his principles may have been, he has hewn some vast vistas through the forest and lent spice to history. We have only to think of Herder.

For that matter, every method is open to criticism, and none is universally valid. Every individual approaches this huge theme of contemplation in his own way, which may be his spiritual way through life: he may then shape his method as that way leads him.

Our task, therefore, being a modest one inasmuch as our train of thought lays no claim to system, we can (fortunately for us!) be thrifty. Not only may and must we leave out of account all hypothetical primitive conditions, all discussions of origins; we must also confine ourselves to the active races, and among these, to the peoples whose history yields us pictures of civilization which are sufficiently and indisputably distinct. Questions such as the influence of soil and climate, or of the movement of history from east to west, are introductory questions for the philosophers of history, but not for us, and hence quite outside our scope. The same holds good for all cosmologies, theories of race, the geography of the three ancient continents, and so on.

The study of any other branch of knowledge may begin with origins, but not that of history. After all, our historical pictures are, for the most part, pure constructions, as we shall see more particularly when we come to speak of the State. Indeed, they are mere reflections of ourselves. There is little value in conclusions drawn from people to people or from race to race. The origins we imagine we can demonstrate are in any case quite late stages. The Egyptian kingdom of Menes, for instance, points to a long and great previous history. How dark is our vision of our contemporaries and neighbors, and how clear our vision of other races, etc.!

What is absolutely necessary here is a discussion of the great general task of the historian, of what we really have to do.

Since mind, like matter, is mutable, and the changes of time bear away ceaselessly the forms which are the vesture of material as of spiritual life, the task of history as a whole is to show its twin aspects, distinct yet identical, proceeding from the fact that, firstly, the spiritual, in whatever domain it is perceived, has a historical aspect under which it appears as change, as the contingent, as a passing moment which forms part of a vast whole beyond our power to divine, and that, secondly, every event has a spiritual aspect by which it partakes of immortality.

For the spirit knows change, but not mortality.

And beside the mutable there appears the multitudinous, the mosaic of peoples and civilizations, which we see mainly as mutual contrasts or complements. We should like to conceive a vast spiritual map on the projection of an immense ethnography, embracing both the material and the spiritual world and striving to do justice to all races, peoples, manners and religions together. Nevertheless, in late, derivative times, the pulse of humanity actually or seemingly beats in unison now and then, as it did in the religious movement of the sixth century B.C., which spread from China to Ionia, and in the religious movement of Luther's time in Germany and India.

And now the central phenomenon of history. A historical power, supremely justified in its own time, comes into being; all possible forms of earthly life, political organizations, privileged classes, a religion closely knit together with secular life, great possessions, a complete code of manners, a definite conception of law, are developed out of it or associated with it, and in time come to regard themselves as props of that power, or even as the sole possible exponents of the moral forces of the epoch. But the spirit works in the depths. Such forms of life may resist change, but the breach comes, whether by revolution or gradual decay, bringing with it the breakdown of moral systems and religions, the apparent downfall of that power, or even the end of the world. But all the time the spirit is building a new house whose outward casing will, in time, suffer the same fate.

Faced with historical forces of such a kind, the contemporary individual feels utterly helpless; as a rule he falls into the bondage either of the aggressor or of the defender. Few are the contemporaries who can attain an Archimedean point outside events, and are able to "overcome in the spirit." Nor is the satisfaction of those who do so, perhaps, very great. They can hardly restrain a rueful feeling as they look back on all the rest, whom they have had to leave in bondage. Not until much later can the mind soar in perfect freedom over such a past.

What issues from this main phenomenon is historical life, rolling on in a thousand forms, complex, in all manner of disguises, bound and free, speaking now through the masses, now through individuals, now in hopeful, now in hopeless mood, setting up and destroying states, religions, civilizations, now a dark enigma to itself, moved by inchoate feelings born of imagination rather than thought, now companioned only by thought, or again filled with isolated premonitions of what is fulfilled long afterwards.

While, as men of a definite epoch, we must inevitably pay our passive tribute to historical life, we must at the same time approach it in a *spirit of contemplation.*

And now let us remember all we owe to the past as a spiritual *continuum* which forms part of our supreme spiritual heritage. Anything which can in the remotest way serve our knowledge of it must be collected, whatever toil it may cost and with all the resources at our disposal, until we are able to reconstruct whole spiritual horizons of the past. The attitude of every century to this heritage is itself knowledge, that is, a *novum* which the next generation will, in its turn, add to its own heritage as something which belongs to history, i.e. which has been superseded.

The only peoples to renounce that privilege are, firstly, barbarians, who, accepting their cake of custom as preordained, never break through it. They are barbarians because they have no history, and vice versa. They possess such things as tribal lays and a sense of the contrast between themselves and their enemies; these might be called the beginnings of history and ethnography. Yet their activity remains racial; it is not self-determined. The shackling of custom by symbols, etc., can only be loosed by knowledge of a past.

Further, Americans renounce history; peoples, that is, of unhistorical cultures who cannot quite shake off the old world. It clings to them parasitically in the shape of such things as the crests of the New York plutocracy, the most absurd forms of Calvinism; spiritualism, etc., and finally in the formation of a neo-American physical type (from a motley immigration) of uncertain character and durability.

The human mind, however, is well equipped by nature for such a task.

Mind is the power of interpreting all things in an ideal sense. It is of its nature ideal; things in their outward forms are not.

Our eye is sun-like; otherwise it could not see the sun.[1]

The mind must transmute into a possession the remembrance of its passage through the ages of the world. What was once joy and sorrow must now become knowledge, as it must in the life of the individual.

Therewith the saying *Historia vitae magistra,* (History is the guide of life) takes on a higher yet a humbler sense. We wish experience to make us, not shrewder (for next time), but wiser (for ever).

How far does this result in scepticism? True scepticism has its indisputable place in a world where beginnings and end are all unknown, and the middle in constant flux, for the amelioration offered by religion is here beyond our scope.

At certain times the world is overrun by false scepticism,

[1] Cf. Plotinus, Enneads I, 6, 9.

and that is no fault of ours; and then it will suddenly go out of fashion again. Of the true kind there can never be enough.

Our reflections, properly understood, need do no violence to the true, the good, the beautiful. The true and the good are in manifold ways colored and conditioned by time; even conscience, for instance, is conditioned by time; but devotion to the true and the good in their temporal form, especially when it involves danger and self-sacrifice, is splendid in the absolute sense. The beautiful may certainly be exalted above time and its changes, and in any case forms a world of its own. Homer and Pheidias are still beautiful, while the good and the true of their time are no longer in all respects ours.

Our study, however, is not only a right and a duty; it is also a supreme need. It is our freedom in the very awareness of universal bondage and the stream of necessities.

Yet we are often rudely reminded of the general and individual shortcomings of our capacity for knowledge, and of the other dangers by which knowledge is threatened.

Here we must first consider the relation between the two poles, knowledge and purpose. Even in history, our desire for knowledge is often baulked by a thickset hedge of purposeful interpretations which seek to pass themselves off as records. Nor can we ever rid ourselves entirely of the views of our own time and personality, and here, perhaps, is the worst enemy of knowledge. The clearest proof of it is this: as soon as history approaches our century and our worthy selves we find everything more "interesting"; in actual fact it is we who are more "interested."

Yet another enemy is the darkness of the future in the

fate of the individual and of the community; yet we keep our gaze fixed steadily on that darkness, into which the countless threads of the past stretch out, distinct and evident to our prophetic souls, yet beyond our power to follow.

If history is ever to help us to solve even an infinitesimal part of the great and grievous riddle of life, we must quit the regions of personal and temporal foreboding for a sphere in which our view is not forthwith dimmed by self. It may be that a calmer consideration from a greater distance may yield a first hint of the true nature of life on earth, and, fortunately for us, ancient history has preserved a few records in which we can closely follow growth, bloom and decay in outstanding historical events and in intellectual, political and economic conditions in every direction. The best example is Athens.

Bias, however, is particularly prone to make its appearance in the guise of patriotism, so that true knowledge finds its chief rival in our preoccupation with the history of our own country.

There are certainly things in which the history of a man's own country will always take precedence, and it is our bounden duty to occupy ourselves with it.

Yet it should always be balanced by some other great line of study, if only because it is so intimately interwoven with our desires and fears, and because the bias it imparts to our mind is always towards intentions and away from knowledge.

Its greater intelligibility is merely apparent, and arises in part from an optical illusion, namely our own much livelier readiness to understand, which may go hand in hand with great blindness.

Our imagined patriotism is often mere pride towards other peoples, and just for that reason lies outside of the path of truth. Even worse, it may be no more than a kind of partisanship within our own national circle; indeed, it often consists simply in causing pain to others. History of that kind is journalism.

Vehement proclamations of metaphysical notions, vehement definitions of good and right, condemning everything outside their limits as high treason, may subsist side by side with the most platitudinous round of life and money-making. Beyond the blind praise of our own country, another and more onerous duty is incumbent upon us as citizens, namely to educate ourselves to be comprehending human beings, for whom truth and the kinship with things of the spirit is the supreme good, and who can elicit our true duty as citizens from that knowledge, even if it were not innate in us.

In the realm of thought, it is supremely just and right that all frontiers should be swept away. There is too little of high spiritual value scattered over the earth for any epoch to say: we are utterly self-sufficient; or even: we prefer our own. That is not even the case with the products of industry, where, given equal quality, and due account being taken of customs dues and freight charges, people simply take the cheaper, or, if the price is the same, the better. In the realm of mind we must simply strive for the higher, the highest we can attain.

The truest study of our national history will be that which considers our own country in parallels and in relation to world history and its laws, as a part of a great whole, illumined by the same heavenly bodies as have shone upon other times and other peoples, threatened with the same pitfalls and one day to be engulfed in the same eternal night and perpetuated in the same great universal tradition.

Ultimately, our pursuit of true knowledge will make it necessary for us to eliminate the notions of fortune and misfortune in history. The reasons for this must be reserved for the last chapter. Our immediate task is to deal with the peculiar qualifications of our time for the study of history, which compensate these defects and dangers.

It is questionable whether we possess specifically superior historical insight.

Lasaulx[1] is even of the opinion "that so much of the life of the present-day European peoples is already past that the lines converging on *one* goal can already be discerned and even conclusions drawn for the future."

To know the future, however, is no more desirable in the life of mankind than in the life of the individual. And our astrological impatience for such knowledge is sheer folly. Whether we imagine a man, for instance, knowing in advance the day of his death and the situation it would find him in, or a people knowing in advance the century of its downfall, both pictures would bear within themselves the inevitable consequence—a confusion of all desire and endeavor. For desire and endeavor can only unfold freely when they live and act "blindly," i.e. for their own sakes and in obedience to inward impulses. After all, the future is shaped only when that happens, and if it did not happen, the future life and end of that man or that people would be different. A future known in advance is an absurdity.

Foreknowledge of the future, however, is not only un-

[1] See pp. 59 f.

desirable, it is probably beyond our power as well. The main obstacle in the way is the confusion of insight by our wishes, hopes and fears; further, our ignorance of everything which we call latent forces, physical or mental, and the incalculable factor of mental contagions, which can suddenly transform the world. Nor must we forget the acoustic illusion in which we live. For four centuries past, thought and argument, multiplied to ubiquity by the press, have drowned every voice but their own, and seem to hold even material forces in dependence on themselves. And yet it may be that those very forces are on the eve of a triumphant expansion of another kind, or that a spiritual current is at the door, ready to carry the world in the opposite direction. If that current wins the day, it will take thought and its trumpets into its service until another comes to take its place. And finally, as regards the future, we must not forget the limitations of our knowledge of racial biology from the physiological side.

On the other hand, if we turn to the knowledge of the *past*, our time is certainly better equipped than any previous one.

As regards material advantages, travelling, the learning of languages and the great development of philology have opened up all literatures to our modern world; records have become available, travel and reproduction, especially photography, have brought monuments within the reach of everybody, while we have at our disposal the vast publication of documents by governments and learned societies, which are certainly more open-minded and more bent on pure history than was the case with the Congregation of St. Maur or Muratori.

In addition, we possess advantages of a spiritual order. First the negative ones: the most important is the indifference of practically all governments to the results of any research which gives them no cause to fear for their existence; their present temporal form (monarchy) has enemies infinitely nearer and more dangerous than research can ever be. Indeed, the practice of *laisser-faire* and *laisser-dire* is now universal because far more important events from daily life must be allowed to appear in every newspaper. (And yet it might be argued that France has been too lax in this respect. The radical branch of French historiography has had a great influence on subsequent events).

Further, we must refer to the impotence of existing religions and creeds in face of any discussion of their present situation or their past. A vast amount of research has been expended on those epochs, peoples and conditions in which the original ideas took shape which helped to mould or actually created religions. A great comparative mythology and history of religions and dogmas could not, in the long run, be suppressed.

And now our positive advantages. The enormous changes which have taken place since the end of the eighteenth century are of such a nature that they imperatively demand the consideration and investigation of what went before and has come after, quite apart from any question of justification or indictment.

A period so agitated as these eighty-three years of a revolutionary epoch must, if it is not to lose its reason altogether, create some counterpoise of the kind.

Only the study of the past can provide us with a standard by which to measure the rapidity and strength of the particular movement in which we live.

Further, the spectacle of the French Revolution, and the discovery of its origins in what went before, has opened men's eyes not only to material, but more especially to spiritual causes and their visible transformation into material effects. The whole of history, wherever sources are at all copious, might teach the same lesson, but it emerges most directly and distinctly from that time. Hence it is an advantage for historical study in our own day that pragmatism is conceived in a much higher and wider sense than it used to be. History has become infinitely more interesting in principle and presentation.

Further, the exchange of literatures and the cosmopolitan intercourse of the nineteenth century have multiplied to infinity the number of possible standpoints: instead of a single branch of knowledge confined to the curiosities of remote times and places, we have the demand for a total picture of mankind.

Finally, we must not forget the great currents in modern philosophy, significant in themselves and throughout associated with historical views.

Thus the studies of the nineteenth century have been able to take on a universality they never had before.

What, then, is the task before us, in view of the vastness of the study of history, which embraces the whole visible and spiritual world and goes far beyond the bounds of any former notion of "history"?

Not a thousand human lives, though gifted with supreme talent and working with supreme energy, could cope with it fully.

For the most extreme specialization is actually the order of the day, down to monographs on the merest minutiae. In such things, even the most well-meaning of men will sometimes lose all sense of proportion, forgetting how minute a fraction of his life on earth a reader (unless he has a definite and personal interest in the subject) can devote to work of that kind. Anyone setting out to write a monograph should have the *Agricola* of Tacitus always at hand, and say: the longer-winded, the shorter-lived.

The merest text-book on a single period or a single branch of historical knowledge opens up a vista into an infinity of established facts. A desperate prospect at the beginning of the study of history!

We need not, however, trouble about the student whose purpose it is to devote his whole life to that study, or even to the writing of history. Our aim is not to train historians, let alone universal historians. Our standard will be the capacity which any academically trained mind should develop up to a certain point.

It has already been said that our theme is not so much the study of history as the study of the historical.

Any specialised knowledge of facts possesses, in addition to its value as knowledge or thought in a particular field, a universal or historical value, in that it illuminates one phase of the changeful spirit of man, yet, placed in the right connection, it testifies at the same time to the continuity and immortality of that spirit.

Beside the direct exploitation of knowledge for one's own special subject, there is another, which must be referred to here.

An essential condition of scholarship is a definite branch of study: theology, jurisprudence, or whatever it may be, must be taken up and carried through to its academic conclusion, and that not only for private, professional reasons, but in order to acquire the habit of steady work, to learn respect for all branches of a particular subject, to fortify the seriousness necessary to learning.

Side by side with it, however, we must continue those

preliminary studies which give access to all that comes later, in particular the various world literatures, i.e. the two classical languages and, if possible, two modern ones. We can never know too many languages. And however much or little we may have known of them, we should never quite let them lapse. All honor to good translations, but none can replace the original expression, and the original language, in word and phrase, is historical evidence of the first rank.

Further, we should avoid anything which exists simply as a *pastime,* for time should be welcomed and turned to account, and secondly we should maintain an attitude of reserve towards the present-day devastation of the mind by newspapers and novels.

We are only concerned here with such minds and hearts as cannot fall victim to common boredom, which can carry through a train of thought, and have imagination enough to be able to do without the concrete imaginings of others or, if they do turn to them, are not enslaved, but can keep their own integrity.

In any case, we should be capable from time to time of turning completely away from purpose to knowledge simply because it is knowledge. In particular, we should be able to contemplate the process of history even when it is not concerned with our own well or ill being, directly or indirectly. But even when it is, we should be able to behold it with detachment.

Further, intellectual work must not aim at pure enjoyment.

All genuine records are at first tedious, because and in so far as they are alien. They set forth the views and interests of their time *for their time,* and come no step to meet us. But the shams of today are addressed to us, and are therefore made amusing and intelligible, as faked antiques generally are. This is especially true of the historical novel, which so many people read as if it were history, slightly rearranged but true in essence.

For the ordinary half-educated man, all poetry (except political verse), and, in the literature of the past, even the greatest creations of humor (Aristophanes, Rabelais, Don Quixote, etc.) are incomprehensible and tedious because none of all this literature was written specifically for him, as present-day novels are.

Yet, even to the scholar and thinker, the past, in its own utterance, is at first always alien, and its acquisition arduous.

A complete study of the sources of any important subject according to the laws of scholarship is an enterprise which demands the whole of a man.

For instance, the history of one single theological or philosophical doctrine would require years for itself alone, while theology as a whole, even excluding the ecclesiastical and constitutional history of the Church, and conceived simply as the history of dogma and religion, stands revealed in all its vastness when we think of all the parties, councils, bulls, scholiasts, heretics, homilists and philosophers of religion. It is true that, if we go deeper into the matter, we shall find them copying each other. We can, moreover, recognize their methods and guess the whole from a part, yet in doing so we run the risk of overlooking the crucial half-page buried in the welter, unless a happy prescience directs our eye upon it, seemingly by chance.

There is a further danger. The man who walks one road of limited interest too long may fall by the wayside. Buckle's study of the Scottish divines of the seventeenth century caused him his paralysis of the brain.

This is quite peculiarly the case with the polyhistorians, who, in the present-day acceptance of the term, ought really to study everything. For everything is source—not only the historians, but the whole realm of literature and monuments; indeed, for the remotest epochs, the latter are the only source. Everything which has come down to us, in whatever form, is in some way connected with the mind of man and its changes, and is their record and expression.

For our purpose, however, we have only to deal with the reading of selected sources, but *as* sources. The theologian, the lawyer, the philologist should master individual writings of early epochs, not only as contributions to his subject, but also for their historical value, as testifying to single, definite phases in the development of the human mind.

For the man determined really to learn, that is, to become rich in mind, a single source, happily chosen, can do duty, to a certain extent, for the whole multitude, since, by a simple function of his brain, he can discern and feel the general in the particular.

If the beginner also takes the general for the particular, or the common for the specific, there is no great harm done. As he goes on, such errors will correct themselves, and the consultation of a single second source, a comparison of likenesses and divergences, will lead him to conclusions more fertile than twenty folios would have yielded.

But he must *want* to seek and find, and *bisogna saper leggere* (must know how to read). He must believe that every dust-heap contains jewels of knowledge, whether of general value or of personal value to us. A single line from an otherwise worthless author may kindle a light to guide all our further steps.

Now a source, as compared with a treatise, has its eternal advantages.

First and foremost, it presents the fact pure, so that *we* must see what conclusions are to be drawn from it, while the treatise anticipates that labor and presents the fact digested, i.e. placed in an alien, and often erroneous setting.

Further, the source gives the fact in a form not far removed from its origin or author, and indeed is often that author's work. Its difficulty lies in its language, but so do its stimulus and a great part of the value which makes it superior to any treatise. Here again we must bear in mind the importance of original languages and the knowledge of them as against the use of translations.

Further, our mind can only enter into a real, chemical combination, in the full sense of the word, with the original source; we must, however, note that the word "original" is here used in a relative sense, since, when the original source is lost, it can be replaced by one at second or third remove.

Sources, however, especially such as come from the hands of great men, are inexhaustible, and everyone must re-read the works which have been exploited a thousand times, because they present a peculiar aspect, not only to every reader and every century, but also to every time of life. It may be, for instance, that there is in Thucydides a fact of capital importance which somebody will note in a hundred years' time.

What changes most of all is the picture created in us by the art and poetry of the past. Sophocles may affect those now entering the world in a way totally different from his effect on us. Nor is that a misfortune. It is simply a result of perpetually living intercourse.

But beyond the labor we expend on sources the prize beckons in those great moments and fateful hours when, from things we have imagined long familiar, a sudden intuition dawns.

Now comes a difficult question. What is the non-historian to note and extract from selected sources?

As regards the actual facts they contain, countless textbooks have long since turned them to account. If he begins to collect those facts, he will pile up notes which he will, in all probability, never look at again. And the reader has not yet a specific goal.

He may, however, discover one if he reads a considerable way into his author without making notes; he should then re-read from the beginning, making notes relevant to that one goal, but should at the same time make a second series of notes on anything which strikes him, if only the titles of chapters and the numbers of pages, with a word or two on their contents.

As work progresses, a second and third goal may then emerge: parallels and contrasts with other sources will come to light, and so on.

Of course "such maxims propagate pure *amateurism*, which takes its pleasure in what is, for others, a commendable ordeal."

The word "amateur" owes its evil reputation to the arts. An artist must be a master or nothing, and must dedicate his life to his art, for the arts, of their very nature, demand perfection.

In learning, on the other hand, a man can only be a master in one particular field, namely as a specialist, and in some field he *should* be a specialist. But if he is not to forfeit his capacity for taking a general view, or even his respect for general views, he should be an amateur at as many points as possible, privately at any rate, for the increase of his own knowledge and the enrichment of his possible standpoints. Otherwise he will remain ignorant in any field lying outside his own specialty and perhaps, as a man, a barbarian.

But the amateur, because he loves things, may, in the course of his life, find points at which to dig deep.

Finally, we must say a word or two here about our relationship to science and mathematics, the only disinterested comrades we have. For theology and law are out to master us, or at any rate to use us as an arsenal, while philosophy, striving to stand above all, borrows from all.

We will not enquire whether the study of mathematics and science excludes from the outset any historical consideration. In any case, the history of ideas should not allow itself to be shut out of those schools.

One of the most tremendous events in the history of the mind of man was the rise of mathematics. We wonder whether number or line or surface first detached itself from things. And how was the necessary consensus on the subject formed in the various peoples? At what moment did this crystallization take place?

And science—when and where did it first relieve the mind of the fear of nature and its worship, from natural magic? When and where did it first become anything like a free goal of the mind?

Science too has seen its changes, its times of bondage and its systematic restriction and perilous sanctification within imposed limits—among priests.

What we have most to deplore is the impossibility of a history of the development of thought in Egypt; it could at best be written hypothetically—perhaps in the form of a novel.

With the Greeks, science and the age of freedom dawn. Yet they did relatively little for science, since all their energy went into the State, speculative thought and art in its plastic expression.

After the Alexandrine, Roman and Byzantine-Arab epoch there follow the Western Middle Ages, and the bondage of science to scholasticism, which supported only what was recognized.

Since the sixteenth century, however, science has been one of the paramount criteria of the genius of an age. Those who occasionally check its advance are the academicians and professors.

The predominance and popularization of science in the nineteenth century is a fact which makes us wonder, in spite of ourselves, what will be its outcome, and in what way it is involved with the fate of our time.

And now there is a friendship between science and history, not only because, as we have already seen, science demands nothing from history, but also because these two branches of learning are alone capable of a detached, disinterested participation in the life of things.

Yet history is not the same thing as nature, and it creates, brings to birth and abandons to decay in a different way.

Nature displays supreme perfection in the species as a whole and a supreme indifference towards the individual. It even suffers hostile, combative organisms which, almost equal in organic perfection, exterminate each other, struggle for existence between themselves. Even human races in a state of nature come in here; their existence may have resembled that of animal states.

History, on the other hand, is the breach with nature caused by the awakening of consciousness. Nevertheless, there are enough vestiges of the original condition for us to be able to denote man as a beast of prey. High refinement in social life and the State exists side by side with a total absence of safeguards for individual life and the perpetual urge to enslave others in order to avoid being enslaved by them.

In nature, there exist *regnum, genus, species;* in history, the race, the family, the group. By a primordial instinct, nature creates in consistently organic fashion with an infinite variety of species and a great similarity of individuals. In history, the variety (within the one species *homo,* of course) is far from being so great. There are no clear lines of demarcation, but individuals feel the incentive inequality—inciting to development.

While nature works on a few primeval models (vertebrates and invertebrates, phanerogams and cryptogams), in the people, the body social is not so much a type as a gradual product. It is the peculiar spirit of the people in its gradual development.

Every species in nature possesses complete what it needs for its life; if this were not so, the species could not go on living and reproducing itself. Every people is incomplete and strives for completion, and the higher it stands, the more it strives.

In nature, the process by which the species comes into being is obscure; its basis may be the aggregation of experiences which are added to the structure, though much more slowly and primevally. The process by which a people is born and modified is demonstrably based partly on its abilities, and also partly on the accumulation of experience, but since conscious mind is here at work, the process is much more rapid than in nature, and the effect of the contrasts and affinities encountered by the people is evident.

In nature, individuals, particularly among the highest species of animals, mean nothing to other individuals except perhaps as stronger enemies or friends. The world of man is constantly acted upon by exceptional individuals.

In nature, the species remains relatively constant: hybrids die out or are sterile from the outset. Historical life teems with hybrids. It is as if they were an essential element of fecundation for great mental processes. The essence of history is change.

In nature, annihilation only comes about by the action of external causes, catastrophes of nature or climate, the overrunning of weaker species by bolder, of nobler by baser. In history, the way of annihilation is invariably prepared by inward degeneration, by decrease of life. Only then can a shock from outside put an end to the whole.

II

The Three Powers

Our theme is the State, Religion and Culture in their mutual bearings. We are fully aware of the arbitrariness of the division into three powers. It is as if we were to remove a number of figures from a picture, leaving the rest where it was. The division, however, is a mere device to enable us to cover the ground. Indeed, any historical study separating history into subjects *must* proceed in this way (research by subjects always regarding its own subject as quintessential).

The three powers are supremely heterogeneous to each other and cannot be co-ordinated, and even if we were to co-ordinate the two constants, State and Religion, Culture would still be something essentially different.

The State and Religion, the expressions of political and metaphysical need, may claim authority at least over their particular peoples, and indeed over the world.

For our special purpose, however, Culture, which meets material and spiritual need in the narrower sense, is the sum of all that has *spontaneously* arisen for the advancement of material life and as an expression of spiritual and moral life—all social intercourse, technologies, arts, literatures and sciences. It is the realm of the variable, free, not necessarily universal, of all that cannot lay claim to compulsive authority.

A question of priority might arise among the three, but it is idle. We can dispense with it, as with any speculations on origins.

Our principal theme will consist in a brief characterization of all three, followed by a discussion of their reciprocal influences.

At times they seem to function alternately. There are primarily political and primarily religious epochs, and finally epochs which seem to live for the great purposes of culture.

Further, their relation to each other as determined and determinant is subject to rapid alternation. Appearances are often so deceptive that we long remain in error as to which is the active and which the passive factor.

Indeed, during epochs of high civilization, all three powers exist simultaneously at all stages of mutual interaction, especially when the cultural heritage of such epochs is a stratification of many ages.

THE STATE

All our efforts to reconstruct the beginnings and origin of the State are vain. Hence, unlike the philosophers of history, we are under no necessity to rack our brains over such questions. Yet in order to have light enough to see the abyss at our feet, we must ask the question—how does a people become a people, and how does it become a State? What are its birth-throes? At what point of its growth can we begin to call it a State?

The hypothesis of the State as founded upon an antecedent contract is absurd. Rousseau makes use of it merely as an ideal, an expedient. His purpose is not to show what happened, but what, according to him, should happen. No State has ever yet been created by a genuine contract, i.e. a contract freely entered into by all parties (*inter volentes*); for cessions and settlements like those between the trembling Romans and triumphant Teutons are no genuine contracts. Hence no State will come into being in that way in the future. And if ever one did, it would be a feeble thing, since men could quibble for ever over its principles.

Tradition, which draws no distinction between the People and the State, is prone to dwell on the idea of racial origin. Eponymous heroes and partly eponymous State-builders are current among the people as mythical representatives of its unity, or it possesses some ancient lore, either of a primitive plurality (the Egyptian nomes), or of a primitive unity which later fell to pieces (the Tower of Babel). But all such lore is brief and mythical.

What kind of light is thrown on the beginnings of the State by national character? Such evidence is in any case very relative, for only an indeterminable part of that character is given by nature. The rest is accumulated past, the results of experience, and thus first arose through the subsequent vicissitudes of State and people.

Often the physiognomy of a people is completely at variance with its political fate owing to a forced change of habitat or as the result of violence suffered at a late stage of its history.

Further, it is true that a State may be powerful in proportion as it corresponds homogeneously to one race. Such a correspondence is, however, rare, and as a rule the State is equated with a dominant ingredient, a particular region, a particular tribe, a particular social stratum.

Or can we assume that the need of justice would of itself have created the State? That, alas! would have taken time—until violence had so far purged itself that, for its own advantage, and in order to enjoy its own in peace, it consented to give others security for despair. We cannot share even that invitingly optimistic view according to which society came into being first, and the State arose as its protector, its negative aspect, its warden and defender, the State and criminal law springing from the same root. Human nature is not like that.

What were the first forms of the State, imposed by necessity? That is a thing we should like to know, for instance, in the case of the lake-dwellers. To draw deductions from negroes and Red Indians is of as little use as to draw deductions from negro religions to throw light on religion. The white and yellow races must have gone different ways from the beginning, and the black races can cast no light of authority on that beginning.

Further, we see another, essentially different kind of State in the insect societies, which are far more perfect than the human State, but are not free. The individual ant functions only as part of the ant State, which must be regarded as a single body. Its life as a whole is disproportionately superior to that of the individual—a life in many atoms. But even the higher animals live only in families, or at most in packs. The human State alone is a society, that is, a union in some way free, based on conscious reciprocity.

Thus there are only two probable theories: (*a*) Force always comes first. We need never be at a loss as to its origin, since it is spontaneously engendered by the inequality of human gifts. In many cases, the State may have been nothing more than its reduction to a system. (*b*) Or we feel that an extremely violent process, particularly of fusion, must have taken place. A flash of lightning fuses several elements into one new alloy—perhaps two stronger ones with one weaker, or vice versa. In this way, the three Dorian races and the three Gothic tribes may have fused for the purpose or on the occasion of a conquest. An example of a terrible power fusing with an existing people and then becoming strong can be seen in the Normans in Lower Italy.

An echo of the terrible convulsions which accompanied the birth of the State, of what it *cost*, can be heard in the enormous and absolute primacy it has at all times enjoyed.

We see this primacy as an established, indisputable fact, while it is assuredly to some extent veiled history, and the same holds good of many things, for a great mass of tradition is handed on unexpressed, by mere procreation, from generation to generation. We can no longer clearly distinguish such things.

Where the convulsion was a conquest, the primordial principle of the State, its outlook, its task and even its emotional significance was the enslavement of the conquered.[1]

In the earliest pictures of the State, the oldest records are not necessarily the most primitive. Desert peoples, even of superior race, whose individual members are at once assimilated to modern life when they enter a different environment, have preserved up to the present day a very primitive organization, namely the patriarchal State, while even the oldest examples of States of which we have knowledge (India before the Ganges epoch, the Jews, the Egyptians) reflect a highly derivative form which has left the conquest of nature far, i.e. thousands of years, behind it. All that we know of them seems to have already passed through thought and to have reached us in a later version, and in the sacred laws of these peoples (Manu, Moses, Zendavesta) many things are unquestionably written which ought to be rules of life but are no longer observed. Thus while the Egypt of Menes (*circa* 4000 B.C.) only began when patriarchal conditions were long since superseded, close beside it, in Arabia, they have survived till our dav

The classical world confined itself to the discussion of

[1] Cf. the *Skolion* of Hybreas (*Oxford Book of Greek Verse in Translation*, p. 246).

the three Aristotelian constitutions and their degenerate subsidiary forms.[1] The real range of variation, however, is much vaster, and cannot be reduced to that classification. Quite a peculiar phenomenon, for instance, is to be seen in the medieval monarchy, since it (1) was strictly hereditary, succumbing but rarely to changes of dynasty and usurpations; (2) was a personal privilege and possession, and the negation of popular sovereignty, so that the people appears in no sense as the source of power; (3) bestowed privileges upon individuals the observation of which could be extorted by feuds and the refusal of taxes and military service; (4) commanded a very restricted sphere of activity, being surrounded by the Church, universities, knightly orders, cities and corporations, all of which were republics protected by privileges and statutes; (5) possessed an inextinguishable royal privilege which could not lapse and did not expire even in times of deepest abasement. Other points which might be discussed here would be world monarchies, "United States", the various forms of conquest, i.e. genuine conquest, with the eviction or assimilation of the conquered, and false conquest, leading only to superficial dominion; further, colonial possessions and the difference between mere trade dominion and genuine colonial empire, and finally the law of colonial emancipation.

States vary enormously in their original disposition and subsequent experiences, and in the way they are acted upon by Culture and Religion: hence we shall have to deal with these points when we come to speak of the two latter powers. Here we need only refer to the difference

[1] For their alleged rotation, see Lasaulx, *Neuer Versuch einer alten auf die Wahrheit der Tatsachen gegründeten Philosophie der Geschichte,* p. 105 f. Cf. Aristotle, *Pol.,* p. 1279*a.*

between the great and the small State and the relation of each to its inner nature.

The great State exists in history for the achievement of great external aims, for the maintenance and protection of certain cultures which would founder without it, for the advancement of passive sections of the population which, left to themselves as small States, would atrophy, and for the undisturbed development of great collective forces.

The small State exists so that there may be a spot on earth where the largest possible proportion of the inhabitants are citizens in the fullest sense of the word, a goal which the Greek City State more nearly attained in its heyday, in spite of the slavery system, than all the republics of today. Small monarchies should approximate to that condition as nearly as possible. Small tyrannies, like those of classical antiquity and the Italian Renaissance, are the most insecure forms of the State and always tend to become absorbed in a bigger whole, for the small State possesses nothing but real, actual freedom, an ideal possession which fully balances the huge advantages of the big State, even its power. And any decline into despotism cuts the ground from under its feet, even should it be the despotism from below, for all its clamor.

Whatever the origin of a State may have been ("The political epitome of a people"), it will only prove its viability if force is transformed into strength.[1]

Every power, of course, as long as its period of growth lasts, aims at completion and perfection within and without, and has no regard for the rights of the weaker.

Here peoples and dynasties proceed in exactly the same fashion, only that in the former, the decisive factor is

[1] We might again refer here to the Normans in Lower Italy.

rather the appetite of the masses, in the latter, reasons of State. It is not mere lust of conquest, but so-called necessity: the Carolingian Empire may serve as an example.

Apart from its internal activity, such as the abolition of all inherited special rights and the extension of its concept of power to one and all, ostensibly in the public interest and even to the ultima ratio, *l'état c'est moi,* the behavior of power towards the outside world can be seen in its most naïve form in the ancient world potentates, who conquered and enslaved and plundered and pillaged far and wide, who, followed by their booty and their slaves, entered Thebes or Nineveh in triumph and were regarded by the people as the beloved of God—till a new and yet more powerful potentate arose. In latter-day Europe, on the other hand, we see periods of prolonged peace alternating with periods of territorial crisis due to the upset at some place or other of the Balance of Power (which has never existed).

Now the truth is—we have only to think of Louis XIV, Napoleon and the revolutionary popular governments—that power is in itself evil. Utterly regardless of all religion, the privilege of egoism, which is denied to the individual, is bestowed on the State. Weaker neighbors are subjected and annexed, or in some way deprived of their independence, not in order to forestall hostilities on their part, for that hardly costs a thought, but to prevent another taking them and turning them to his own political ends. And once on that road, there is no stopping. There is an excuse for everything, since "mere peaceableness would have led nowhere and we should have been devoured by other ruffians," and "the others do the same."

The next step is that such things are done in advance, without any real motive, on the principle: "If we take it in time, we shall avert the danger of war in the future." Ultimately a permanent appetite for territorial "rounding-off" is created, which devours whatever happens to lie convenient and can be laid hands on, in particular "indispensable access to the sea"; in which process the aggressor takes advantage of all the weakness, all the internal disorders and external enemies of the victim. The lure of joining up small territories becomes irresistible, especially if it means a quadrupling of value by a mere doubling of area. It may even be that the peoples concerned, particularly if they belong to small States without freedom, are desirous of union, since it implies the removal of customs barriers, and the expansion of their industrial sphere—quite apart from the factitious grievances of which we hear so much to-day.

Ill deeds should, as far as possible, be committed naïvely, for the aesthetic effect of legal justifications and recriminations on both sides is deplorable. Men are ashamed of the power they have craved to possess and spared no crime to obtain; the name of law is still numinous and nobody would wish to abolish its influence on mankind. In this way men arrive at the kind of sophistry indulged in by Frederick II of Prussia in the First Silesian War, and the upshot of the whole process is the beautiful theory of "unjustified existences."

The subsequent amalgamation of the spoils which is actually achieved constitutes no moral exoneration of the robber. No good results can exculpate an evil past.

But men must come to terms even with the greatest horrors, once they have happened; they must rally such sound strength as is left in them, and go on building.

The State founded on sheer crime is compelled in the course of time to develop a kind of justice and morality, since those of its citizens who are just and moral gradually get the upper hand.

Ultimately, there is a great, indirect vindication of the evil-doer, namely that, without his foreknowledge, great historical purposes lying in the remote future were furthered by his deeds.

This is, in particular, the argument of those who come later in time, who know that they owe their material benefits to all that came of the crime. But the counter-questions arise: "What do we know about purposes? And if they exist, could they not be accomplished in other ways? And are we to take no account of the blow dealt to morality by any successful crime?"

One thing, however, is admitted by most people—the sovereign right of civilization to conquer and subdue barbarism, which must then abandon its bloody, internecine warfare and abhorrent customs and bow to the moral principles of the civilized State. Above all, the barbarians must be deprived of their dangerousness, of the potential power of aggression. It is, however, open to question whether civilization really penetrates below the surface of barbarism and what good can come of the posterity of conquering peoples and conquered barbarians, especially when they are of different race, whether it is not better for them to retire and die out (as in America), and whether the civilized human being flourishes everywhere on the alien soil. In any case, the methods by which barbarism is subdued should not rival those previously in use among the barbarians themselves.

As regards the internal policy of the State, it was not engendered by the abdication of the egoisms of its individual members. It *is* that abdication, it *is* their reduction to a common denominator, in order that as many interests and egoisms as possible may find permanent satisfaction in it and, in the end, completely fuse their existence with its own.

Its supreme achievement is to bring to birth a sense of duty among the better citizens—that is, patriotism, which, in its two stages, namely that of the primitive and that of the derivative cultures, makes its appearance among the people almost spontaneously as a high racial virtue. It is nourished in part by the hatred for all who are not ourselves, but, in trained minds, appears as a need for devotion to a general goal, a way of rising above the self-seeking of the individual and the family, in so far as this need is not provided for by religion and society.

It is a degeneration, it is philosophic and bureaucratic arrogance, for the State to attempt to fulfil moral purposes directly, for only society can and may do that.

The State is certainly the "standard of the just and good" [1] which must be set up somewhere; it is no more than that. "The realization of ethical values on earth" by the State would simply be brought to grief again and again by the spiritual inadequacy of human nature in general, and even of the best of humanity in particular. The forum of morality lies quite outside the State, and we may even wonder that it can do as much as to uphold conventional justice. The State will be most likely to remain healthy when it is aware of its own nature (and maybe of its essential origin) as an expedient.

The benefit conferred by the State consists in its being

[1] As regards the programmes of power dictated to the State by society, and indeed the whole present ferment in the idea of the State under the influence of Culture, see the chapter on the State as determined by Culture.

the guardian of the law. The separate individual is subject to laws and judges armed with compulsive powers, who safeguard not only the private obligations incurred between individuals, but also general necessities, and that far less by the actual exercise of power than by the wholesome fear of it. The security necessary to life consists in the belief that this will continue in the future, i.e. that it will no longer be necessary for men within the State, as long as it exists, to take up arms against each other. Every man knows that, far from increasing his possessions or power by force, the use of force only precipitates his ruin.

Further, it is the business of the State to prevent the various conceptions of civil life from coming to blows. It has to stand above parties, in spite of the fact that every party strives to get the State into its power and to proclaim itself the community.

Finally, in late, mixed forms of the State, in which different and even hostile religions or religious ideas find a home (and in this sense there is religious toleration in all civilized States), the State at any rate sees to it that not only the various egoisms but also the various metaphysics shall carry on no blood-feuds (a thing that would inevitably happen even today without the State, for the fanatics would begin and the others follow suit).

RELIGION

Religions are the expression of human nature's eternal and indestructible metaphysical need.

Their greatness is that they represent the whole supersensual complement of man, everything he cannot give to himself. At the same time, they are the reflection of whole peoples and epochs of civilization in a great "other," or the impress and contour which those peoples and epochs project upon eternity.

That impress and contour, however, though it regards itself as stable and perdurable, is subject to change, partial or whole, gradual or sudden.

We cannot establish a comparison of greatness between the two processes—the rise of a State and the rise of a religion.

A dual feeling, however, overcomes the mind when it contemplates religion; as it considers, compares and analyses, it is aware of greatness, it receives the vast image of a thing which was perhaps individual in its origin, and became, in its expansion, worldwide, universal, age-old. Here we have the supreme matter in which to study the supremacy of a general idea over countless minds, a supremacy so complete as to beget an utter contempt of all earthly things, whether for themselves or others, i.e. to the point of suicide by asceticism and martyrdom sought with joy, but also imposed on others. The metaphysical temper and destinies of nations vary, of course, extremely. We may at once exclude here the religions of lesser races, those of the negro peoples, etc., of the savages and semi-savages. The primordial elements of the spiritual life can be deduced from them even less than the origins of the State from the negro State. For such peoples are from the outset a prey to everlasting fear; their religions do not even give us a standard for the first signs of the birth of the spirit, because among them the spirit is destined never to come to spontaneous birth.

Even among more highly civilized peoples, however, the content of religion reveals a whole gradation from the worship of imperial gods, imposed upon conquered peoples without any spiritual intent, from orgiastic and bacchantic rites and similar forms of possession by the god to the purest worship of God and men's sense of themselves as children of a heavenly Father.

The relationship of religions to morality varies just as widely. A religion gives us no standard by which to assess the moral nature of the peoples confessing it. Among the Greeks, for instance, morality was practically independent of religion and in all probability more closely connected with the ideal of the State.

Nor must we regard people who have never "advanced" beyond a national religion as possessing a meaner spiritual or moral endowment. It was their fate that their religion became crystallized at a very undeveloped stage of their history, and that later no headway could be made against it. For the moment of crystallization is of momentous importance in religion as in the State, and is independent of the will or progress of the people.[1]

As regards the rise of religion, our minds seem to be incapable of imagining the birth of the spirit at all, for we are latecomers and the heirs of time. Renan contests the *primus in orbe deos fecit timor*[2] by pointing out that, if religion had been originally born of the calculation of fear, man would not be religious at his supreme moments; nor were religions invented by the poor in spirit and the weak, as the Italian sophists of the sixteenth century taught, otherwise the noblest natures would not be the most religious. On the contrary, he says, religion is a creation of the normal human being. That is true, yet there are plenty of religions of fear. Among primitive peoples we find a cult, compounded of worship and dread, of natural objects, natural powers and natural phenomena; then come ancestor-worship and the cult of fetishes, in which men project their feeling of dependence into a single object belonging to them personally. In part these religions consist of the propitiation of the dread denizens of childish nightmares, and in part of the wonder awakened by the heavenly bodies and the elements. Among nations still ignorant of writing, they may be the only witness to the spirit.

There is a conjecture more probable than that of an original awareness of God, namely that of an ancient, unconscious metaphysical need. A great or terrible moment, or a man endowed with the qualities of the founder of a religion, brings that need to consciousness. The thing that

[1] Certain peoples have, it is true, been able to "put their religious ideas back into the crucible" (Quinet): e.g. in very early times the Hindus and Zends, who officially revolutionized their quondam (common) polytheism into Brahminism and dualism.

[2] "Fear first created gods on earth." Statius, *Thebais,* 3, 661.

was already obscurely alive among the more gifted of the tribe finds expression. The process may be repeated when peoples mingle or separate.

The decisive factor is most probably the feeling of dependence on a greater power, the dread which overcomes men even in the full consciousness of their own strength and brutality.

Since the causes of fear, and hence the occasions for propitiation of the terror, are many, there is the strongest presumption that polytheism came first, and that the unity of the primitive awareness of God is nothing but a dream.

The original feeling of dread may have been splendid, for its object was infinity; the beginning of religion, on the other hand, admitted a limitation, a reduction, a definition, which may have been experienced as a great benefit. It may be that men suddenly seemed to know where they were. Fear may then have sought a new home in the service of fetishes and demons.

How far are religions *founded?* One thing is certain, that they came into being as the sudden creation of individual men or moments. These are the moments of crystallization and radiation.[1] Part of humanity is moved to join because the founder or the event has touched to the quick the metaphysical need felt by the most vital spirits; the rank and file follow, because they cannot resist, and because the definite has royal rights over the vague, uncertain and anarchistic. It is true that those masses are later prone to cling most tenaciously to the external form and rites of the religion concerned, and maintain them (for the heart of any religion is a sealed book to them)

[1] A distinct sign of a unique foundation, incomprehensible in any other circumstances, is, for instance, the rise of the twelve zodiacal gods.

until they are subjected by some stronger power which has acquired a carapace for them to cling to, whereupon they cling to that.

We can hardly imagine that religions came into being gradually, otherwise they would not display the triumphant brilliance of their bloom, which is the reflection of a great, unique moment. Those known to us name their founder or reformer (that is, their guide at moments of great crisis), and even the partially natural and polytheistic religions may have simply arisen from the fusion of earlier cults which had been founded at definite moments. Religions know transformations and fusions, some sudden, some gradual, but no gradual coming to birth.

Sometimes their rise is involved with that of a State; religion may even found the State (Temple States). Whether it enters the service of the State at a later stage, and what is its relationship to the State in other respects, are questions which will be discussed later.

What peoples and stages of civilization are predisposed to the rise of religion? All peoples and all ages feel the metaphysical need, and all cling to a religion once adopted.

If a higher religion is to take firm root, however, peoples absorbed in life and work in this world offer less favorable ground than contemplative peoples, whose livelihood requires less labor and whose culture is therefore generalized, and free of our present-day division into educated and uneducated. So with peoples of great sobriety and nervous sensitivity, in whom a sensitive, precise mind can predominate without prejudice to miracles, to the supernatural, to visions. Among such peoples, a lengthy preparation, a religious gestation can take place. The secret of Renan's great importance is that he knew such conditions at first hand, and based his history of primitive Christianity on them.

Peoples whose life and work are centred in this world will, of course, accept religion from the hands of ecstatic and contemplative peoples and gradually infuse it with their spirit. Thus, for instance, the Reformation in England and Holland, which produced no original reformer, yet took the lead in Protestantism. Even the Greeks and the Romans, as peoples of secular life, were unable, or at least no more able than the Hindus, to revolutionize their religions from within, but had to turn to the Jews (Christians) for that revolution.

It is difficult for us to grasp the great religious crises; hence our everlasting disputes over speculative ideas in religion. To some they will always appear primordial, to others a later importation, and the two will never come to terms. The former will always see in them vestiges of a primitive wisdom, or even of a brighter youth of the human race, the latter, a laborious acquisition.

But although we can hardly imagine the state of exaltation which accompanies the birth of a religion, and more especially the absolute absence of the critical spirit at such times and in such peoples, that state, however short-lived it may be, is of decisive importance for the whole future. It imparts to the religions then founded their temper and their myths—indeed, in some cases, even their rites and their hierarchy.

The later "institutions" of a religion are isolated vestiges or echoes of the state of things prevailing at their birth, e.g. the monasteries were the vestiges of the original communal life of the primitive community.

Further, the founders and witnesses of the birth of a religion sometimes form a permanent college which may fulfil the need of a corporation to perform the sacred rites, and gradually acquires the sole right of sacrifice, excommunication and so on.

In later religions we can sometimes trace the history of such developments. The ancient religions, on the other hand, reach us as an almost indecipherable palimpsest of metaphysics, ancient debris of earlier cultural and historical tradition, ancient folk-memories of all kinds,[1] which had long since formed one whole for the peoples who practised them and were, indeed, to their eyes, fused into one indivisible symbol of their soul.

Religions are divided by Lasaulx into the three following great groups: (*a*) the pantheistic systems of the East and the polytheistic systems of the West, the former with the Hindus, the latter with the Hellenes as their highest representatives: (*b*) the monotheism of the Jews and its camp-follower, Islam (Lasaulx might have put the dualism of the Persians under this heading): (*c*) the doctrine of the Trinity, which set itself up from the first not as a national but as a world religion. (This first emergence as a world religion, however, is also characteristic of Buddhism.)

This classification according to fundamental principles and origin, however, might be paralleled by more than one other,[2] first and foremost by a classification not only grouping the religions on a different principle, but taking sections through the various phases and social strata of

[1] Though the gods must not be directly interpreted as history, after the fashion of Euhemeros.

[2] Especially if the criterion were the status of sin and atonement, or the prevailing temper of the best of those peoples as revealed in literature, which gives so much more vivid a picture than any official one. This might lead us to a division of religions into optimistic and pessimistic.

the devotees of one and the same religion. We should then have: (*a*) religions with an emphasis on a future world of rewards and punishments, and possessing, perhaps, an eschatology also; and (*b*) those in which such elements are largely or wholly absent, for instance, the religion of the Greeks, who, with their clear insight into humanity and the limits of the individual, presupposed only a colorless world to come and spent little thought on it, leaving eschatology as a physical problem to the philosophers. Those philosophers, however, adhered in part to the third solution, namely (*c*) metempsychosis, the explicit or implicit corollary of which is the immortality of the world. This is the central tenet of the Hindu faith, which attempted to make its way into the Western world through the Albigenses. Buddha, however, sought to deliver mankind even from this form of immortality by (*d*) Nirvana.

A very curious point is the extraordinarily far-reaching agreement between the Christians and the Scandinavians in their conception of the end of the world. It is the more striking since the latter made no special use of the immortality of the individual, reserving their Valhalla to fallen heroes. The general ideas of medieval Christianity regarding the life to come are reflected in the superb and comprehensive eschatology which we find in Otto of Freising,[1] based on the Biblical doctrine of the reign of Antichrist immediately before the end of the world or the release of Satan after his thousand years of captivity.[2] According to the Scandinavian tradition,[3] a period of three years of extreme moral degeneration will precede the

[1] *Chron.* I, viii. English trans. (*The Two Cities*), C. C. Mierow, in Columbia University Records of Civilization, 1928.

[2] Rev. xx., and also in 2 Thess. ii, 3: "the man of sin, the son of perdition."

[3] Cf. Simrock, *Deutsche Mythologie,* pp. 136 ff.

great world catastrophe. This twilight of the moral powers is the twilight of the gods, Ragnarok, which thus denotes, not the consequence, but the cause of the end of the world. The gods and the heroes assembled by them in Valhalla fall in the battle with the powers of night; then comes the world conflagration, whereupon indeed a newborn world emerges, with a new, unnamed supreme god and a rejuvenated race of men. Between the two worlds is Muspilli,[1] where Elias struggles with Antichrist, but, though he slays him, he himself is wounded, and his blood, dripping on to the earth, sets fire to the world. The idea common to Christians and Scandinavians is this: the ideal knows, as it were, that, even when it has been realized, it is threatened by mortal enemies who, stronger than itself, will encompass its downfall. That downfall, however, is followed by a general retribution (according to Cyril of Jerusalem after three and a half years, and according to Otto of Freising forty-two months, of the reign of Antichrist). The ideal feels that it is too holy for this world.

The power of the priesthood stands as a rule (though not always) [2] in direct proportion to the place in doctrine accorded to the future life and last things. The priests have, more or less, the access to that world in their hands. Priestly power may, it is true, have other sources and causes in this world, such as the power of ritual to compel the gods, theurgy, trial by ordeal for the discovery of crime, and finally the association of the priesthood with medicine, arising in part from the closer relations of the priests with the gods, in part from priestly science, and in

[1] Cf. the *Edda* for this "Day of Judgment."

[2] The Scandinavians, who, for all their superb eschatology, have no doctrine of personal immortality, have no hierarchy: the Jews have a hierarchy, but no doctrine of a future life.

part from the idea that sickness is a punishment for sins committed—even in a former life—or the work of demons with which the priest can deal.[1] Finally, the power of the priesthood in state or national religions requires no explanation.

Only other-worldly religions proselytize, and not even all of them. The Egyptians and Zends, for instance, did not proselytize. Missionary zeal is not merely the product of the intensity of a religion, for religions of great intensity often confine themselves to contemning, destroying, or at best pitying what is not themselves. Missions are the product of the content of religion, and actually of its other-worldly content, since no one would expend so much effort for the sake of life in this world, nor would many converts be made.

Hence the question arises whether Judaism, when it spread in the Near East and the Roman Empire between 50 B.C. and A.D. 50 did not include some Pharisaic doctrine of a future life. Or did conversion go on without missions? Was the future life replaced by the hope of an earthly Messiah? In any case, all the Oriental mystery cults which found their way into the Empire pointed to another world. And the main appeal of Christianity for the Romans was its promise of immortal bliss.

It may well be that only other-worldly religions which are at the same time strongly equipped with dogma produce enough of those zealous *personalities* which must either win men or destroy the world. It is the converts themselves, particularly those who were once bitter adversaries, who become the most zealous apostles.

[1] Struggles for whole nations may take place between two thaumaturgies, e.g. the struggle between St. Hilarion and the Marnas priests for the people in and about Gaza. Cf. J. Burckhardt, *Die Zeit Konstantins des Grossen,* Gesamtausgabe II, p. 320 f.

It is quite logical, and only apparently a paradox, if we speak here of the missionaries of Buddhism, which promises to bring to a standstill the cycle of metempsychosis, the future life in its Oriental form.

The perfect contrast to the missionary religions is offered by classical polytheism, especially in its Roman form, which certainly disseminated its gods over the Western world, but for the most part invited the gods of other peoples into its pantheon. It was a national religion which became an imperial religion, though undergoing considerable modification in the process.

And here we arrive at the contrast between national and world religions, which partly coincides with their outlook on the future life.

They render the human-superhuman on quite different planes, the one in veiled, the other in unveiled form.

The national religions come first. They are closely interwoven with the memories, culture and history of their peoples. The function of their gods is to protect or terrorize their particular people or particular State. Such religions are heroic and proud in their attitude as long as the people flourishes, admit at any rate a general hope, for instance that one day all the nations shall gather on Mount Moriah to worship Jehovah, but are for the time being subject to national restrictions, indeed are fortified within and cut off from the outside world by a sacred language, and also for the time being do not proselytize. Towards others, as we saw was the case with the Greeks and Romans, they soon became polytheistically friendly, inviting, recognizing affinities, ready to exchange gods, prone to contempt, yet, with the exception of the Persians, not given to persecution.

Contrasted with these there stand the world religions, Buddhism, Christianity, Islam. They are late arrivals on the scene; their most potent vehicle is usually social, since they imply the abolition of castes and proclaim themselves the religions of the poor and of slaves, and are hence of their very nature international, while Islam is a religion of conquerors.

They dispense with a sacred language and translate their scriptures, with the exception of Islam, which keeps its Arabic Koran and compels the peoples to acquire some knowledge of Arabic.

The Latin employed in the Catholic liturgy can only be regarded as a sacred language in a restricted sense, for it has a magnificent practical purpose, while we can see an isolated case in the remarkable fate of Coptic, which became a sacred language owing to the fact that the Copts, who can now speak and understand Arabic only, have retained the scriptures and liturgies long ago translated into Coptic, a national language they can no longer understand.

It is the world religions which provoke the greatest historical crises. They know from the outset that they are world religions, and intend to be world religions.

The part played in life by the various religions varies enormously in importance. If we begin by comparing them with each other, we shall find some which are practically devoid of recognizable dogma. They have either never had, or have lost, their scriptures and adopted art and poetry instead. They are equally satisfied with laxer or stricter forms of worship and propitiation of the gods, with ceremonies more splendid or more sober. Life is not ordered by religion to any great extent. Philosophy and reason can soon disintegrate such a religion and betray all its secrets, so that we know all about it we wish to know.

The other religions have scriptures, a priesthood, a liturgy strictly prescribed down to the smallest details. Their dogmatism may be a very artificial one, may pass into sectarianism on the one hand, into philosophy on the other—the people, largely ignorant of such things, are content with the outward husk. Yet the liturgy of such a religion may enclose its living body like a carapace—as in the case of the Brahmins, for instance.

Finally, we have the great, essentially dogmatic world religions, in which dogma, and not, as in the others, ritual, claims to dominate the individual soul, leaving the values of earthly life to come to terms with it as best they can.

A much more difficult point is the assessment of the hold which one and the same religion has at different times on different sections of its adherents.

In the time dimension, we should have to distinguish between the primary stage of the nascent faith, that is, the naïve stage, then the secondary, when faith has become tradition, and the tertiary, when it can already appeal to its antiquity, when it has become the repository of national memories, or even, here and there, the national stay.

As regards the hold of a religion on the various strata of its adherents, we might perhaps say that the religions of the more highly civilized peoples exist simultaneously on all three planes according to the variations of social stratification and cultural influences. We might think here of the polytheism of the educated Romans, or of the Christianity of today, which is institutional for some, dogmatic for others, devotional for yet others, while here and there it has faded into mere religiosity.

A great uncertainty vitiates our judgment. We cannot, for instance, judge how far the Byzantine religion was still religiosity at a time when the dogmatic wrangling of the clergy existed side by side with extreme institutionalism, expressed in ritual and the emotional worship of symbols, with a despotic degradation of the human being. Yet we must not rush to conclusions; the best qualities of the Byzantines were none the less rooted in that religion which still deserves to be called the salt of its own earth.

And now we come to the breakdown of religions and the resistance they offer to it. For instance, early in its life a religion establishes a sacred law, i.e. it enters into an intimate association with a whole public order, which it safeguards, or it establishes its hierarchy side by side with the State, but in political relationship with it. These visible institutions, closely interwoven with all secular life, and finding their support in the inertia of the masses, may preserve the outward life of a religion indefinitely, just as old trees, completely decayed within, can subsist on their bark and their foliage, and still look great. But the spirit has, for the most part, fled from them, though it has not yet found a new, clearly conscious metaphysical element to form the foundation of a counter-religion strong enough to struggle and conquer.

During that time, the isolated creative efforts of the spirit are called heresy, or at any rate are execrated as such.

Even peoples living under the strictest tutelage, whose whole mind has seemed carefully trained in the dominant religion, will, now and then, fall victim to heresy group by group. We have only to think of the Mazdak heresy in the Sassanian Empire, which arose under the influence of

Manichaeism, of the State-founding heresies of Islam, of the Albigenses of the twelfth and thirteenth centuries—neo-Manichees, with their belief in the transmigration of souls which tempts one to wonder if metempsychosis may not be destined to cross the path of Christianity again. Every time heresy appears, it is a sign that the dominant religion no longer quite fulfils the metaphysical need from which it sprang.

The power of resistance of a religion varies exceedingly according to the class or power defending it. Small states, whose sacred things are closely knit together with the people and the State, can, perhaps, ward off a new heresy or religion better than great world empires with a standardized culture and general intercourse, which have subjected small nations because those nations were already tired. Such empires may have found it easier to subject the individual peoples *just because* they left them their religion. Christianity would have found difficulty in penetrating the City State of the fifth and fourth centuries B.C. The Roman Empire opened all its gates to Christianity, and the opposition it later set up was purely political.

Now there have been very easy and rapid mass-movements from one religion to another; [1] in theory, however, all religions claim to be at least as durable as the visible world, and each bears within it a lasting human value which partially justifies the claim.

Of all struggles, the most appalling are the *wars of religion,* more especially those between religions in which the thought of a future life predominates, or in which morality is in other ways completely bound up with the existing

[1] We might think of the first century of the Hegira, but also of the manner of religious conversion immediately preceding Mohammed.

form of religion, or in which a religion has taken on a strong national coloring and a people is defending itself in its religion. Among civilized peoples they are most terrible of all. The means of offence and defence are unlimited, ordinary morality is suspended in the name of the "higher purpose," negotiation and mediation are abhorrent—people want all or nothing.

As regards the rise of *persecutions,* we may first note an initial stage in the punishment of blasphemy; it is feared that the blasphemies of the enemies of God will provoke the punishment of God, and the blasphemer must therefore be delivered up to it, so that nobody else shall suffer with him. Such things may happen under the most tolerant forms of polytheism—witness the sacrilege trials in Athens—as soon as a direct defiance is manifested.

The world religions and other-worldly religions proceeded in a radically different way.

They not only countered attacks which had already been delivered, but, with all their power and as long as they could, combated the mere existence, even in secret, of a metaphysic differing from their own.

The Zend religion made no effort to convert, but displayed the most violent hatred of everything that was not the doctrine of Ormuzd. Cambyses destroyed the Egyptian temples and killed the Bull Apis. Xerxes laid waste the holy places of Greece.

Islam, too, proselytized either not at all or only at times and in places. As long as it could, it spread not by mission, but by conquest. It even welcomed the presence in its midst of infidel tax-payers, though killing them by means of contempt and ill-treatment, or even massacring them in outbursts of fury.

Christianity, however, from the fourth century onward, claimed possession of the soul and conscience of the individual for itself alone, and without hesitation enlisted the secular arm in its cause against the heathen, and more especially against Christian heretics. (This point will be discussed later.) The very religion whose victory was a triumph of conscience over violence set upon men's consciences with fire and sword.

To its believers, Christianity lent a frightful strength. The martyr who survived his torture quite logically turned into a persecutor, not so much for the sake of revenge as because the cause meant more to him than anything else. His earthly life was perhaps of no great value to him in any case; he even desired to suffer and die. (Such things happen even outside of Christianity without providing any proof of the objective worth of the cause concerned.)

With its infinite solicitude for the soul of the individual, the Church left him only the choice between its dogma (its syllogisms) and the stake. Its terrible assumption was that man must have power over the opinions of his fellows.

We often find it admitted, overtly or covertly, that heresy is tantamount to eternal damnation, hence that it must at all costs be prevented from infecting innocent souls, still more whole peoples, that death is of no account in comparison with the eternal damnation of nations.

While the masses are generally presumed to be the victims of mere crude ignorance of the truth, leaders of heresies are always credited with sheer malevolence, the true faith being self-evident. *On est bien près de brûler dans ce monde-ci les gens que l'on brûle dans l'autre.* The salvation of souls takes precedence of all else, even to the point of kidnapping and forced education.

Among the Church Fathers, we already find St. Augustine in favor of the bloody persecution of the Donatists.[1] "Not we have persecuted you, but your own works" (i.e. because you have separated yourselves from the Church by your own godlessness). "What injustice can there be in punishing for their sins, by order of the government, those whom God warns by this present judgment and chastisement to flee eternal fire? Let them first prove that they are not heretics and not schismatics, and then complain." St. Hilary and St. Jerome speak in no milder accents, and in the Middle Ages Innocent III called the temporal lords to arms with threats, and preached a crusade against the heretics, with grants of land and indulgences, as if it had been for the Holy Land. It is true that the adversary—heathen or heretic—was actually only disposed of by virtual extermination. The Albigenses *were* exterminated.

The nemesis which overtook the Church was that it became more and more a police institution, and that its prelates stank of the police-court.

The *Reformers'* conception of eternal damnation was no different from that of the Catholic Church, but, in practice, they left the matter to God, with the possible exception of grave cases of blasphemy; at that point they regressed into the primitive stage of persecution.

The great intellectual movement of the eighteenth century brought a great breach in the persecutions. In the first place, the secular arm refused further service, a new conception of the State having arisen. The decisive factor, however, probably lay elsewhere. Under the influence, among other things, of the Copernican system, the preoccupation with a life to come declined, it became bad form and the sign of a hard heart for men to be always

[1] St. Augustine, *contra litt. Petil.*, II, 42 f. See *Post-Nicene Fathers*, 1st Series.

thinking about the "eternal" damnation of other souls, while it gradually became possible to postulate a temperate bliss for everyone.

The eighteenth-century philosophy of reason and "tolerance," which found zealous, convinced adherents and even martyrs, and transformed the spiritual world, was, of course, a kind of religion too, though no human being swore allegiance to it. The same might be said of certain philosophies of the ancient world, e.g. stoicism—or rather, to give the phenomenon its general name, mere philosophical tendencies, without dogma, assemblies and special obligations, and with a great variety of adherents, can assume the full value of a sect or religion.

And now the decline of religion. This is by no means accomplished only by what is called inner disintegration, the spiritual alienation of individual categories of the people (whether as sects within the people or as educated, thinking groups). Indeed, not even the presence of a new religion better fulfilling the metaphysical needs of the time is enough.

Sects can be persecuted and stamped out, or left to their own instability and metamorphoses. The educated classes which have been deflected by cultural influences from the dominant religion will probably return to it (the fate of almost all the Latin peoples), or come to terms with it again for reasons of prudence (while among the people religion has from all time been the essential stuff of civilization). A new religion can arise beside the old one and divide the world with it, but can never oust it, even if it has conquered the masses, unless the State intervenes.

It may be that every fully developed religion of a higher type is relatively eternal (i.e. as eternal as the life of the peoples confessing it), unless its opponents are able to mobilize the power of the State against it. All succumb to force if it is consistently applied, and especially if it is embodied in a single, inescapable world power like the Roman Empire. Without force, or at any rate without the steady application of force, religions continue to live. The spirit of the people is their perpetual fount of strength, indeed, in the end they again win over the secular arm to their side. This was the case with the religions of the East. In India, with the help of the State, Brahminism was able to exterminate Buddhism. Without the imperial legislation from Constantine to Theodosius, the Graeco-Roman religion would still be alive today. If there had not been occasional complete, if temporary, suppressions, carried out by the secular arm (if necessary with the utmost violence), the Reformation would have established itself nowhere. It lost all those territories in which it did not command this privilege of the secular arm, and was obliged to allow a considerable body of Catholics to remain alive. Thus even a young and apparently vigorous religion may founder, and in places perhaps for ever. For it is doubtful whether a fresh impetus will coincide with "a favorable moment of crystallization."

CULTURE

Culture may be defined as the sum total of those mental developments which take place spontaneously and lay no claim to universal or compulsive authority.

Its action on the two constants is one of perpetual modification and disintegration, and is limited only by the extent to which they have pressed it into their service and included it within their aims.

Otherwise it is the critic of both, the clock which tells the hour at which their form and substance no longer coincide.

Culture is, further, that millionfold process by which the spontaneous, unthinking activity of a race is transformed into considered action, or indeed, at its last and highest stage, in science and especially philosophy, into pure thought.

Its total external form, however, as distinguished from the State and religion, is society in its broadest sense.

Each one of its elements has, like the State and religion, its growth, bloom and decay, and its perpetuation in a general tradition (in so far as it is capable and worthy of it). Countless elements also subsist in the unconscious as an acquisition bequeathed to mankind perhaps by some forgotten people. An unconscious accumulation of vestiges of culture in peoples and individuals should always be taken into account.

This growth and decay follows higher, inscrutable laws of life.

The spearhead of all Culture is a miracle of mind—speech, whose spring, independently of the individual people and its individual language, is in the soul, otherwise no deaf-mute could be taught to speak and to understand speech. Such teaching is only explicable if there is in the soul an intimate and responsive urge to clothe thought in words.[1]

Further, languages are the most direct and specific revelation of the spirit of the nations, their ideal image, the most perdurable material in which they enclose the content of their spiritual life, especially in the sayings of their great poets and thinkers.

An immense field of study has been opened up here, reaching backwards to the original and fundamental meaning of words (in etymology assisted by comparative philology) and forwards to their grammatical and syntactical development, starting out from the root which can be traced through the verb, noun, adjective and their infinite inflections.

As a whole, we may say that the earlier the language, the richer it is; supreme intellectual culture and its masterpieces only make their appearance when it is already in its decline.

At the beginning, in its unfolding, the play of language must have been exquisitely graceful. All the organs of

[1] Sufficient proof of this is actually given by the mere possibility of learning foreign languages to the point of the expression of ideas. (Cf. Ennius' *tria corda.*)

man, and especially the ear, seem to have been more sensitive, even among the Greeks and the Germanic peoples. The great wealth of inflections must have been at latest coeval with the names of things—it may even have existed earlier. Thus men probably possessed the instrument in its perfection before they put it to use, so that they were already in a position to say a great deal when they still had very little to say. It was the rough-and-tumble of historical life, and the overwhelming of language by things, by use, which dulled their senses.

The influence of an existing language on the people which speaks it, however, is incalculably great.

According to Lasaulx this was the order of cultural development: mining (i.e. some form of metal-working) was followed by stock-breeding, agriculture, shipping, trade, industry and material welfare; only then did the arts emerge from the crafts, and ultimately science from art.[1] This is an apparent confusion, some of these things having their origin in material, some in spiritual necessities. Yet the connection is actually very close and no separation of the two needs is possible. In the course of any material activity carried on with independent power, and not merely slavishly, a spiritual surplus is generated, be it ever so little. The same faculty thus functions in rapid succession in two kinds of service.

This spiritual surplus either enriches created form as ornament, as supreme external perfection—the arms and utensils in Homer are magnificent before there is any question of the divine image—or it becomes conscious thought, reflection, comparison, speech—the work of art—and before man himself realizes it, there has awakened in him a need

[1] Here Lasaulx follows Bacon: *De dignitate*, iv. 2, and *Essays*, 58.

totally different from that with which he began his work. It is this new need which continues to grow and make itself felt.

In man, no one side is ever active to the exclusion of the rest; the whole is always at work, even though some elements may function in a weaker, unconscious fashion.

In any case, we should not judge these things from the standpoint of the present day with its infinite division of labor and specialization, but with reference to times when all activity was more coherent.

And finally, it is unnecessary to find a material occasion for *every* spiritual birth, even though it might ultimately be possible to do so. When mind has once become conscious of itself, it continues to create its own world without extraneous aid.

The arts, more enigmatic than the sciences, are probably the most extraordinary creations of the spirit. Here no distinction can be drawn between the three visual arts, poetry and music.

All five seem to have emerged from religious ritual, and even, in early times, to have been connected with it, though they also existed without and before it. Fortunately, even here we can dispense with speculation on origins.

Schiller's *Künstler*[1] is not quite the last word on the position of art in the culture of the world. It is not enough to show the beautiful as an antecedent phase of, an education for, the true, since art exists mainly for its own sake.

The sciences, on the other hand, are the spiritual aspect of practical necessities and the systematic aspect of the

[1] Transl. Forster, *The Artists,* Dole ed., Vol. III, pp. 165 f.

infinite multiplicity of things; that is, they collect and classify *what already exists without their aid;* on the other hand, they forge ahead and discover it, whether as concrete fact or as law. Finally, philosophy sets out to fathom the supreme laws of all being, but again as that which has existed from all time, without and before itself.

The arts are quite different; they have nothing to do with what exists without them, nor have they any laws to discover (just because they are not sciences); they have to body forth a higher life which would not exist without them.

They arise from mysterious vibrations communicated to the soul. What is released by those vibrations has ceased to be individual and temporal and has become symbolically significant and immortal.

The great men of old knew nothing about us, and it is open to question how far they themselves thought about posterity, but: "The man who has done justice to the best of his time has lived for all time."

From the world, from time and nature, art and poetry draw images, eternally valid and universally intelligible, the only perdurable thing on earth, a second, ideal creation, exempt from the limitations of individual temporality, an earthly immortality, a language for all the nations. Hence they are, no less than philosophy, great exponents of their epochs.

The outward form of their work is subject to the vicissitudes of all earthly things, but enough subsists into far distant ages to bring them freedom, inspiration and spiritual unity.

In this, we, the later-born, are fortunate in our capacity for restoration, which, with the assistance of analogy, divines a whole from fragments. For art is still art, even in the excerpt, the outline, the mere allusion; indeed, it is particularly poignant in the fragment, whether it be an ancient sculpture or a snatch of melody.

We shall have to speak later of our assumption of the happiness of the creative spirit.

In most arts, and even in poetry, their substance (the ideal, the terrible, the sensuously desirable) may play a very important part in the total effect both on the artist and the beholder. Indeed, most people believe that art is the imitation of physical existence, individual and defective as it is, and that its real function is to give memorable form to, to "immortalize," things that seem to them important for other reasons.

Fortunately for us, however, we have architecture; here the instinct for ideal creation finds its purest expression, free of any other consideration. Here we can see most clearly what art is, even though we cannot deny that it is subservient to purpose and often reposes for long periods on conventional repetitions. The supreme, as it was the earliest, allegiance of the arts, and one to which they could submit without degradation, was to religion. It is true that religion would not always foster the arts, for the metaphysical need it represents can be of such a nature that it is partially (as in Islam) or wholly (as in Puritanism) devoid of the artistic instinct, or hostile to art.

In all earthly occasions, however, true art finds stimuli rather than tasks; it surrenders freely to the vibrations it has received from them. Art bound down to facts, still more to thoughts, is lost.[1]

Here poetry is most instructive; it will rather create a new world than narrate pre-existing facts, and in its man-

[1] Of course, anyone who finds "ideas" represented in ancient works of art must require of modern ones that they should represent "thoughts."

ner of thought and feeling presents the supreme contrast and supreme complement to philosophy.[1]

How would the thoughts of the *Prometheus* of Aeschylus sound in philosophy? In their poetic presentation, at any rate, they awaken in us the sense of the tremendous.

Within culture, the different domains dislodge, supplant and modify each other. There is a perpetual flux.

Individual peoples and individual epochs show outstanding gifts and preferences for the several elements.

Powerful individuals appear and lay down lines which are followed by whole epochs and peoples to the point of complete one-sidedness.

On the other hand, it is sometimes very difficult for us to decide how far an element of culture which now, to our eyes, colors a whole epoch, really dominated *life* at that time. Philistinism and force have always existed side by side with culture, and we must always be on our guard against optical illusions in appraising spiritual greatness in its own time.[2]

The various elements of culture and the various stages of culture reached at different places interacted at first mainly through trade, which disseminated the products of the more highly developed and specialised communities among the others. Not that the zeal to do likewise was always awakened. The Etruscan and Pontic peoples bought or ordered the beautiful things of Greece and the matter went no further than mere barter. Yet the history

[1] Cf. again Schiller's *Künstler*.

[2] Cf. the Brahminic philosophy of Brahmin India. This was a scholastic exegesis of religion, and it colored all intellectual life. Its centres were the royal courts. Speculation was perhaps never so much common property as there, so that the conflict with Buddhism was quite as much philosophic as religious in kind.

of culture is rich in magnetic and fateful contacts between peoples, crafts, minds. Every endeavor stimulates endeavor, or at any rate the boast: "We can do it too," till at last the various civilized peoples display with relative uniformity that infinite complexity of all activity, that common field of interaction which we of today take as a matter of course.

And finally we shall deal with the great centres of intellectual exchange, such as Athens, Florence, etc. Such places give birth to a strong local prejudice, namely, that there was nothing they could not do, and that the best society, and the greatest, or even the sole stimulation of and respect for culture was to be found there.

Hence these places produced from among their own citizens a disproportionate number of great individuals, through whom they continue to act on the world. That is not the result of "great educational facilities," as in the big or even middle-sized cities of our day; all "great educational facilities" can produce their inflated nonentities, monopolizing leading positions by dint of waiting and their own social claims, and beyond that, mere universal fault-finding. What happened was the stimulation of supreme powers by the exceptional; no "talent" was brought to birth, but genius called to genius.

Apart from such centres of exchange, one of the main prerequisites of any more perfected culture is social intercourse. It forms the right contrast to the caste-system, with its one-sided, though relatively high, partial culture, which, in technology, in the acquisition and perfection of craftsmanship, may be justified, but in the spiritual world, as we can see by the example of Egypt, always leads to stagnation, narrowness and pride towards the outside world.

We must not, however, forget that the hereditary system in the crafts may have offered the only safeguard against the relapse into barbarism.

Social intercourse, however, even where the castes are preserved, brings all the elements of culture more or less into touch, from the highest intellectual to the meanest mechanical activity. Thus they form a great chain, a thousandfold entwined, which is more or less affected at all its parts by *one* electric shock. *One* important innovation in the domain of mind and spirit may implant even in men who seem to have little share in it a new conception of their ordinary, everyday doings.

Finally, what is called high society forms an indispensable forum, more particularly for the arts. The latter should not be essentially dependent on it, especially not on its false satellites, on the chatter of modern salons and so on, but should, it would seem, find in social intercourse *the* standard of intelligibility without which they run the risk of losing touch with earth or falling victim to little esoteric circles of devotees.

And now, finally, the relationship, real or ostensible, of culture to morality. Gustav Freytag (*Bilder aus der deutschen Vergangenheit*), for instance, draws a contrast between our own time and the sixteenth and seventeenth centuries, based on the growth of "a sense of duty and honesty," or "substance, efficiency and honesty." Yet arguments based on the corruption, debauchery and more especially the violence of times past, or on the cruelty and perfidy of barbarians, are misleading. For we judge everything by that standard of security without which *we* could no longer exist, and condemn the past by pointing out that our atmosphere did not exist in it, forgetting that even now, the moment security is suspended—in war, for instance—every conceivable horror shows its head. Neither the spirit nor the brain of man has visibly developed in historical times, and his faculties were in any case complete long before then.[1] Hence our assumption that we live in the age of moral progress is supremely ridiculous when we look back on those perilous times out of which the free strength of ideal desire rises to heaven in the lofty spires of a hundred cathedrals. The matter is made worse by our vulgar hatred of everything that is different, of the many-sidedness of life, of symbolic rites and privileges half or quite in abeyance, by our identification of the moral with the precise and our incapacity to understand the multifarious, the fortuitous. We need not wish ourselves back into the Middle Ages, but we should try to understand them. Our life is a business, theirs was living. The people as a totality hardly existed, but that which was of the people flourished.

Thus what we are wont to regard as moral progress is the domestication of individuality brought about (*a*) by the versatility and wealth of culture and (*b*) by the vast increase in the power of the State over the individual, which may even lead to the complete abdication of the individual, more especially where money-making predominates to the exclusion of everything else, ultimately absorbing all initiative. The loss of initiative is exactly balanced by our power of offence and defence.

Morality as a power, however, stands no higher, nor is there more of it, than in so-called barbarous times. We may be sure that even among the lake-dwellers men gave their lives for each other. Good and evil, perhaps even fortune and misfortune, may have kept a roughly even balance throughout all the various epochs and cultures.

[1] Cf. Buckle, *History of Civilization in England,* I, Ch. IV.

Even progress in intellectual development is open to doubt, since, as civilization advanced, the division of labor may have steadily narrowed the consciousness of the individual. In the sciences, a host of discoveries of isolated facts already threatens to obscure any general outlook. In no sphere of life does individual ability develop uniformly with the expansion of the whole; culture might easily stumble over its own feet.

In detail, the point at issue is not the shades of meaning by which the notions "good" and "evil" are modified (for that depends on the prevailing culture and religion), but whether men, as they are, do their duty and sacrifice their self-seeking according to those notions.

For that matter, it is not until after Rousseau that we find a moral dream of the past *en bloc*, starting out, of course, from the assumption that all men are by nature good, but that their goodness had simply not been able to find expression till his time, and could not but reveal itself in all its glory if only they had the power in their hands. The corollary of this was (in the French Revolution) that men took upon themselves the right to indict the past as a whole. The arrogant belief in the moral superiority of the present, however, has only fully developed of late years; it makes no exceptions, even in favor of classical antiquity. The secret mental reservation is that money-making is today easier and safer than ever. Were that menaced, the exaltation it engenders would collapse.

Christianity had, it is true, regarded itself as the one pathway to salvation, though only for its own devotees; hence it had all the more rigorously condemned the world around it as evil, and made the flight from that world its prime condition.

A peculiarity of higher cultures is their susceptibility to renaissances. Either one and the same or a later people partially adopts a past culture into its own by a kind of hereditary right or by right of admiration.

These renaissances are to be distinguished from the politico-religious restorations with which they nevertheless coincide here and there. We might ask how far this was the case at the restoration of Judaism after the Exile, and at the restoration of Persia by the Sassanidae. Under Charlemagne the two coincided—the restoration of the late Roman Empire and the renaissance of late Roman art and literature.

A pure renaissance, on the other hand, may be seen in the Italian and European movement of the fifteenth and sixteenth centuries. Its specific characteristics were its spontaneity, the verification of experience through which it triumphed, its extension, to a greater or less degree, to every possible domain of life, e.g. the idea of the State, and finally, its European character.

If we now turn to the culture of the nineteenth century, we find it in possession of the traditions of all times, peoples and cultures, while the literature of our age is a world literature.

In this, it is the beholder who profits most. There exists a magnificent, general, tacit agreement to approach everything with impartial interest, to take intellectual possession of the whole world, past and present.

Even in straitened circumstances, a man of finer culture now enjoys his few classics and the scenes of nature much more profoundly, and the happiness life offers much more consciously, than in bygone times.

State and Church now impose little restraint on such endeavors, and gradually adjust their outlook to very manifold points of view. They have neither the power nor the desire to suppress them. They believe their existence less menaced by an apparently limitless development of culture than by its repression. In what way culture actually proves serviceable in this point will be discussed later.

The benefit to the wage-earners, who are the essentially progressive element, is less obvious. They strive with elemental passion for (1) a still greater acceleration of communications, (2) the complete abolition of such frontiers as still exist, i.e. the universal State. The retribution which overtakes them is the enormous competition in every detail of life, and their own unrest. The man of culture who earns his living would like to snatch his share of all kinds of learning and enjoyment, yet must, to his distress, leave the best to others. Others must be cultured for him, just as others had to pray and sing for the great noble of the Middle Ages.

A large contingent, of course, is provided by people of American culture, who have to a great extent foregone history, i.e. spiritual continuity, and wish to share in the enjoyment of art and poetry merely as forms of luxury.

Art and poetry themselves are in our day in the most wretched plight, for they have no spiritual home in our ugly, restless world, and any creative spontaneity is seriously menaced. That they (i.e. real art and poetry, for the false take life easy) continue at all notwithstanding can only be explained by the great power of the instinct.

The greatest innovation in the world is the demand for education as a right of man; it is a disguised demand for comfort.

ON THE HISTORICAL CONSIDERATION OF POETRY

THE rivalry between history and poetry has been finally settled by Schopenhauer.[1] Poetry achieves more for the knowledge of human nature; even Aristotle said, "poetry is more philosophical and profound than history," and that is true, because the faculty which gives birth to poetry is intrinsically of a higher order than that of the greatest historian. Further, the end to which it is created is much sublimer than that of history.

Hence history finds in poetry not only one of its most important, but also one of its purest and finest sources.

Firstly, it is indebted to poetry for insight into the nature of mankind as a whole; further, for penetrating light on times and peoples. Poetry, for the historical observer, is the image of the eternal in its temporal and national expression, hence instructive in all its aspects and, moreover, often the best, or only thing to survive.

Let us first consider its status at various epochs, among various peoples and classes, asking each time—*who* is singing or writing, and *for whom?*—then its matter and spirit.

First and foremost, poetry appears in all its significance as the *voice of religion.*

[1] *Die Welt als Wille und Vorstellung,* Vol. I, pp. 288 ff.; Vol. II, p. 499: trans. *The World as Will and Idea,* Vol. I, Sect. 51; Vol. II, Chap. 38.

The hymn not only glorifies the gods, but points to a definite stage of the cult, to a definite degree of pre-eminence of the priesthood, whether we think of the Aryan hymns to the Indus, or of the Psalms, or of the early Christian hymns, or of the Protestant hymn as the supreme religious expression, especially of the seventeenth century.

One of the freest and greatest utterances of the whole ancient world was the theocratic and political exhortation of the Hebrew prophet.

The Greek theogonist (Hesiod) represents the moment at which the nation desired and received a coherent form for its boundless wealth of myth.

The *Voluspa* (words of the *Völe* = revelations of the prophetess), which can be traced back to the early eighth century, is a mighty witness to the mythological hymn among the Scandinavians; in addition to a whole mythology, it embraces the end of the world and the birth of a new earth. But even the later mythological lays of the *Edda* are extremely rich in myth and figures and endless catalogues of names. The picture of the earthly and heavenly world, again interspersed with theogonic elements, is reflected in the strangest imaginings.[1] The tone is wilfully enigmatic—it is the genuine accent of the seer.

Then comes the epic with its bards. It replaces history as a whole, and revelation to a considerable extent, as an expression of national life and a first-class testimony to the need and capacity of a people to see and represent itself in a type. The bards endowed with this capacity in its supreme degree were great men.

[1] For instance, *Grimmismal* and *Vafthrudnismal.* In the latter, there is a discussion on mythological and theogonic mysteries between Odin, who pretends to be Gangradr, and the giant Vafthrudnir. Ultimately the giant realizes that Odin means to slay him. Transl. Bellows, *The Poetic Edda,* London, 1923.

The status of the epic shows a fundamental change as soon as the epoch is a literary one, and poetry has become a form of literature, so that what was once recited before an audience is read in private. But that change is only accomplished when a barrier has arisen between the highly educated and uneducated classes. It is a matter for great surprise that Virgil, in these circumstances, could occupy his high rank, could dominate all the age which followed and become a mythical figure.

How infinitely great are the gradations of existence from the epic rhapsodist to the novelist of today!

The lyric poetry of classical times is to be found in every conceivable company: ministering to religion in the collective lyric, ministering to the symposium as social art, then (with Pindar) as the herald of victory in combat, and, at the same time (among the Aeolians), as the subjective lyric, till here, too, poetry became a species of literature, as the Roman lyric and elegy were.

In the Middle Ages, the lyric became a vital expression of the great cosmopolitan nobility. It was practised in kindred form in the south of France, the north of France, Germany and Italy, and the way it was carried about from Court to Court is itself a fact of great importance in the history of culture.

Among the Meistersinger, we can discern the effort to keep poetry working as long as possible on pedantic, objective lines. But finally, side by side with a steady current of popular poetry, in which the objective seems to take on subjective form, there came the complete emancipation of the subjective lyric as we understand it today, involving a dilettante freedom of form and a new relationship to music, and fostered in Italy under the surveillance of Academies.

It will be better to postpone the discussion of drama. The fate of modern poetry as a whole is the consciousness, born of the history of literature, of its relationship to the poetry of *all* times and peoples. On that background, it appears as an imitation or an echo. As regards the poets, however, it will be worth while to investigate for its own sake the personality of the poet in the world and the vast change in his status from the time of Homer up to the present day.

Looking at poetry from the standpoint of its *matter* and *spirit,* the first conclusion we come to is this: it is in any case for long periods the only means of communication, so that we might speak of poetry in bondage. It is itself the most ancient form of history; for the most part, mythology comes to us in poetic garb. Further, as gnomic, didactic poetry, it is the most ancient vehicle of ethics. In the hymn it glorifies religion. Finally, in the lyric, it is a direct revelation of what men have found great, lovely, glorious and terrible.

But then came the great crisis in poetry. In its earlier phases, its matter and its necessarily strict form were closely fused. The whole of poetry was *one* national and religious revelation. The spirit of the people seems to speak to us directly, objectively, so that we feel Herder justified in his description of the folksong and the popular ballad as "The Voice of the Peoples in Song." Their style seems to be self-created, indissolubly blended of matter and spirit.

In all peoples of superior culture whose literature we know with anything approaching completeness, there then followed, at a certain stage of development—among the Greeks, Pindar might be taken as the dividing line—the transition of poetry from necessity to choice, from the general and popular to the individual, from the economy of types to infinite diversity.

From that time on, poets were the spokesmen of their time and people in quite a different sense. They no longer gave a direct revelation of the spirit of that time and people, but expressed their own personality, which often conflicted with it. As documents in the history of culture, however, they are no less instructive than their forebears, though from a different angle.

This comes out most clearly in the free choice of their matter, or even its creation. Previously, the matter had rather chosen the poet, the magnet had, so to speak, attracted the man. Now it was the other way about.

At this point, a fact of great historical importance is the penetration of the Arthurian cycle into the epic poetry of the Western nobility. It largely overshadowed the whole ancient national saga of the Teutons, the Charlemagne cycle of the French. The style persisted, but in the matter the poets escaped from the strictly national. And among the poems of the Arthurian cycle we find a German *Parzival.*

In subsequent times, what any century, any nation, wanted, read, recited, sang, is one of the most important testimonies to its character.

The old German cycle, the cycle of Charlemagne and the cycle of Arthur, then passed through many vicissitudes in France, Germany and Italy. To a certain extent, the legend persisted side by side with them, and we can observe at the same time the rise, and here and there the predominance, of the *fabliaux,* tales, farces, *conti* and bestiaries, etc., while the fairy-tale is of particular importance in the history of modern Oriental culture. Finally, the Charlemagne cycle received a quite unprecedented stylistic treatment at the hands of the great Italians (Boiardo, Ariosto). We find here an almost completely free development of the subject-matter in classical form.

Ultimately, the epic issues into the novel, which helps to characterize its whole epoch by its relative importance, its subject-matter and the composition of its reading public. It is essentially a form for solitary reading. Here, however, the quantitative hunger for new matter sets in. It is probably the only form in which poetry can make a direct appeal to those masses which it desires as readers, namely, as the broadest picture of life in constant touch with reality, i.e. with what we call realism. This property even allows it to command an international reading public; no single country can supply the demand and the public is over-stimulated. Hence there exists an exchange (though a very unequal one) between France, Germany, England and America.

And now we must turn to drama, not only as regards its status, but also as regards its subject-matter and spirit. By its mere existence, and by the manner of its authority, drama reflects a definite state of society; it does so, as a rule, in connection with the cult. Its subject-matter, however, makes of it one of the greatest witnesses to the peoples and times which gave it birth; though not unconditionally, since it requires a coincidence of fortunate circumstances, and even in a supremely gifted people may be inhibited, or even killed, by external circumstance. At times—we have only to think of England under the Commonwealth—it has its deadly enemies, even though that, in its turn, is a proof of its power and importance. Further, before it can exist, there must be theatres and performances. Drama would never have come into being merely to be read.

The dramatic instinct lies deep in man, as can be seen

even in the drama of half-civilized peoples, which here and there strives to achieve a grotesque imitation of reality by pantomime, accompanied by howls and contortions.

Chinese drama stopped short at bourgeois realism; Indian drama, which developed late, and perhaps first under Greek influence, is, as far as we know it, an artistic product, short-lived in its bloom. Its origin is again religious, namely the rites of Vishnu, yet it did not create a theatre. Its chief limitation—and in this it is instructive—consists in the slight value it placed on earthly life and its conflicts, and in an inadequate awareness of strong personality wrestling with fate.

Attic drama, on the other hand, casts floods of light on the whole life of Attica and Greece.

Firstly, the performance was a social occasion of the first magnitude, an ἀγών in the supreme sense of the word, the poets contesting with each other, a fact which certainly very soon brought amateurs into the ranks of the competitors.[1] Further, as to its subject-matter and treatment, we are faced here with that mysterious rise of drama "from the spirit of music." The protagonist remains an echo of Dionysus, and the entire content is pure myth, avoiding history, which often tries to force its way in. It is dominated by the steady determination to present humanity only in typical, and not in realistic figures, and, connected with this, the conviction of the inexhaustibility of the golden age of gods and heroes.

What more was needed for the Lesser Dionysia to develop into an old Attic comedy, that living mouthpiece of a time and place in a condition of unprecedented intellectual ferment? It cannot be transplanted to a later theatre. The first comedy capable of a cosmopolitan appeal

[1] The "throng of little lads": Aristophanes, *Frogs*, 89 f.

was the middle and later comedy, with class humor and love intrigue. These passed into Roman hands, and ultimately helped to form the basis of later polite comedy, yet nowhere did they become vital organs without which we cannot imagine a people. Among the Romans, in any case, the theatre was invaded by a coarse lust for the spectacular, which is the death of dramatic poetry.

When it reawakened in the Middle Ages, the only themes it could use were religious. Since the time of the early Church, the classical stage had been anathema; actors (*histriones*) existed, but they were to all intents and purposes outlaws.[1] In the monasteries, and in city churches or market-places, Christmas or Nativity plays (*ludi de nativitate Dei*) were performed. Thus a religion which was moved to find the most diverse visual expression (picture cycles, sculptures on church portals, church windows, etc.) also turned to the dramatization of holy story and legend with utter simplicity. The theological mentors of that drama imparted to it a strong allegorical bias.

Compared with Attic comedy in its relation to myth and in liberty of form, such drama was not free. The aim of Attic drama was to make ideal figures speak with the voice of all mankind. The medieval mystery play (properly, *ministerium*) was and remained part of the liturgy and bound to a definite story.

The secular spirit of the actors (townsmen and craftsmen) and of the spectators could not possibly find satisfaction in it in the long run. The allegorical and satirical "morality" arose; then came plays from the Old Testament and secular history; the sacred story itself was invaded by popular scenes, even of an indecent description, till the

[1] Capitulare anni 789. Cf. also St. Thomas Aquinas.

farce, etc., was sufficiently developed to split off as a separate form.

Meanwhile, in Italy, the separation from the mystery play was being accomplished in the main through the imitation of classical tragedy and by a type of comedy formed on the model of Plautus and Terence. And then, in the course of time, there came everywhere the transition from the occasional, festal performance to the regular professional stage, from the citizen as player to the professional actor.

If we now ask how far and in what sense the theatre has become national, or at any rate popular, in the various occidental countries, we shall first have to turn once more to Italy. Yet, in spite of the proverbial Italian gift for acting, the later Italians never brought serious drama to its bloom; its place was taken by opera. Elsewhere the profession of actor remained dishonorable, and hence the theatre-going classes of the public dubious. Not everybody was carried over his misgivings by the example of the Court. Even Shakespeare's position (according to recent researches) was very relative. The English theatre was confined to London and the Court, so that the term "national theatre" cannot stand. In London it was eschewed by the better class of citizens, supported only by young men of fashion and the lower kind of craftsmen, and mortally hated by those who were soon to have the State in their hands. And even before that, Shakespeare's own manner of drama had been superseded by another (Beaumont and Fletcher's comedy of character).

A much more national phenomenon in all its aspects (including the *autos sagramentales*), and in this the perfect counterpart of Greek drama, is the drama of Spain, so that we cannot imagine the Spanish nation without its drama.

The Court certainly had its company of actors, but the stage was not dependent on the Court, nor even on the luxury of the great cities, but on the taste of the nation, in which, as in Italy, histrionic talent is general. Further, the *autos* were always (even in our own century) associated with the liturgy, though that did not prevent them from developing into a wealth of comedy with modern characters.

As regards the European drama and stage in the eighteenth century, the striking facts are the decrease of its popularity, and its increasing restriction to the larger cities (in France, practically to Paris alone). At the same time, however, famous actors, soon to achieve European reputation, make their appearance. The actual performances and their requirements begin to be outbalanced by dramatic creation, so that drama becomes a branch of literature apart from the stage, just as in the latter days of Athens there were dramas for reading, or at any rate for recitation. Finally (with Diderot among others), topical drama makes its appearance.

In the nineteenth century, and more especially at the present day, the theatre represents a place of entertainment for the lazy and the tired. Its competitors in the life of the great cities are the theatrical show, the pantomime, and especially the opera. The theatres are becoming huge, and subtler effects are often precluded by mere size; cruder dramatic effects are wanted, and are exaggerated far beyond the demand. Drama has become a business, like the novel and many other things which still bear the name of literature.

We are compensated by our greater theoretical knowledge of what, in the whole of dramatic poetry, was good, and why.

Today it is altogether doubtful how far the spirit of modern nations can be judged by the need they feel for an objective, ideal picture of life presented on the stage.

Here we may add a few words on the historical consideration of the other arts, omitting, however, men's feeling for the music of their own generation, which, in its turn, forms a world of its own.

Yet men's feeling for the visual arts is also a world of its own, and the question arises—how does history speak through art?

It does so primarily in building and monuments, which are the purposive expression of power, whether in the name of the State or of Religion. Yet a Stonehenge can be satisfying until a people feels the need to express itself in form.

This need gives birth to styles, but it is a long road, in religious monuments, from purpose to perfection, to the Parthenon and Cologne Cathedral. Further, the monumentality appears as an expression of luxury in castles, palaces, villas, etc. In such cases it is both the expression and the stimulus of private feeling, the former in the owner, the latter in the beholder.

Thus the character of whole nations, cultures and epochs speaks through the totality of their architecture, which is the outward shell of their being.

In religious, monumental, naïve epochs, art is the inevitable form of everything men feel holy or powerful. Thus what is expressed in *sculpture* or *painting* is primarily religion, first in types, Egyptian, the Oriental, Greek, medieval and even later art each representing the divine, or at any rate the sacred, in the figure of a sublimer type of their own kind of humanity, and secondly in historical pictures, art coming into being, as it were, in order to take over the function of the word in the narration of myth, sacred history and legend. Here lie its greatest, inexhaustible themes. Here it creates its own standard, learns what it can do.

Yet even here, in sculpture and painting, art becomes a luxury. Secular art is born; on the one hand, it is of the secular and monumental order, and the handmaid of power, on the other, the handmaid of wealth. Subsidiary forms such as portrait, genre, landscape, succeed each other, fulfilling the requirements of individual fortunes and patrons. Here, too, art becomes the expression of individual moods, and their stimulus.

In derivative or late epochs, men come to believe that art is at their service. It is used for purposes of ostentation, exploiting at times its subsidiary and decorative rather than its essential forms. Indeed, it becomes a pastime and the theme of idle talk.

Yet at the same time, art becomes aware of its high status as a power and a force *in itself*, requiring from life only occasions and fleeting contacts, but then achieving supremacy by its own means.

It is the awareness of this great mystery that removes the person of the great artist, in whom all is fulfilled, to such a vast height and distance from us, whether the expression be that of the spirit of a people, of a religion, of a supreme good which once held sway—or a perfectly free impulse of a single soul. Hence the fascination (and in our day the high price) of originals.

III

The Reciprocal Action of the Three Powers

The consideration of their six relationships is without systematic value, and even dubious as regards its matter, since determinant and determined change places so rapidly that the true determinant is often difficult to discover, especially for times remote from our own.

Yet this arrangement provides a very convenient framework for a number of historical observations very diverse in kind and covering every epoch, which have a certain value and which it would be difficult to place otherwise. It is—to use another figure of speech—merely the ruffling of the water which makes the ice crystals set.

History is actually the most unscientific of all the sciences, although it communicates so much that is worth knowing. Clear-cut concepts belong to logic, not to history, where everything is in a state of flux, of perpetual transition and combination. Philosophical and historical ideas differ in essence and origin; the former must be as firm and exclusive as possible, the latter as fluid and open.

Thus the very innocence of this arrangement from the point of view of method, may serve to commend it. For the rapid movement from one time or people to other times and peoples yields genuine parallels, such as a chronologically ordered philosophy of history cannot provide. The latter lays more stress on the contrast between successive times and peoples, *we* lay more stress on their identities and kinships. In the former, the main point is change, for us it is likeness.

The same phenomenon will occasionally be found to recur with startling exactitude in times and places far remote from each other, though in very different guise.

Nothing wholly unconditioned has ever existed, and nothing that was solely a determinant. At the same time, one element predominates in one aspect of life, another in another. It is all a question of relative importance, of the dominant at any particular time.

The best order would apparently be: (1) Culture determined by the State; (2) the State determined by Culture; (3) Culture determined by Religion; (4) Religion determined by Culture; (5) the State determined by Religion; (6) Religion determined by the State. The advantage of this arrangement would be that each consideration would be followed by its inversion.

Yet there are greater advantages in the arrangement by which each element is shown in its two relationships successively, beginning with Culture, to be followed by the State and finally Religion. This is a more chronological procedure; without pressing the point, the earlier may be said in a general way to stand at the beginning and the later at the end.

It will much simplify matters if we confine ourselves in each case to this simple transposition, leaving out of account X as simultaneously determined by Y and Z. It lies in the nature of our theme, however, that repetitions are unavoidable, whatever order we adopt.

CULTURE DETERMINED BY THE STATE

We shall again waive any discussion of origins, and even the question of which came first, State or culture, or whether they must be taken as coeval. Nor can we do more than allude to the question of how far law may be regarded as the reflection of the State in culture. Since law may have power in the guise of custom even when the State is practically non-existent and incapable of seconding it (e.g. among the primitive Teutons), we can hardly assume the State to have been its sole origin.

Further, we shall confine ourselves to fully civilized peoples, leaving out of account, for instance, nomads who come into contact with culture on its fringes, at isolated markets, ports, etc., as well as derivative States with a kind of semi-culture, e.g. the Celts.

Our chief example is unquestionably offered by Egypt, which may have been the origin and model of other Asiatic despotisms. For purposes of comparison, we may turn to Mexico and Peru.

Wherever in these early stages a complete culture has developed to the point of the refinements of city life, the State will always be found to have played a preponderating part. Whether it came first, as has already been pointed out, is of no consequence.

As for the State, we may say that it bears the marks of the thousands of years of unrelenting effort and struggle which brought it to birth, that it is in no wise a spontaneous crystallization, a natural process. Religion supports it with sacred law and bestows upon it an unconditional dominion. All knowledge and thought, all physical strength and splendor, is drawn into the service of this dual power. High intelligence—that of priests, Chaldeans, Magi—surrounds the throne.

The most distinct symptom of its dominion over culture appears when the State imparts to culture a specific bias, or brings it to a standstill. In so far as this happens by way of religion, it will be discussed in the next section. The State as such, however, has a hand in the process.

Here we should deal with the question of closed countries. Are countries closed for reasons of State, or rather for reasons of national pride, or of instinctive hate, fear and repulsion? [1] Culture would, left to itself, tend to expand and create a general level, but it cost so much to bring the State into tolerable order that people expect no good to come from the outside world, but only trouble.

Where this way of thinking prevails at a primitive stage of development, the State will assuredly, in the course of time, make it law. The clearest sign of it is the absence of sea-faring among coast-dwellers, such as the Egyptians and Mexicans, while even peoples in a state of nature (those of the Antilles before the arrival of Columbus) practise it. In Egypt, its place was taken by a very highly developed Nile shipping. The Persians, on the other hand, constructed artificial cataracts along the whole course of

[1] Note that *hospes* (stranger) and *hostis* (enemy) come from the same root.

the lower Tigris to prevent any foreign fleet from entering their country.[1]

As regards the institution of caste, it may have had a double root; priests and warriors may have already existed as a class even at the birth of the State; the remaining castes, corresponding to the other avocations, appear to have been later institutions. And here the decisive fact that every man was bound to follow in his father's footsteps was more probably established by the State than by the priests, for, had they decreed it, they would certainly have abolished intermarriage between the castes. In Egypt, apart from the swineherds, who appear to have formed a class of outcasts, no such prohibition can be discovered, while in India it certainly exists.[2]

This institution, which implies the strongest negation of individuality, may give birth to a relatively high partial culture, which may find its justification in the hereditary perfection of manual skill (even though weaving, carpentry, glass-making, etc., remain perfectly stationary), but, in intellectual life at any rate, produces stagnation, narrow-mindedness and pride towards the world outside. For the freedom of the individual, which is here crushed, in no way implies the free right of every man to *do* as he likes, but the unimpeded right to know and communicate knowledge, and the freedom of the creative impulse, and that is what is arrested.

[1] Arrian, VII, 7, 7, *History of Alexander,* where we read how Alexander scoffed at the idea. For the revolution in Egypt under Psammeticus and the ensuing prosperity of the country, cf. Curtius, *Griechische Geschichte,* Vol. I, pp. 345 ff.; Eng. trans. A. Ward, 1873, Vol. II, Book II, Chap. 5, p. 119 f.

[2] The chief castes are the Vaisyas and Sudras, the great mass of the Aryans and non-Aryans.

In Egypt, this tendency was reinforced by the fact that the two higher castes shackled art and science in the most dangerous fashion by declaring them sacred. The State, with its sacred law, thus enclosed permitted knowledge and permitted art in a system, reserving all the essentials to a definite caste. Art, of course, continued to serve the monarch in every way and with supreme devotion, achieving thereby the highest expression of monumental form, and, within the confines of an art whose progress was arrested, an unerring sense of style. Its corollary, however, was slow inward decay without any possibility of regeneration.

What methods were applied by the State in Assyria, Babylon, Persia, etc., to check the development of the individual, which at that time was, most probably, simply synonymous with evil? There is every likelihood that individuality sought to raise its head wherever it could, and succumbed to civil and religious restrictions, caste institutions, etc., leaving not a trace behind. The greatest technical and artistic geniuses were powerless to make any change in the utterly uncouth royal fortresses of Nineveh. The meanness of their ground-plan and the slavishness of their sculptures were law for centuries.

We cannot dismiss the possibility of active coercion; even in the monarchies of the ancient world, a phenomenon of the type of Peter the Great may have existed. A potentate may have *imposed* a culture, learned abroad, on his unwilling subjects, and forced them to become a world power.

In contrast to these despotisms, there stands the free City State of the classical world, after it had overcome an actual, though not permanent, caste system and possibly a code of sacred law. Its sole known forerunners were the

Phoenician cities. What stands out in the polis is the process of conscious change in manifold life able to know and compare and describe itself, while no books with an established doctrine of State and culture are extant. There, at any rate, occupation was independent of birth; the purely technical was certainly scorned as philistine, but agriculture and, on the whole, commerce also were held in honor.

It is true that at a relatively late stage an influence came from the East, seeking to restrain the expression of individuality by a priestly covenant based on the thought of the other world in the guise of metempsychosis, but Pythagoras's success in Croton and Metapontum was short-lived.

Culture, however, was to a high degree determined and dominated by the State, both in the positive and in the negative sense, since it demanded first and foremost of every man that he should be a citizen. Every individual felt that the polis lived in him. This supremacy of the polis, however, is fundamentally different from the supreme power of the modern State, which seeks only to keep its material hold on every individual, while the polis required of every man that he should serve it, and hence intervened in many concerns which are now left to individual and private judgment.

Sparta, however, stood utterly apart, upholding artificially and with cruelty the status created by an ancient conquest. It was that, with a growing inward hollowness masked by false rhetoric, and a manner of life consciously maintained, which was the basis of her peculiar type of foreign policy.

Having unfettered the individual, Greek public life was marked by a peculiar violence both in love and hate which dealt repeated blows to Greek culture. Every breach was terrible and often led to bloody party conflicts aiming at the extermination of the other side and the eviction of whole sections of the population, especially those whose culture was most advanced. And yet, in the end, the brilliance of glory and culture outweighs everything else. It was only in a *Greek* cosmos that all the powers of the individual, released from his bonds, reached that pitch of sensitiveness and strength which made it possible to achieve the highest in every sphere of life. It must, however, be said that culture as a whole, and art and science in particular, flourished more under durable tyrannies than in freedom; indeed, without such pauses, which sometimes lasted a century, it would hardly have reached its zenith. Even Athens needed the age of the Peisistratidae.

We may, perhaps, formulate the following axiom: Culture, as part of civic duty, fostered the creative spirit (in an infinitely wide and very intense sense) rather than knowledge, which grows by leisurely addition.

The latter came into its own in the general idleness which prevailed under the Diadochi, when political life was at a standstill, for Polybius could say (mainly with a view to geography): "Since men of action have been liberated from their ambitious preoccupations with war and politics, they have used the occasion to devote their minds to scientific pursuits." (Polybius, *Histories,* III, 59 and XII, 28.)

Rome then *salvaged* all the cultures of the ancient world, in so far as they were still in existence and in any condition to be salvaged. Rome was primarily a State, and the study of it stands in no need of commendation, for here at last the polis was created which did not only, like fifth-century Athens, rule a clientèle of fifteen to eighteen million souls, but in course of time dominated the world, and that not by virtue of the *form* of the State (which was poor enough in the century preceding Caesar), but by virtue of the *spirit* of the State, and the overwhelming prejudice of the individual in favor of citizenship of a world power. The huge power of offence and defence which developed between the Samnite War and the war of Perseus and heralded a new era in world history was still making itself felt. It did not, as among the Greeks, erupt sporadically, but became concentrated in a Caesar who was capable of making up for great sins of omission, of saving Rome from the barbarian invasions and of reorganizing it. The Empire which then followed was in any case vastly superior in strength to all the ancient monarchies, and indeed the only one to merit the name, for all its shortcomings. The question at issue here is not whether world monarchies are desirable institutions, but whether the Roman Empire actually fulfilled its own purpose, namely, to subsume the ancient cultures and to spread Christianity, the only institution by which their main elements could be saved from destruction by the Teutons.

It is supremely significant that the Empire, torn by factions as it was, always strove to regain its unity; at the crisis following the death of Nero, that unity was still unquestioned; after the deaths of Commodus and Pertinax it was rescued by fierce battles, but even after the Thirty Tyrants it was again restored to brilliance by Aurelian and safeguarded against many usurpers by his successors. It reappeared under Justinian, theoretically at any rate, and again became a reality, though in different form, under Charlemagne. Nor were such results brought about by mere lust of power. The parts themselves strove to reunite. Meanwhile the Church had grown up and, from the tombs of the Apostles, had proclaimed Rome the mistress of the world in a new sense.

If now we enquire into Rome's education for this huge task in her earlier history, we find a people living almost exclusively for the State, war and agriculture, with a very mediocre culture.

The great blessing for the culture of the world lay in the philhellenism of the Romans—coupled, it is true, with a marked fear of the disintegrating foreign spirit. To that philhellenism alone we owe the continuity of intellectual tradition.

The attitude adopted by the Roman Empire towards culture *qua* culture was purely passive. The State certainly desired a general activity, if only because of the *vectigalia* (taxes), but could give it no particular encouragement. Rome was occupied with the business of government alone, and merely took good care that everything and everybody should be tributable to her.

Under the good Emperors, she gave the weary world peace in private life, and, in practice, took up a liberal attitude to all things of the mind and the arts in so far as they served to glorify her power.

Bad Emperors murdered the rich in Rome and the provinces, and robbed culture of its security, though only temporarily. Domitian had many vineyards uprooted, but Trajan had them replanted.

Thus under the almost general tolerance, cultures and religions could become generalized. The Empire did not prove destructive to culture till the fourth century, which brought the evils of the financial system by which the *possessores* (landed proprietors) were liable for the taxes of their districts. The result was the flight to the barbarians, while at the same time other abuses were causing depopulation.

The dominion of barbarian conquerors over civilized peoples is sometimes very lasting, as we can see by the example of the Turks. If this was not the case in the States of the *Völkerwanderung*,[1] the reason is that conquerors and conquered did not remain separated by religion. Hence intermarriage was possible, and on the degree and nature of intermarriage, in such circumstances, everything depends. The new State, however, retarded Culture, which is not always a misfortune. It did so by a new institution of castes. Of these, one, the clergy, was pre-existent and inherited; the other, the nobility, developed from the clients of the Germanic chieftains, was new.

Between and beside these two castes, which possessed their special culture, it was very difficult for the main exponent of the new culture to rise. This was the city, which, for the first time since the fall of the Roman Empire, united and represented *all* branches of culture. After the twelfth century, it even took art out of the hands of the hierarchy, for the great works of art of the late Middle Ages were created by laymen. Soon after, in Italy, science also emancipated itself from the Church. Thus there came a time when general culture was represented solely by individual petty States, while the specific cultural world of the nobility and clergy was passing into its decline and the Courts were mere assembly-places for the nobility.

Here we see the bright side of the dismemberment and medley of petty States created by the medieval feudal system. The Carolingian State had given rise to a type of State and life, at once national and provincial, which it

[1] The great migration of the Germanic tribes.

would be idle either to praise or to blame. And that had continued on a small scale. Every possible kind of privilege, at every stage of power, was bestowed in return for certain services, so that a perpetual devolution prevailed in which the idea of office evaporated. It was the most uncertain and unwieldy method imaginable of drawing income from capital and service from gifts, a fragmentation and delegation of power which, to our power-drunk century, would look like madness, while government in our sense was impossible. But things which are without significance for the culture of their times are never long-lived, and the feudal system lived long. The men of that epoch developed their own virtues and vices within the system of their time; personality had free play and could put good-will into action. Therein lay its emotional appeal. And at the same time, in the cities, culture found terrible barriers in the decadence of the gild system; there, however, it was not the State, but culture itself which created self-imposed limitations in the form of corporations.

But now, with Frederick II and his Lower Italian Empire, there dawns on the horizon the modern, centralized Power State, based on the practice of Norman tyranny and on Mohammedan models, exercising terrible dominion over culture too, especially by its trade monopolies, which Frederick reserved for himself—we have only to think of his own privilege of trade with the entire Mediterranean. Here the State intervened in all private affairs, so that the royal *bajuli* (bailiffs) even regulated wages; the old taxes on the various occupations were swelled by a mass of new and very irksome impositions; where the tax-gatherers were not harsh enough, Frederick, as an ultimate means of pressure, put Saracens in their place, and in the end even made use of Saracen justiciaries. The defaulting taxpayer was sent to the galleys; tax-resisting districts were occupied by Saracen or German garrisons. Other abuses were the system of exact cadastral survey, secret police, forced loans, blackmail, prohibition of marriage with foreigners without special permission, the obligation to study at the University of Naples, and lastly the debasement of the coinage and the swelling of the monopolies, so that 75 per cent. of salt, iron, silk, etc. went to the State. The great general crime against culture, however, was the disastrous seclusion of Lower Italy from the West. We must beware of liberal sympathies with the great Hohenstaufen!

Frederick's successors, the Italian tyrants, must at least have proceeded with greater caution and avoided plunging their subjects into despair. In the rest of Europe, however, it took a long time for power to attain to such concentration. And when that happened, we have one safe standard by which to judge whether its concern for the public interest was serious, namely, that the State separated law from power, handled, in particular, the exchequer with impartiality, and admitted suits against the exchequer and complaints against the clergy before independent courts.

Here we might make mention in passing of Spain as a purely consuming and destructive power, or one in any case in which spiritual and temporal were differently blended. The first *perfected* example of the modern State with supreme coercive power exercised on nearly all branches of culture is to be seen in the France of Louis XIV and in his imitators.[1]

In essence, that power was a restoration by violence, and counter to the true spirit of the age, which had

[1] Cf. Buckle, *op. cit.* Vol. I, Chap. XI.

seemed, since the sixteenth century, to be striving towards political and intellectual freedom. It was born of the union of the French conception of monarchy with Roman law under Philip the Fair and with the political ideas of the Renaissance, which tended now to democratic Utopias and now to absolutism. It was reinforced by the French bias towards uniformity, docility to tutelage and predilection for an alliance with the Church. That more Mongolian than occidental monstrosity which bore the name of Louis XIV would certainly have been excommunicated in the Middle Ages, but in his own time it was possible for him to set himself up as the sole possessor of rights and the sole proprietor of bodies and souls.

It is a great evil that, where one begins, the others must follow suit, if only for the sake of their own safety. This Power State was imitated, on a big and small scale, as far as it lay in men's ability to do so, and persisted even when Reason and Revolution had given it quite a new meaning and its name was no longer Louis, but Republic. Not until the nineteenth century, as we shall see later, did culture harness that State to its own service, and the dispute begin as to which should lay down the law to the other. That dispute is the great crisis which the conception of the State is going through today.

As regards its relationship to trade and commerce, Louis himself turned Colbert's system into one of sheer exploitation. There were forced industries, forced agriculture, forced colonies, a forced navy, things which the German sultans emulated with might and main, yet the general oppression and blackmail was only a check, and not a spur to activity. At all points, genuine initiative was baulked.

We can see the vestiges of this system even today in the

protective tariff industries, the State apparently acting in the interests of those industries, but actually in its own.

At the same time the State acquired the habit of an aggressive foreign policy, of large standing armies and other costly instruments of force, in short, of a separate life completely divorced from its own higher aims. It became a mere dreary self-enjoyment of power, a pseudo-organism existing by and for itself.

And now comes its relationship to intellectual life. Here the most important and characteristic event of Louis XIV's reign was the revocation of the Edict of Nantes and the great expulsion of the Huguenots, the greatest human sacrifice ever offered to the Moloch of "unity"; in other words, to the royal conception of power.

First and foremost, the State (with *l'état c'est moi*) set up a doctrine of itself which was in conflict with general truth and the antithesis not only of culture but also of religion itself.[1]

Further, exclusion and promotion were turned into a system, the former carried to the point of the persecution of certain types of cultured minds, while care was taken that any who were not persecuted should be sickened of any free impulse.

In this process, intellect came half-way to meet power. What power could not attain by violence, intellect freely offered, in order to remain in its good graces. This would be the place to say a few words on the worth and worthlessness of all academies.

Literature and even philosophy became servile in their glorification of the State, and art monumentally servile; they created only what was acceptable at Court. Intellect

[1] Cf. also Napoleon's *Catéchisme de l'Empire* and, in anticipation, the Spanish monarchy with its claim to equality with God.

put itself out to board in every direction and cringed before convention.[1]

With creative activity in this venal condition, freedom of expression was only to be found among exiles, and probably among the entertainers of the common people.

At the same time, Courts became the model for the whole of social life; their taste was the sole arbiter.

Further, in the course of time the State set up its own academies, tolerating no competition except that of the Church, which it had to tolerate. It could not, of course, abandon intellectual life entirely to society, because society at times tends to weary in well-doing and would allow certain branches of culture to die out if there were no stronger will to sustain them. In late, exhausted epochs, the State may, in an emergency, act as the heir and protector of things belonging to the realm of culture which would perish without it. We can see, for instance, how many things are lacking in America, where the State has not taken over this function. That is the late determination of culture by the State, which is quite different from that of primitive times.

The gradual habituation to total tutelage, however, in the end kills all initiative; people expect everything from the State, and the result is that at the first shift of power they demand everything from the State, casting all their burdens upon it. We shall have to return to this new phase, in which culture dictates programmes to the State (quite particularly such as are really incumbent on society), sets out to transform it into an agent of morality and operates a profound change in its principle.

Faced with this development, sovereign and coercive power forcibly maintains its position with the help of its

[1] In modern times, regents are replaced by publishers or the public.

tradition and its accumulated means of compulsion, and relies on habit. This dynamic central will, however, is and remains a very different thing from the common and total will of the nations, since it comprehends the concentration of power in a totally different way.

The modern trend of the nations is towards unity and the great State, which, even when its territorial unity is threatened (as in the American Union) and it seems to be heading for separation, upholds its unity with all the means in its power. The causes of that trend, however, are still under dispute and its outcome unpredictable.

Among other things, certain supreme achievements of culture (as though culture were the guiding principle) are put forward as the purpose of that trend—unrestricted traffic and freedom of movement, the ennobling of all endeavor by its dedication to national ends, concentration instead of dispersal, with a resulting gain in value, simplification instead of complication. Indeed, there are wiseacres enough who imagine that *they* would dictate the programme of culture to the State, once it was completely united.

First and foremost, however, what the nation desires, implicitly or explicitly, is power. Its previous dismemberment is abhorred as a brand of shame. The individual cannot find any satisfaction in such a service; his one desire is to participate in a great entity, and this clearly betrays power as the primary and culture as a very secondary goal at best. More specifically, the idea is to make the general will of the nation felt abroad, in defiance of other nations.

Hence, firstly, the hopelessness of any attempt at decentralization, of any voluntary restriction of power in favor of local and civilized life. The central will can never be too strong.

Now power is of its nature evil, whoever wields it. It is not stability but a lust, and *ipso facto* insatiable, therefore unhappy in itself and doomed to make others unhappy.

Inevitably, in its pursuit, peoples fall into the hands both of ambitious dynasties seeking to maintain themselves, and of individual "great men," etc., i.e. of the forces which have the furtherance of culture least at heart.

But the man who desires power and the man who desires culture—it may be that both are the blind tools of a third, still unknown force.

CULTURE DETERMINED BY RELIGION

RELIGIONS have high claims to be regarded as the mothers of culture; indeed, religion is a prime condition of any culture deserving the name, and hence may coincide with the sole existing culture.

It is true that the two arise from essentially different needs: metaphysical on the one hand, intellectual and material on the other. What actually happens, however, is that the one carries the other along with it and presses it into its own service.

A powerful religion permeates all the affairs of life and lends color to every movement of the spirit, to every element of culture.[1]

In time, of course, those things come to react upon religion, and indeed its living core may be stifled by the ideas and images it once took into its sphere. The "sanctification of all the concerns of life" has its fateful aspect.

Every religion would, if left to its own devices, harness both State and culture entirely to its own ends, i.e. turn them into mere bulwarks of itself and re-create all society from its own centre. Its representatives, i.e. its hierarchy,

[1] How far are inferior peoples held in their uncivilized condition by their religions of fear? Or do those religions subsist *because* the race is uncivilizable?

would completely supplant any other rulers. And then, when faith had petrified into tradition, it would be useless for culture to attempt to maintain itself as progress and change; it would remain fettered.

This danger is particularly great in States with a sacred code of law. There it is the united power of State and religion which holds culture in check.

Further, the very *substance* of a religion, its doctrine, can impose strict and definite limits on culture, even where that culture is of a very high order.

First and foremost, the preoccupation with a future life may completely overshadow this world. At the very beginning of history we encounter Egypt with its cult of tombs, which imposed upon the Egyptian such enormous sacrifices for his burial; while, again, at the end of the ancient world we find gloom and asceticism carried to extremes, namely, to the point of disgust with earthly life.

Thus Christianity began not only to permeate but also to replace Roman culture. In the fourth century, the Church overcame the Arian schism, and with Theodosius the Empire and orthodoxy became synonymous. That meant not only that the unity of the Church was exalted above the unity of the Empire, but the Church ousted all non-religious literature. We learn practically nothing more of secular thought; outwardly, asceticism colored the whole of life; there was a rush to the cloister. The cultured ancient world, which the State had mishandled too, seemed to have condemned itself to celibacy and decay. The only voices we hear seem to be those of barbarism and religion. The hierarchs were the most powerful of men, liturgy and dogmatic controversy the main occupation even of the people.

Yet even in such circumstances there was one incalculable blessing for culture, namely that, in the West at any rate, State and Church did not fuse into one oppressive whole (while in Byzantium they did to a certain extent). The barbarians established secular empires, at first predominantly Arian.

In Islam, where this fusion took place, the whole of culture was dominated, shaped and colored by it. Islam has only one form of polity, of necessity despotic, the consummation of power, secular, priestly and theocratic, which was transferred as a matter of course from the Caliphate to all dynasties. Thus all its parts were mere replicas of the world empire on a small scale, hence Arabized and despotic. All power came from God in the same sense as among the Jews.

This aridity, this dreary uniformity of Islam, which is so terribly limited on the religious side, probably did more harm than good to Culture, if only because it rendered the peoples affected by it quite incapable of going over to another culture. Its simplicity much facilitated its expansion, but was marked by that extreme exclusiveness which is a feature of all rigid monotheism, while the wretched Koran stood, and still stands, in the way of any political and legal growth. Law remained half priestly.

The best that might be said of the cultural influence of the Koran is that it does not prohibit activity as such, fosters mobility (by travel)—hence the unity of this culture from the Ganges to the Senegal—and excludes Oriental jugglery and magic in their crudest forms.

Yet Christian contemplation even at its gloomiest was less pernicious culturally than Islam, as will at once appear from the following consideration.

Quite apart from the general servitude imposed by despotism and its police, from the lack of any sense of honor in anyone connected with power, for which the absence of a nobility and clergy offers no compensation, a diabolical pride is engendered towards non-Islamic populations and countries, involving a periodical renewal of the Holy War, and that pride cuts it off from what is, after all, far and away the greater part of the world and from any comprehension of it.

The sole ideals of life are the two poles—the monarch and the cynically ascetic dervish-sufi, to which we may perhaps add the vagabond after the manner of Abu Said. Freedom and personality may, it would seem, find a refuge in satire, vagabondage and a life of penance.

In Islamic education, we are struck by the predominance of linguistics and grammar over substance, by the sophistical nature of philosophy, of which only the heretical side is free and significant, further, by the poor quality of historical learning—poor because everything outside of Islam is indifferent and everything within Islam a prey to parties and sects—and by a scientific teaching the defects of which immediately become apparent when it is compared with free and unrestricted empiricism. Men were not able to investigate and discover nearly as much as they might have done in freedom. What was lacking was a general impulse to fathom the world and its laws.

Islamic poetry is mainly characterized by its repugnance to the epic, born of the fear that the souls of the several peoples might continue to live in it; Firdausi[1] only exists as contraband. It has, further, a didactic bias which is mortal to the epic, and a tendency to value narrative only as the shell of a general thought, as a parable. For the rest, poetry took refuge in the tale, thronged with figures but

[1] Cf. note p. 198.

devoid of characters. Further, there was no drama. Fatalism makes it impossible to show fate as born of the interplay of passion and justification—indeed, it may be that despotism of its very nature checks the objective poetic expression of anything at all. And no comedy could come into being, if only because there was no mixed social intercourse and because all comic feeling was consumed by the joke, the lampoon, the parable, the juggler, etc.

In the visual arts, architecture alone developed, firstly through Persian builders and subsequently with the help of Byzantine and any other styles which lay to hand. Sculpture and painting were practically non-existent, because the decree of the Koran was not only observed but carried far beyond its letter. What the intellect forfeited in these circumstances may be left to the imagination.

Side by side with this picture, there exists, of course, another—that fiction of flourishing, populous, busy Islamic cities and States with poet-princes, noble-minded grandees and so on, as for instance in Spain under and after the Umayyads.

Yet it was not possible to pass beyond those barriers to the totality of intellectual life, and as a result it was beyond the power of Islam to change, to merge into another, higher culture, and the situation was aggravated by its political and military weakness in face of the Almoravides, Almohades and Christians.

The influence of religions on cultures depends, of course, to a large extent on their significance for life as a whole. It is not, however, only their present significance which counts, but that which they once enjoyed. At the critical moment of a people's mental development, a religion imprints upon it a mark which it will never cease to bear. And even if, later, all the gates into a free culture are thrown open, the impulse, or at any rate the best impulse, towards what was once admired is spent. For the moment when that particular branch of culture might have bloomed as part of a general efflorescence of national life never returns. Just as great forests grow once, but never rise again if they have been felled, both men and peoples possess or acquire certain things in youth or never.

For that matter, as regards culture in general, it is doubtful whether we are justified in regarding its unchecked expansion at any stage as desirable, whether what is here blighted, to die undeveloped, is not destined to come to light among future peoples and cultures as something utterly unprecedented and new-born, so that it may *once* exist in a pristine state.

It was the classical religions which placed the fewest obstacles in the way of culture, for they had no priesthood, no scriptures and no outstanding emphasis on a future life.

The Greek world of gods and heroes was an ideal reflection of the human world, with divine and heroic models for every high endeavor and for every enjoyment. It was a divinization and not a petrifaction of culture when the fire-god became the skilful smith, the goddess of lightning and war the protectress of all culture, art and clear-thinking men, and the god of the hearth the lord of roads, messages and traffic. The Romans completed this divinization of all mundane activity down to the *pulchra Laverna* (goddess of gain, honest or no: hence of thieves).

Among the ancients, religion thus offered little resistance to the development of intellect; at the point where poetry, as the educator of man, dismissed him, philosophy was waiting to receive him and lead him on to monotheism, atheism and pantheism.

Inevitably, religion, which subsisted nevertheless, became a hollow shell, a mere mass creed, which, after the second century, enfolded a weary culture with its black pinions. The conflict with an invading Christianity could only end in its overthrow.

Art, in its relation to religion, must be dealt with separately.

Whatever their origin, the arts, in the critical early stages of their growth, were at the service of Religion.

What must or may have existed even before were copies of real objects, plastic or flat, with color, the decoration of buildings, the beginnings of narrative and of emotional expression in song, and possibly even a very formal kind of dance. Even if a religion existed simultaneously with these things, they were not yet its servants.

Yet religion and the cultus could alone call forth those solemn vibrations in the soul through which men's highest powers could be poured into such things; through them alone could the consciousness of higher laws mature and impose upon the individual artist, who would otherwise have given free rein to his imagination, a *style*. What style means is that a degree of perfection once achieved is retained in opposition to the popular taste persisting beside it (which may always have had a bias towards the pretty, gaudy, ghastly, etc.).

Here lay man's first experience of release from religious terror. The sculptures of the gods meant salvation from the grisly idol; the hymn purified the soul.

Even despots may have exploited for their own ends an art which owed its origin to the priests.

Art, however, as time goes on, is not merely maintained at a certain level; it is also fixed, the higher developments being temporarily checked by priestly arrest; what had once been achieved with enormous effort was pronounced sacred, as can be seen in Egypt at the beginning and Byzantium at the end of the ancient world.

Egypt came to a stop there, was never allowed to take the step to individual expression, and became incapable of any development or transition to new forms. *Sint, ut sunt, aut non sint* must be said of her artists.

The greatest enslavement of an art once great, which might, in freedom, still have been capable of great things, is to be seen in Byzantium. Practically only the sacred was permitted, and that only in a selection and form of representation dictated by convention and executed with unchanging methods. Art became more formal than at any other time and place.

Elsewhere, as in Islam, art was forcibly stunted or even negated by religion, as it was in Puritanism and Calvinism, in which iconoclasm inevitably spread from the churches to the whole of life.

The various stages of the detachment of the individual arts from the cultus may have been as follows:

The first to become really free was poetry, which developed a neutral, heroic, lyrical world of beauty. Among the Hebrews and Greeks we even find didactic poetry at a very early date. Poetry is the first art which religion outgrows and dismisses, for religion has long since been provided with the verse necessary to its ritual, and probably prefers to retain that which arose in its primitive stages. Side by side with this a free poetry of a devotional kind may subsist, since the free play of the imagination on sacred themes causes no misgivings. Further, the popular epic remained a receptacle for myth where myth existed, because myth cannot be separated from the mere popular saga. Secular poetry, however, now became all the more a necessity, in that there was no medium but poetry for any record destined to be preserved and handed down.

Then one branch of knowledge after the other detached itself from religion, except where the latter maintained its dominion by sacred law, and ultimately science arose without any connection with religion at all.

Yet there remains with us the feeling that all poetry and all intellectual life were once the handmaids of the holy, and have passed through the temple.

Visual art, on the other hand, remained longer at the service of religion, and indeed an important part of it remained permanently, if not in that service, at any rate closely associated with it (for, as we shall see later, the matter has two sides).

To architecture, Religion offers a supreme aim; to sculpture and painting, an approved, universally intelligible range of ideas, an occupation homogeneously distributed over many lands.

The value of uniformity for the development of styles, however, is incalculable. It challenges art to remain eternally youthful and fresh within the circle of ancient themes, yet at the same time monumental and adequate to the sanctuary. Hence it comes that the Madonnas and Descents from the Cross, a thousand times repeated, are not the most effete, but the best productions of the best period.

No comparable advantage is offered by secular themes, since they are, of their very nature, in constant change.

No style could have been formed by them; the secular art of the present day lives partly on the fact that sacred styles have existed and still exist. We may say that, if it had not been for Giotto, Jan Steen would have been a different, and probably a lesser, artist.

Finally, religion offers music an incomparable emotional sphere. It is true that what music creates within that sphere, being only half explicit, long outlives religion itself.

THE STATE DETERMINED BY RELIGION

Late in time, it was recognized that religion is the main bond of human society [1] as the sole guardian of that state of morality which holds society together. In the same way, it is certain that religion was a powerful contributing factor when States were founded, presumably after frightful paroxysms. For that reason it has claimed a lasting influence on the whole subsequent life of the State.

This connection between the State and religion explains why a sacred code of law came to be established by the priesthood; its object was to secure to the State the greatest possible degree of durability. At the beginning, it rendered equal services to rulers and priests.

Yet even if this dual power had not of itself invited a dual abuse, the misfortune was that it checked all individuality. Every breach with the established order was regarded as sacrilege and hence avenged by cruel punishments and refined tortures. In this sacred petrifaction, all further development was arrested.

The bright side of the process was that, at times when the individual is suppressed, really great things can be

[1] Cf. Bacon, *Sermones Fideles. Religio praecipuum humanae societatis vinculum* and *Essay* III. For the sense of honor as the modern substitute, cf. Prévost-Paradol, *France Nouvelle,* p. 357 ff.

achieved through the power of the priests and the State, great aims can be realized, much knowledge gained, the whole nation can discover its form of self-expression, its own source of feeling and its own national pride. The peoples ruled by sacred law have really existed to some purpose and left mighty traces behind them; it is of the utmost importance to study at least one of them, and to observe how the personality of the individual is fettered and only the whole is personal.

Sacred law is, in the absolute sense, part of the lot of such peoples as have ever served it. It is true that they never again become capable of freedom. The bondage of the first generations runs in their blood till today. How far intellectual culture is hampered in that condition we have already seen in the example of ancient Egypt.

Sacred books are instructive in the highest sense of the word, not in themselves, but for the assessment of what has been frustrated and suppressed in such peoples.

Further, despotism gets the upper hand sooner or later, and abuses religion by using it as a prop.

The Temple and Oracle States of Asia Minor, including the shrine of Ammon, present special variants. In these States, though only for a small circle, Religion was the foundation of life and sole ruling power. They seldom possessed a body of citizens, but as a rule a body of temple slaves, recruited partly from gifts, partly from tribes who had been pressed into the service of the god after holy wars, or in other ways.

Delphi and Dodona may also be mentioned here as Oracle States of a peculiar kind. The constitution of Delphi was of such a kind that, from a number of families descended from Deucalion—"nobles of Delphi, the lords," the five ruling priests were chosen by lot; then came the Amphictyonic Council as the superior authority.

We might mention here Diodorus's [1] interesting account of the secularization of a priestly State of this kind in Meroe by Ergamenes, and finally the Dacian-Getian theocracy which flourished about 100 B.C., in which a god (i.e. a human being in the guise of a god) functioned side by side with the King.[3]

The greatest, historically most significant and strongest theocracies, however, were not to be found at all among the polytheistic religions, but among such religions as had, possibly by a sudden, violent wrench, broken away from polytheism, which were founded and revealed and instituted by a reaction.

Thus we can see the Jews, through all the vicissitudes of their history, perpetually striving to establish a theocracy, as can be seen most clearly in their later restoration as a Temple State. They hoped less for the world dominion of their nation than of their religion; all the peoples were to gather together to worship on Mount Moriah. It is true that, with David and Solomon, the Jewish theocracy was temporarily transformed into a secular despotism, but periodically the Jews sought to eliminate from their national being any element which the State and universal by side with the King.[2]

Aryan polytheism, in its reversion to pantheism, was the source of the religion of the Brahmins; the Zend religion, on the other hand, transformed it into an unparalleled dualism. And that change can only have been effected in one sudden movement by one great (very

[1] Diodorus, *Historical Library,* III, 6.
[2] Strabo, *Geography,* VII, 3, 5.

great) individual. Hence there can be no doubt of Zarathustra as an individual historical personality.

It was, in the extreme sense, theocratic in intention. The whole world, visible and invisible, and even past history (*Shahnama*),[1] was divided between two personified principles and their trains (hardly personified at all). And that in a predominantly pessimistic sense, so that the one-time ruler, beloved of the gods, ends his life evilly in the toils of Ahriman.

Yet at this very point, we must again note how easily religion and the State change places in their mutual interaction. All this did not prevent the actual monarchs of Persia (the Achaemenidae at any rate) from arrogating to themselves the representation of Ormuzd on earth and believing themselves to stand under his special and permanent guidance, while the monarchy itself was in reality a horrible Oriental despotism. Indeed, on the strength of that delusion, the monarch assumed that he could do no wrong, and subjected his enemies to the most infamous tortures. The Magi, whose power in life was incomparably less than that of the Brahmins, appear only as the wardens of one courtly superstition after the other, not as guides and warners. On the whole, State and religion were here associated to the great detriment of both.

Morality does not seem to have profited in any way by this dualism. There seems to have been no intention that morality should be free, for Ahriman befooled the hearts of the good until they acted evilly. And retribution, all the same, came in the next world.

So great was the power of this religion, however, that it inspired the Persians with a haughty hatred of idolatry.

[1] The *Book of Kings,* Firdausi's epic; adapted by Matthew Arnold (*Sohrab and Rustum*), trans. Atkinson and others.

It was closely bound up with national feeling, and hence strong enough to produce a renaissance. The Macedonians and Parthians were followed by the Sassanidae, who turned that feeling to their own great political ends, and seemed to restore the old faith in its purity. Dualism, however, could not stand its ground against Islam. Though it had itself been a violent simplification, it succumbed, quite logically, to a still more violent one. What happened was that one abstraction made way for a second, still greater abstraction.

In connection with the renaissance of the Zend religion in the Sassanian epoch, we might now briefly review such restorations in general. We shall take no account of the restorations which simply follow civil wars, nor shall we discuss the restoration of Messenia at the time of Epaminondas, nor the restorations of 1815, in which the State made the first advances to the Church, nor, finally, restorations which are still to come: for instance, that of the Jews, who, having lost their temple twice, have centred their aspirations on a third one, and that of the Greeks, which turns on the Hagia Sophia. The restoration we have in mind nearly always takes the form of the re-establishment of a past form of a people or a State by religion, or at any rate with its help, and the chief examples, apart from the Sassanian one already mentioned, are those of the Jews under Cyrus and Darius, the Empire of Charlemagne, in which the intention of the Church seems to have been a condition similar to that under Constantine and Theodosius, and the establishment of the Kingdom of Jerusalem by the First Crusade. The greatness of these restorations is not to be measured by their success, which is generally less than the optical illusion of their beginnings gave reason to hope. Their greatness lies in the effort they evoke, in the power to realize a cherished ideal, which is not the actual past, but its image transfigured by memory. The result is necessarily somewhat strange, since it is established in a changed world. What remains of it is the ancient religion in a stricter form.

And now we must again turn back to Islam, with its stranglehold on national feeling and its miserable constitutional and legal system grafted on to religion, beyond which its peoples never advanced. The State, as a political picture, is here supremely uninteresting; in the Caliphate, practically from the outset, a despotism without responsibility to heaven or earth was taken for granted, and even, by a highly illogical twist, by its renegades. What is supremely interesting is how this organization came into being and could not but come into being, given the nature of Islam and of its rule over Giaours. There lies the explanation of the great similarity of Islamic States from the Tagus to the Ganges, the only difference being that the latter were ruled with more, the former with less steadfastness and talent. A kind of division of power can be dimly descried only among the Seljuk nobility.

It would seem that the belief in a future life was never of great consequence among the Moslems from the beginning. No interdict in the Western sense had any power, no moral qualms could afflict the potentate, and it was easy for him to remain orthodox or adhere to whichever of the sects happened to predominate.[1] It is true that, from time to time, benevolent despots were regarded with great affection, but even their sphere of influence was re-

[1] But it sometimes happened that a fanatic gathered zealots under some standard or other, e.g. the Wahabis, whose doctrine is a hotch-potch utterly unintelligible to us.

stricted to their immediate entourage. Now the question may arise how far Islam (like the more ancient Parsee religion and Byzantium) represented a State in any sense whatever. Its pride was simply that it was Islam, nor could this simplest of all religions be attacked through its own devotees. Sacraments could not be withheld from the evildoer, whose fatalism made him impervious to many things, while every one of its members was familiar with violence and corruption. Whoever was either unable or unwilling to exterminate the Moslems found it best to leave them in peace. Their empty, arid and treeless lands might perhaps be taken from them, but obedience to a non-Koranic dispensation could never be enforced. Their equanimity gave them a high degree of individual independence; their slave system and their subjection of the Giaours inspired them with that contempt of all labor, except agriculture, which is the basis of their communal feeling.

A peculiar steadfastness is to be seen in the Ottoman State. It may perhaps be explained by the fact that the powers necessary for usurpation are exhausted. Any importation from Western culture, however, seems to be detrimental to the Moslems, from loans and national debts onward.

A perfect contrast to the political and religious systems of the ancient East is offered by the Graeco-Roman world at the time of its highest development. The religions of that world were mainly determined by the State and Culture. They were State and Culture religions, the gods were State and Culture gods, while the State was not a theocracy; hence the absence of a priesthood in these religions.

Since religion was thus determined by the State—for that reason we shall have to return to classical antiquity later—the Christian Empire meant a revolution of which we may say that it was the greatest that had ever happened. We have already seen how profoundly culture was determined by religion in the period immediately following, namely, that of the Christian Emperors and its prolongation in Byzantium. Soon the State was almost in the same position, and from that time onward to the present day, we find metaphysics constantly intervening in politics, wars, etc., in some fashion and at some point, and where the main issue is not metaphysical, metaphysics nevertheless take a hand in resolve and decision, or are invoked as an afterthought.

Byzantinism developed analogously to Islam and frequently in interaction with it. But in Byzantium, the basis of the whole power and policy of the priesthood was at all times the great stress laid on the doctrine of the future life. This had been a feature of later paganism, but among the Byzantines it was reinforced *in concreto* by the Church's power of interdict even after death. At that time, Byzantium was the impregnable capital of an extremely miscellaneous, or even nationless residue of the Roman Empire, with a great concentration of material means and of political and military ability. It proved itself capable of assimilating a great immigration of Slavs and of regaining piecemeal much that had been lost. The relationship between State and religion, however, fluctuated. Until the dispute over iconoclasm, the Church was, in the main, predominant, judging the Empire entirely according to its subservience to ecclesiastical ends, while the writers judged the Emperors simply and solely by the favors they bestowed on the orthodox Church. Even Justinian had for the most part to make himself felt as a representative of orthodoxy, as its sword and missionary.[1] According to that standard, the Church secured to the Empire the obedience of peoples and happiness on earth. After Constantine, all the Emperors had to take their share in theological controversy.

This state of affairs lasted until Leo the Isaurian began to theologize independently. It may even be in his time, but in any case no later than that of Copronymos and his successors, that the political motive came to the fore. Their aim was to get the helm of State into their own hands, and to force the clergy and the monks to give them elbow-room. In a general way, the Empire resumed the decisive rôle it was obviously playing by the time of the Macedonians and Comneni; the higher spiritual impetus of the Church died down, as we can see by the extinction of any important heresies. From that time forth, it was taken for granted that the Empire, State and orthodoxy were identical. Orthodoxy was no longer a danger to the Empire, but rather its supporting soul. Religion served it as a source of collective emotion, directed rather against the Franks than against the Mohammedans.

In any case, religion now entered upon its curious last phase. Once more (1261) it helped to restore the State. Then, in 1453, having become a national concern, it began to take the place of the submerged State and to work ceaselessly for its restoration. The fact that it continued to exist among the Turks without a State can be taken as a proof either of its vitality or of its complete inanition.

In the Teutonic States at the time of the great migra-

[1] Cf. Gibbon, *Decline and Fall of the Roman Empire*, ed. Bury, Chap. XV.

tions we encounter first the remarkable attempt to elude a sharing of power with the priests by the adoption of Arianism.

This attempt failed everywhere in the course of time; the *orthodox* Church became mistress and forced itself into a position of political command, hence we shall have no further need to distinguish between the Church and its hierarchical development. The only question is, *who is* the Church at any given moment?

In the West, the identification of religion and the State was happily avoided. A very peculiar and extremely wealthy corporation was created, outside of life, yet part and parcel of it, and enjoying a share of the supreme power of the State and the Law, with full sovereignty at certain points.

More than once the Church entered upon a decline, which always consisted in the intrusion of worldly covetousness and the tendency to exploit it in piecemeal fashion. But the secular powers as a rule came to the help, if not of the Church, then at least of its central institution, the Papacy. Some rescued and reformed it: for instance, Charlemagne, Otto the Great, Henry III. Their intention in doing so was to make use of it subsequently as an instrument of Empire over the whole of the West.

In every case the upshot was the contrary. Charlemagne's Empire broke up, and the Church became mightier than ever. Torn from the depths of abasement by Henry III, it rose against and towered above his successors and all other secular powers. For the feudal State actually existed only piecemeal, while the Church (*a*) as regards estates and privileges was also part of that State, but (*b*) was as a rule too strong for the monarchies, hence was only a part and yet the whole.

Thus, in its unity and spirit, the Church stood in contrast to the weakness and multiplicity of the States. Under Gregory VII it set about absorbing them, and although under Urban II it relaxed that effort to a certain extent, it nevertheless ordered the Western world to turn toward the East.

From the twelfth century onward, the Church felt the after-effects of having grown into a huge "kingdom of this world," a kingdom which was by way of outstripping its own clerical and spiritual strength. It was confronted not only by the Waldensian doctrine of the Primitive Church, but by pantheism, and (in Amalrich of Bena and the Albigenses) a dualism associated with the doctrine of metempsychosis.

The Church then forced the State to lend it the support of the secular arm as a matter of course. As soon as any power can command that arm, it is no far cry from: "One thing only is needful" to "One thing only is permissible." Thus Innocent III carried the day by virtue of the threats and promises contained in his decretals.

After him, however, the Church stood as a triumphant, ruthless reaction against the true spirit of the age. It was a police force, habituated to the most extreme methods, which artificially re-established the Middle Ages.

Its system of possessions and power, however, bound it to the secular world by a thousand ties. It had actually to hand over its most lucrative offices to the nobility of various countries; even the Benedictine Order degenerated into a petty nobility. The lower ranks were given over to the race for benefices and the wrangling of the canonists and schoolmen. Knights, lawyers and sophists were the men who counted, and the Church, as the victim of a general exploitation, presented the supreme example of a religion overwhelmed by its institutions and representatives.

Inasmuch as the maintenance of the orthodox faith was by now purely a police matter, to which those in power were spiritually indifferent, it is open to question whether the institution which perpetuated its temporal sway can be regarded as representing a religion at all. The position was rendered more acute by the peculiar relationship of the ecclesiastical State to Italian politics. Real worship had taken refuge with the stricter orders, with mystics and scattered preachers.

At that time the Church must have already adopted its attitude of absolute conservatism; any kind of change must have caused it uneasiness and every movement suspicion, since its complicated system of possession and power might always suffer in some way.

Above all, it opposed the rise of States with centralized power (in Lower Italy and in France under Philip the Fair) and restricted confiscations, at any rate on a large scale—though always with exceptions. It clung passionately to the past in its power and possessions, and just as passionately in the rigor of its doctrine, save that the theory of powers was strained still further, while any increase of its own revenues was greedily accepted. Ultimately it possessed a third of all there was to possess.[1] Yet only the lesser part of that third was actually possessed by the Church itself for its spiritual purposes, the lion's share falling to the great men who had imposed themselves upon it.

Since the Church had long been guilty of this flagrant negation of the religion it was supposed to represent, it

[1] Seyssel, *Histoire du roy Louis XII,* alleges that the clergy possessed more than a third of the revenues of the kingdom.

ultimately stood in open conflict with the political ideas and cultural forces surrounding it. Hence its occasional concordats with the State, which were, in actual fact, partial cessions—for instance, the concordat with Francis I. Yet there is this to be said, that they saved the Church from the Reformation in the countries concerned.

From the Reformation onward, the Church again turned seriously to dogma in one direction. The Church of the Counter-Reformation, however, was to be much more openly reactionary than that of Innocent III. The character of Catholicism since that time—with exceptions, such as the demagogy of the Ligue—has been marked by the covenant between throne and altar. Both recognize the complicity of their respective forms of conservatism as opposed to the spirit of modern nations. The Church, it is true, loved no State, yet inclined towards that system which was most willing and able to carry out persecutions for it. It adjusted itself to the modern State as it had once adjusted itself to the feudal system.

On the other hand, it holds the spirit of modern national politics in absolute abhorrence, refusing to have any truck with it,[1] though permitting certain of its outposts [2] (clergy and laymen who do not know what heresy they are committing thereby) to do so and to lend their authority to all kinds of leniencies and compromises.

It denies the sovereignty of the people and proclaims the divine right of governments, taking its stand on the sinfulness of men and the necessity of saving souls [3] at all costs. Its real creation is the modern conception of legitimacy.

[1] This is what is called in France *l'antagonisme entre l'église catholique et la révolution française*. Cf. also the Syllabus of Errors.

[2] I.e. till 1870. What is to happen now, time alone will tell.

[3] Cf. Bossuet, "the polity derived from the very words of Holy Writ."

In the Middle Ages, it adapted itself to the Three Estates, of which it was one. On the other hand, it abhors modern constitutional representation and democracy. In itself it has become steadily more aristocratic and, in the end, more monarchist.

It practises tolerance only in so far as it absolutely must, and persecutes with the utmost rigor any intellectual movement which causes it the slightest qualms.

The Protestant Churches in Germany and Switzerland, like those in Sweden and Denmark, were from the beginning State Churches, because the governments were converted first and established the Churches. Calvinism, at first the Church of those Western peoples which possessed Catholic and persecuting governments, was also later organized as a State Church in Holland and England, although in England it was organized as an estate with independent means and representatives in the House of Lords. Calvinism was there grafted on to a remnant of feudalism.

The schools in the Catholic and Protestant countries oscillate between State and Church control.

After so close a connection and such manifold interactions between State and religion, the problem of our time is the separation of Church and State. It is the logical outcome of toleration, i.e. of the actual, inevitable indifference of the State, connected with the growing theory of the equality of all men, and as soon as a State exists which permits freedom of speech, that separation comes about of itself, for it is one of the firmest convictions of our time that difference of creed should no longer be allowed to determine a difference of civic rights. Those civic rights are also becoming very extensive. They include general access to office and exemption from taxation for the upkeep of institutions in which the taxpayer does not participate.

At the same time, the idea of the State has been modified from above by its rulers and from below by the people. So changed, the State is no longer a fitting consort for the Church. That the substance of religion remains unchanged is of no avail, since the State is no longer the same; for religion cannot of itself compel the State to maintain the old relationship.

Further, the government, especially in Germany and Switzerland,[1] is undenominational, for since the beginning of the century, as the result of fusions, cessions, peace treaties, etc., the State has included so-called "subjects" of different denominations, often in large numbers on both sides, and must now guarantee equal rights to its population. It begins by taking over two or more State religions, pays their clergy—which it must, having previously swallowed their previously independent estates—and hopes to manage in that fashion—indeed, would be able to do so if there did not exist within all individual religious communities the great rift between orthodoxy and rationalism, and it is *there* that the maintenance of religious parity becomes so infinitely harassing. For it serves no purpose to bestow privileges on "majorities," since those majorities are not in authority, nor can they be verified in practice.

Secondly, looked at from the standpoint of the people, it is culture (in the broadest sense of the word) which increasingly replaces religion as soon as the question arises

[1] Other countries have at any rate to grant equal rights to their religious minorities.

which shall influence the State. In a general way, culture is already dictating to the State its present programmes.

The Churches, however, will in time abandon their connection with the State as gladly as the latter has abandoned its connection with them. If they now resemble a ship which once rode the waves but has long grown used to lying at anchor, they will learn to float again as soon as they take to the water. Even Catholicism has already learnt to do so in America. Then they will once more be elements and proofs of liberty.

THE STATE DETERMINED BY CULTURE

WITH respect to culture, the State, in its earlier phases, and especially when it is associated with religion, plays the dominating rôle. Since the State came into existence through the co-operation of very various factors, more especially of an extremely violent though temporary character, nothing is further from the truth than to conceive it as a reflection or creation of the culture then prevailing among the people who created it. Hence the earlier stages have been fully discussed in the first of these relationships.[1]

As far as our knowledge goes, however, the Phoenician cities are the first thing to claim our attention. Their very polity—moderately monarchistic or republican, aristocratic or plutocratic, with ancient hereditary oligarchies functioning beside the King—would of itself reveal a cultural intention. Their rise was to a certain extent steady and systematic; they knew neither sacerdotal law [2] nor caste system.

[1] Here we must leave out of account the negation or arrest of culture, as when, for instance, nomads prohibit the ruling class from carrying on agriculture and leave it entirely to slaves.

[2] A possible, if obscure exception may have been Tyre. In 950 the Hiramidae were overthrown by Ithobal, the priest of Astarte, but in Ithobal's own house his great-grandson Pygmalion murdered his grandson (Pygmalion's uncle), Sicharbaal, the priest of Melkart, and was proclaimed king by the people, who rejected co-government by the priest. This may possibly mean that a priestly dominion aimed at from the beginning was frustrated.

Their practical intelligence and self-knowledge already appear in their colonization. Even in the mother country, some cities were colonies of others; thus Tripolis was founded equally by Tyre, Sidon and Aradus. The important point, however, is that these cities give us the first examples of genuine overseas colonies founded by genuine City States.

For since culture and business were here one, certain interests had to be artificially maintained by propitiating, buying and occupying the masses of the people; among other means to that end, there was their periodical removal to colonies, which is not at all the same thing as forcible deportation, the only thing despotism knows.

The dangers threatening these cities came from mercenaries (even Tyre employed them), condottieri, and probably foreign enemies. They readily submitted to foreign rule, especially when they were allowed to retain their own culture, their most precious possession. At no moment did any sign of tyranny appear, and they maintained themselves, at any rate, for relatively long periods.

We see here, moreover, a high degree of patriotism with absolutely innocuous methods, and pronounced hedonism, yet little effeminacy. Their cultural achievements were immense. Their flags waved from Ophir to Cornwall, and although they were extremely exclusive, and occasionally practised slave-raiding as a trade, they gave the world its first example of a free, unchecked mobility and industry, for which alone the State seems to have existed.

And now comes the City State of the Greeks. We have considered above how far, in the polis, the State dominated culture; yet here, on the whole, we might contend, firstly, that in the colonies culture (trade, industry, free philosophy, etc.) was from the outset the dominating factor, indeed that to a certain extent they came into being for this purpose, since the colonists eluded the rigorous political law of the mother country; and secondly, that the triumph of democracy might be regarded as the conquest of the State by culture, which is here equivalent to thought. Whether the triumph of democracy may be said to occur when culture has ceased to be the prerogative of those social classes or castes which were its exponents, or whether, inversely, culture becomes common property when the triumph of democracy is complete, is of no great importance.

In any case, an epoch followed in which the political life of the Athenians interests us of a later age less than their quality as a focus of culture, and this gives us occasion to dwell particularly on this one city.

Let us consider the value of such a situation in such an archipelago, of the particularly happy, unforced fusion of races,[1] into which freshly immigrated elements brought primarily fresh stimulus, of the high talent and versatility of the Ionian race, of the significance of the conservative control of the Eupatridae, and then again the breach with their overlordship, and of the rise of a body of citizens with equal rights, in which men were citizens and only citizens. With the fervor of civic life the individual too was unchained, to be combated by ostracism, etc., and later by trials on charges of sacrilege and peculation, and the impeachment of military leaders. And thus there developed that indescribable life of the fifth century. Individuals could maintain their position only by unprecedented services to the city (Pericles) or by crime (Alcibiades). This atmosphere of perpetual tension plunged Athens into

[1] For that reason Athens appears in legend as the hospitable asylum.

a terrible life-struggle, in which it succumbed. But it continued to exist as a spiritual force, as a focus of that flame which, independently of the polis, had become a pressing need of Hellas. Intellectual life became cosmopolitan. At this point there is much to be learned from the after-effects of the heroic Salaminic epoch in the time of Demosthenes, where there was purpose but no fulfilment, from the further development and exhaustion of democracy, and from the later Athens, enjoying and enjoyed.

What vast historical insight radiates from that city! In the course of his work, every student must make a halt there and learn to relate details to that centre. Greek philosophy, arising in the various peoples, found its common issue in Athens. In Athens, Homer was put into the shape we know. Greek drama, the supreme representation of the spiritual in a medium both sensuously perceptible and mobile, is the work of Athens. Atticism became the style of *all* later Greeks. Indeed, the enormous predilection of the whole later classical world, even Rome, for the Greek language as the richest and most flexible organ of the mind, rests mainly on the shoulders of Athens. Finally, Greek art, more independent of Athens than any other expression of the Greek spirit, owes to it Pheidias and others numbered among the greatest, and found in Athens its most important centre.

At this point it is worth while to consider in a general way the importance of any recognized centre of intellectual exchange, more particularly when it is *free.* When Timur Leng carried off to Samarkand all the artists, craftsmen and scholars from the countries he had laid waste and the peoples he had destroyed, there was not much for them to do there but die. Nor do the artificial concentrations of good minds in more modern capitals approximate even remotely to the intellectual intercourse of Athens. Men of parts only move to the capital when they are already famous, some of them achieve little afterwards, or at any rate not their best, and one might well imagine that it would be better for them to go back to the provinces. There is not much exchange between them; indeed, given the present-day notions of intellectual property, exchange would be looked at askance. It is only very vigorous epochs that can give and take without wasting words. Today, a man must be very rich to allow others to take from him without protest, without "claiming" his ideas as his own, without squabbling about priority. And then comes the intellectual pest of our time—originality. It supplies the need tired men feel for sensation. In the ancient world, it was possible, under the beneficent influence of a free intellectual mart, once the truest, simplest and finest expression had been found for anything, to form a consensus. The most striking example is to be seen in visual art, which (even at its zenith) repeated the most excellent types in sculpture, fresco, and we may assume in all forms whose monuments have not come down to us. Originality must be *possessed,* not striven for.

To return to the free intellectual mart, however, we must say that by no means every nation has achieved that high privilege. State and society and religion may have taken on fixed, intractable forms before the individually liberated mind could create such a soil for itself. Political power does what it can to falsify the situation. Modern metropolitan concentrations, supported by important official commissions in art and science, promote only individual branches, but not the whole sphere of intellect, which can only be fostered by freedom. Further, however glad men might be to stay there learning for ever, they should nevertheless feel the still stronger urge to go away and give expression in the world to the stimulus they have received. Instead of which they hang on in the capital and are ashamed to live in the provinces, which are thus impoverished, partly because anybody who can goes away, partly because anyone obliged to stay becomes discontented. Pernicious questions of social rank perpetually ruin the best. Even in the ancient world, many a man hung on in Athens, but not as a civil servant looking forward to his pension.

Medieval efforts in a similar direction were all unfree and not aimed at intellectual life as a whole, yet they were relatively energetic and noteworthy. A centre of intellectual exchange was formed by the wandering caste of the knight-errantry with its code of conduct and its poetry, which achieved, if nothing else, great homogeneity and a recognizable and characteristic type.

Medieval Paris can claim primacy in scholasticism associated with a great deal of miscellaneous cultural material and general thought. It formed, however, a caste which, once its members had attained some success in life (i.e. when they had their benefices safe and sound), was no longer very productive.

Nor did the various seats of the Papal Curia, in spite of the fact that there was so much to see and learn, leave much behind them but a dreary trail of backbiting.

Later centres were never anything but Courts, residences, etc. Florence alone could vie with Athens.

What the free intellectual mart really achieves is the clarity of all expression and the unerring sense of what men want. The arbitrary and the strange are shed, a standard and a style won, while science and art can interact. The productions of any age clearly show whether they came into being under such an influence or not. In their meaner form, they are conventional; in their nobler, classical. The positive and negative sides are always interwoven.

In Athens, then, intellect comes out free and unashamed, or at any rate can be discerned throughout as if through a light veil, owing to the simplicity of economic life, the voluntary moderation of agriculture, commerce and industry, and the great general sobriety. Citizenship, eloquence, art, poetry and philosophy radiated from the life of the city.

We find here no demarcation of classes by rank, no distinction of gentle and simple, no painful struggles to keep up with others in ostentation, no doing the same thing "for the sake of form," hence no collapse from overstrain, no Philistia in shirt-sleeves one day and flashy social functions the next. Festivals were a regular feature of life, not a strain.

Hence it was possible to develop that social intercourse which is the background of Plato's dialogues, or, to take another example, of Xenophon's *Convivium.*

On the other hand, there was no exaggeration of music, for us the cloak which covers a multitude of incongruities, nor was there any false prudery covering a mean and secret malevolence. People had something to say to each other, and said it.

Thus a general understanding was created. Orators and dramatists could reckon with an audience such as had never before existed. People had time and taste for the highest and best because mind was not drowned in moneymaking, social distinctions and false decencies. There was comprehension for the sublime, sensitiveness for the subtlest allusions and appreciation of the crassest wit.

Everything we know about Athens shows us even the most practical details of life on an intellectual background, and in intellectual form. Athens has no tedious pages.

Further, we see here more clearly than anywhere else the interaction between the individual and the community. Since a strong local prejudice arose that men must be able to do anything in Athens, and that there the best society and the greatest, or indeed the only stimulus was to be found, the city actually produced a disproportionate number of remarkable men and permitted them to rise. Athens always sought her highest in individuals. Men's supreme ambition was to distinguish themselves there, and the struggle for that goal was terrible. But Athens, from time to time, saw herself embodied in some individual figure, hence her relationship to Alcibiades was such as no city has ever borne to one of its sons. Yet Athens knew all the time that she could never suffer another Alcibiades.

As a result of the crises supervening on the Peloponnesian War, we notice a great decline in that ambition, in so far as it was of a political nature, with a growing tendency towards specialization, especially such as had nothing to do with the State. While Athens was in a position to provide half the world with specialists in any subject, while her name lived more especially in science and art, her politics became the cockpit of official mediocrities. It is a wonder that she later prospered so long after all her politics had sunk into that rapid and notorious decadence, the causes and circumstances of which are so lucidly set forth by Thucydides.

The decadence resulted from the fact that a democracy had tried to carry an empire, a situation in which an aristocracy (such as Rome and Venice) can hold out much longer, and that demagogues exploited the emotions of dominion. There lies the root of all the subsequent troubles and of the great catastrophe.

Everything we see elsewhere mixed and haphazard and confused is in Athens transparent and typical, even the maladies of the State—of which the most striking example is given by the Thirty Tyrants.

And in order that the intellectual tradition shall be complete to the last detail, we have, in addition to all the rest, Plato's political Utopia, i.e. the indirect demonstration of why Athens was lost.

The value to the historian of such a unique paradigm cannot be overrated. Here causes and effects are clearer, forces and individuals greater, and monuments more numerous than anywhere else.

This is no blind worship of an idealized picture of ancient Athens. The actual city we know is a place where knowledge flows more freely than in any other place, a key to open other doors, an existence in which humanity is expressed in more manifold forms.

As regards the Greek democracies as a whole, however, their political life was gradually bereft of its glory and open to question at any moment.

Speculative thought made its appearance in the guise of a creator of new political forms, but actually as a general solvent, at first in words, which inevitably led to deeds.

It appeared on the scene as political theory and took the State to task—a thing that would have been impossible if genuinely creative political power had not been far advanced in decline. At the same time, however, it accelerated that process and completely devoured such formative capacity as still existed, so that it fared very much as art does when it falls into the hands of aesthetics.

But there was a Macedon at hand and a Rome standing ready in the distance. In declining democracies, there are always and inevitably parties in favor of such great powers, nor must they of necessity be corrupt—they only need to be dazzled.

We might certainly ask whether political life was really overwhelmed by culture taking thought to itself, or merely by one-sided party egoism (not to speak of the demagogue as an individual). Some single element or other arises in opposition to principles of life which have been from the outset very complicated, and takes advantage of moments of dismay and fatigue. It professes to be the most important part, or even the whole, of the community, and spreads abroad a dazzlement which is often very general and only fades when the real, old, traditional whole is visibly out of joint, and a prey to the nearest great power.

Rome as a State remained superior to its Culture, and has therefore been discussed already.

What followed was the confused political life of the Germano-Roman Empires of the Völkerwanderung. As States, they were uncouth botches, barbarian and makeshift, and hence, as soon as the impetus of conquest slowed down at any point, subject to rapid decay. For the dynasties were ruthless, barbarous and erratic. Internecine warfare, defiance of the great and attacks from outside were the order of the day. In actual fact, there was no State, no culture and no religion to play the leading rôle. The best among them may have been the countries in which it was possible to restore Teutonic custom, as among the Alamannic tribes in the Frankish epoch.

Although these conditions must in part be ascribed to the reaction of the Latin element, Latin culture or the refinement of its pleasures were without effect; its impulses were just as crude as those of the Teutons, and, as we can see from the tales in Gregory of Tours, worked merely as an elemental force.

The institution which, on the whole, inherited most of the power lost by the State was the Church. Actually, power fell to pieces, and the pieces remained mere raw, shapeless fragments of power.

Then the Pepin dynasty rescued Franconia, if nothing else, from the ruins. With Charlemagne, it rose to be a world monarchy.

We cannot say that, under Charlemagne, the State was determined by culture, for culture came only third after State and Church, nor could it arrest the rapid decay of the Empire. It soon yielded to a barbarism which seems to have been worse than that of the seventh and eighth centuries.

If only we could imagine Charlemagne's Empire lasting in all its glory for a hundred years! Then culture would have become supreme and the first instead of the last. Then urban life, art and literature would have marked the age. There would have been no Middle Ages; the world, overleaping them, would have emerged into the full Renaissance (instead of its infancy). The Church, on the other hand, for all Charlemagne's patronage, would not by far have attained that degree of power it possessed later.

But there were too many barbarian elements whose civilization was only skin-deep. They actually hated the

Carolingians,[1] and all they had to do was to bide their time until the first weak government came. At first these "great ones" had to share their power with the Church, but when dangers began to threaten from the outside, and the Norman epoch proved that all the priests could do was to save their own skins, then that man remained master of each province who gave proof of strength for his own ends and for the protection of others.

Then began the feudal system, which the Church, in the end, adopted in its entirety for the sake of its possessions and privileges.

To a cursory glance, the feudal system looks as if it had merely checked and retarded culture, owing, not to the predominance of the Church, but to its own inefficiency.[2] The Feudal State was obliged openly to confess itself incapable of establishing law and order in its own name, that is, through the King. Its relationship to its constituent elements, big, medium and small, was most dubious and subsisted only by force of habit and its own ineptitude, and probably only with the help and at the desire of the Church. It was a State in which political life in the provinces far outweighed the political life of the capital, indeed which, in Italy, actually dissolved into fully sovereign separate parts, and even elsewhere (in Germany) proved to be incapable of maintaining its integrity against the Hussites, Poles, Swiss and Burgundians.

We have already alluded above to some details of the feudal system. The whole world was articulated into castes. At the bottom was the utterly helpless serf (villein).

[1] *Life of Charlemagne by a Monk of St. Gall;* Book I, 3. English ed. by A. S. Grant, London, 1922.

[2] For the feudal monarchy, cf. *supra* p. 113. It was safeguarded by law against usurpation, but usurpation was really hardly worth while.

Gradually, the burgess made his appearance, his emergence beset with the gravest perils. Then came the nobility, which, on the strength of its system of knighthood, completely ignored the individual State, the individual being ideally relieved of his allegiance to it by a cosmopolitan fiction. As a more highly developed general military class, it represents an apogee of social feeling in the West. Then came the Church in the form of a large number of corporations (colleges, monasteries, universities, etc.). And nearly the whole of this hierarchy was closely associated with inalienable landed property and hereditary handicrafts, and with that indescribable inefficiency of any political activity to which we have already referred. The very study of this infinite dispersion and interdependence is toilsome. It is hardly possible to discover what each man was or represented, what were his rights and claims, and how he stood to his superiors, dependents and equals.

Yet while all power was broken up into fragments, the separate fragments of what has since become national power were strongly influenced by their partial culture, so that the latter appears almost as the dominating element. Each caste, the knighthood, clergy and burgesses, was entirely under the rule of its culture, and most of all the order of knighthood, which existed simply as a form of social intercourse.

The individual, it is true, was still fettered, but not within the intellectual sphere of his caste. There personality could display itself freely and develop good-will, and thus there actually existed a considerable degree of genuine freedom. There was a great wealth, if not yet of personalities, at any rate of grades and forms of life. At certain times and in certain places, there reigned a *bellum omnium contra omnes* (war of all against all), which, however, as was pointed out above, cannot be judged from the standpoint of our modern demand for security.

It may be that our own time is still living on the fact that progress was then retarded, and that no uniform despotism prematurely devoured the strength of the nations. We should in any case suspend judgment on the Middle Ages, because they bequeathed no national debts to their posterity.

Then, step by step, there came into being the modern centralized State, dominating and determining culture, worshipped as a god and ruling like a sultan. Monarchies such as those of France and Spain were disproportionately stronger than culture by the very fact that they were at the same time the head of the chief religious party. They were surrounded by the hereditary nobility, politically powerless, but still socially privileged, and the clergy. Even when, in revolutions, this national omnipotence no longer bore the name of Louis, but of Republic, and everything else changed, one thing never wavered, and that was the idea of the State.

Yet in the eighteenth century modern culture set out on its way, and after 1815 advanced by leaps and bounds towards the great crisis. Even in the Age of Reason, when the State seemed unchanged, it was actually cast into the shade by people who did not care to discuss the events of the day, but ruled the world as *philosophes*—a Voltaire, a Rousseau, etc. Rousseau's *Contrat Social* was perhaps a greater "event" than the Seven Years' War. The State was subjected to the most powerful action of thought, of philosophical abstraction; the idea of the sovereignty of the people emerged,[1] the epoch of money-making and traffic set in, and those interests came to regard themselves more and more as the governing principle of the world.

The State of coercive power had first experimented with the mercantile system, and this was followed by various schools and sects of political economy, which had even recommended Free Trade as an ideal, but it was not until after 1815 that the barriers of all activity—gild systems or forced trades—began to fall. All landed property became transferable and at the disposal of industry, and England, with its world trade and its industry, led the way.

England introduced the mass use of coal and iron, the machine in industry and hence general industrialization. With the steamship and the railway she applied the machine to traffic while physics and chemistry were operating an internal revolution in industry, and obtained the mastery of large-scale consumption in the world by means of cotton. Then came an enormous expansion of the power of credit in the widest sense of the word, the exploitation of India, the extension of colonization to Polynesia, etc. At the same time the United States laid hands on almost the whole of North America, and finally Eastern Asia was opened up to traffic.

Looked at from the standpoint of these facts, it might appear as if the State were merely a police force protect-

[1] "There is no political idea which has had so profound an influence in the course of the last few centuries as that of the sovereignty of the people. At times repressed and acting only on opinion, then breaking out again, openly confessed, never realized and perpetually intervening, it is the eternal ferment of the modern world." Ranke, *History of England,* Vol. III. (In 1648, it certainly came to the surface, but in a form that stultified its principle. The theoretical proclamation of the extreme rights of the independence of the people was coupled in Parliament, after Pride's Purge, with actual subjection to a military power.)

ing this multitudinous activity, which at one time looked to the State for co-operation in many directions, but ultimately only required of it the abolition of restrictions. Further, it aimed at extending its customs radius as far as possible, and therefore desired the State to be as powerful as possible.

At the same time, however, the ideas of the French Revolution were still actively at work, politically and socially. Constitutional, radical, social claims were being put forward, supported by the general equalization of rights, and, by way of the press, were reaching the public on a gigantic scale. Political science became common property, statistics and political economy the arsenal from which everybody took the weapons he could best wield. Every movement was oecumenical. The Church, however, seemed to be nothing but an irrational force; religion was desired, but without the Church.

And on the other hand the State, as independently of all this development as the temporary circumstances permitted, proclaimed its power as a heritage to be increased with might and main. Wherever possible, it reduced the rights of the lower orders to a mere fiction. There were and still are dynasties, bureaucracies and militarisms which are firmly resolved to establish their own programmes, and not to submit to dictation.

All these things have co-operated to produce the great crisis in the idea of the State through which we are now living.

No class of society now admits that the State has any special rights. Everything is open to question. Indeed, political thought expects the State to be as mutable as its own caprices.

At the same time, political thought claims for the State

an ever-increasing and more comprehensive power of coercion, so that it may be in a position to put into practice the completely theoretical political programmes which political thinkers periodically draw up, the most turbulent individuals demanding the most extreme control of the individual and the community.

The State is thus, on the one hand, the realization and expression of the cultural ideas of every party; on the other, merely the visible vestures of civic life and only *ad hoc* almighty. It should be able to do everything, yet allowed to do nothing. In particular, it must not defend its existing form in any crisis—and after all, what men want more than anything else is to retrieve their share of its exercise of power.

Thus the *form* of the State is increasingly questionable and its radius of power increasingly great. The latter also holds good in the geographical sense; the State must now embrace at least the whole nation and something over. The unity of the State's power and its mere area have become a cult.

The more radically the sacred right of the State (its once arbitrary power over life and property) dies out, the more its secular rights expand. The rights of corporations are in any case extinct; nothing now exists which can cause any inconvenience. In the end, people become exceedingly sensitive to any differentiation; the simplifications and standardizations secured by the great State suffice no longer. Money-making, the main force of present-day culture, postulates the universal State, if only for the sake of communications, though that demand finds a powerful counterpoise in the specific character of the individual peoples and their sense of power.

And through it all there can occasionally be heard complaining undertones in favor of decentralization, American simplifications, etc.

The most important point, however, is that the boundaries between the respective duties of State and Society threaten to shift entirely.

The strongest impetus in this direction came from the French Revolution and the Rights of Man, while the State might well be thankful if its constitution survived with a reasonable definition of the rights of the *citizen.*

In any case, as Carlyle rightly points out, some thought should have been spent on the duties and capacities of man, on the natural resources of the country.

The modern version of the Rights of Man includes the right to work and subsistence. For men are no longer willing to leave the most vital matters to Society, because they want the impossible and imagine that it can only be secured under compulsion from the State.

Not only is everything of the nature of an "institution" or a "foundation" promptly noised abroad by the literary and journalistic intercourse of the day, so that there is a general demand for it, but absolutely everything that people know or feel Society will not undertake is simply heaped on to the daily growing burden of the State. At every turn, needs grow, bearing their theories with them, and not only needs, but debt, the chief, miserable folly of the nineteenth century. This habit of flinging away the fortune of future generations is of itself enough to show that a heartless pride is the peculiar characteristic of our time.

Jan. 18th, 1871. A great war has broken out, putting an end to all this activity and thought, setting power against power on the biggest scale and throwing the two greatest nations in Europe back on to their natural resources. At the beginning, both sides categorically declared that this war was only to be waged for the sake of a lasting peace, i.e. in the hope of an undisturbed civilized life.—How do matters stand now?

The end of the story is: somewhere the natural inequality of man will once more be restored to honor. But meanwhile, what the State and the idea of the State have to go through, the gods alone know.

Additional Note, 1870–1871. First and foremost, both governments have led their peoples out of the sphere of rights back to the sphere of duties and are demanding unprecedented efforts from them. Neither thought nor reasoning, but devotion, is the order of the day. Neither the one nor the many counts, but only the one whole.

Not culture, but mere existence, is once more at stake, and for years to come the mere appetite for so-called improvements will be answered by the gesture towards these untold sufferings and losses.

The State will resume its supremacy over culture, and will even re-orient it in many directions. Culture may even ask how it may best please the State.

Firstly, trade and commerce will be rudely reminded that they are not the main object of human life.

A good deal of the extravagant expenditure on scientific research and its communication, and on art, will be cut down. What is left will have to work doubly hard.

The prevailing form of life will be a harsh utilitarianism accompanied by an increase in religious feeling, which need not in any way be regarded as necessarily hostile to culture.

Most important of all, the boundaries between State and

Society will be established for generations to come, and by the State.

The wars still to be fought will do their share in consolidating this situation. The State itself is assuming a physiognomy of such a kind that no other mentality will have power over it for a very long time.

Some kind of reaction towards a free ideal will arise, though at the cost of superhuman strength and effort.

RELIGION DETERMINED BY THE STATE

Among the religions determined by the State, the classical religions hold pride of place. We must not allow ourselves to be misled by frequent expressions of piety, such as Horace's *dis te minorem quod geris imperas* (by esteeming yourself less than the gods you may rule), or Cicero's *De Legibus,* I, 7 (and elsewhere), or the passage in Valerius Maximus, I: *omnia namque post religionem ponenda semper nostra civitas duxit . . . quapropter non dubitaverunt sacris imperia servire* (our State always held that religion should come before everything, so that there was no doubt that the supreme power was at the service of the cult).

Whatever their religious feelings may have been,[1] the world of the Greeks and Romans was entirely secular; they really did not know (at any rate in their time of growth) what a priest was. They had regular ceremonies, but no law and no written revelation to exalt Religion above the State and the rest of life.

Their gods, poetically humanized and capable of mutual hostility, were in part explicitly State gods, and specifically

[1] We must never forget that Fate, which was superior to Zeus himself, could be swayed by no religion, and that little thought was expended on a future life.

bound to protect the State. Apollo was, among other things, the god of colonial enterprise, "the founder," and had to give information on the subject at Delphi.

Though the gods were considered as binding on all the Hellenes, indeed even on the barbarians and the whole world (a thing which offered little difficulty to later thought), they were nevertheless localized by an additional name, and hence pressed into the service of the place which bore it, the State or a particular sphere of life.

If the Greeks and Romans had had priests and a theology, they would never have created their perfect State on the basis of human needs and relationships.[1]

The only case in which the Roman religion developed an active proselytism was in the Romanization of the Gallic and other Northern and Western gods. In the Imperial age, however, the Romans had no real desire to convert the Christians, but simply to restrain them from sacrilege; for that matter, both these things happened in the service of the State.

The rest of the ancient world, the East, the theocracies, etc., was much more determined by Religion, which also imposed limits on their culture, than Religion by them, only that, as we saw above, despotism supervened in the course of time, arrogated divinity to itself, and in doing so, behaved satanically.

Religions best preserve their idealism when their attitude towards the State is one of suffering and protest, though that constitutes their ordeal by fire. Many a fine flight of the spirit has come to grief during such a time,

[1] Renan, *Apôtres*, p. 364 (pp. 288 in English Trans.): *L'infériorité religieuse des Grecs et des Romains était la conséquence de leur supériorité politique et intellectuelle. La supériorité du peuple juif, au contraire, a été la cause de son infériorité politique et philosophique.* The Jews and Primitive Christians based society on religion, like Islam.

for the danger of extermination by the State really exists where the latter represents a different and hostile religion. Christianity *is* suffering, and its teaching a teaching for those who suffer, and of all religions, with the exception of Buddhism, it is perhaps the one least adapted to a union with the State. Its very universality militates against such a union. How did it happen, then, that Christianity entered into the closest possible union with the State?

The foundations were laid very early, soon after the apostolic age. The decisive fact was that the Christians of the second and third centuries were men of the classical world, living, moreover, under a universal State. Statedom, therefore, seduced Christianity into taking on its own form. The Christians, cost what it would, formed a new society, distinguished one doctrine as orthodox from all secondary ideas (as heresies), and even then imposed on their community an essentially hierarchic organization. Much had already become very earthly; we have only to think of the time of Paul of Samosata and the lamentations of Eusebius.

Thus Christianity, even at the time of the persecutions, was a kind of standardized Imperial religion, and when the change came with Constantine, the community suddenly became so powerful that it could almost have absorbed the State into itself. In any case, it now became an over-mighty State Church. Throughout the Völkerwanderung, far into the Byzantine epoch, and, in the West, throughout the Middle Ages, religion, as we have already seen, was dominant. Charlemagne's oecumenical Empire, like the Empires of Constantine and Theodosius, was essentially a Christian Empire, and if the Church had any fear of being used as a tool, that anxiety was short-lived. The Empire fell to pieces, and in the feudal epoch the

Church remained at any rate more powerful than any other institution.

Every contact with the secular, however, reacts strongly upon religion. An inward decay is inevitably associated with the rise of its secular power, if only because quite other men come to the fore than at the time of the *ecclesia pressa* (persecuted church).

The effects of this infection of the Church by the State were the following:

Firstly, in the late Roman and Byzantine Empires, where the Empire was regarded as exactly coincident with the Church, and the Church formed, as it were, a great second political system, this parallelism bred in it a false sense of power. It became itself a State by acquiring a political constitution, and hence a second political power, instead of being a moral force in the lives of the people. Its personnel was therefore of necessity secular-minded. It was power and possessions which, in the Western Church, filled the sanctuary with those who had no call to be there. But power is of its very nature evil.

The second consequence was the enormous over-valuation of the unity once attained. The tradition, as we saw, goes back to the epoch of the Primitive Church and the persecutions. The *ecclesia triumphans*, however, now rallied all its means of power to safeguard its unity, and by virtue of its unity developed more and more means of power, became indeed insatiable in that respect, and in the end filled the whole of life with its moats and bulwarks. That is true both of the Western and Byzantine Churches. Again and again voices were raised proclaiming that the Deity rejoiced in the diversity of worship, but in vain.

No man of Western mind now believes in the dogma of the *ecclesia triumphans,* e.g. of the fifth century. We have gradually grown used to the sight of the manifold in religion, which, more especially in the English-speaking countries, seems compatible with widespread religious feeling, and under our very eyes we see the fusion and parity of religions in mixed populations, a thing of which no one dreamt at that time. The current history of dogma, moreover, does justice to the heresies, of which we know that at times they harbored the best minds and spirits of their age.

But what hecatombs have been offered up to the idea of unity—a genuine *idée fixe.* And that *idée fixe* could only develop fully because the political Church had been overcome by a lust for absolute power. The *dogmatic* basis of unity and its poetic glorification as *tunica inconsutilis* (the seamless tunic) is a mere detail.

With the Reformation, which set in at the time of the rapid rise of the modern Power State, a great general change came over both sides.

In the great Western countries, with the exception of England, the Counter-Reformation sealed the "Covenant between the Throne and the Altar"—that is, the Church, to maintain itself, once more made use of the secular arm in the widest sense of the word. Since then the two have stood in the closest complicity. In the Spain of Philip II, for instance, it was almost impossible to distinguish what belonged to each, and yet the Church, which made huge payments to the State, would have done better to distribute the Spanish bankruptcy over as many countries as possible. Even under Louis XIV, Catholicism was essentially a means of rule, an *instrumentum imperii,* and the King committed his great ecclesiastical act of terrorism,[1] although egged on to it by the clergy, essentially from lust of *political* unity *against* the opinion of the Pope.

In later times, this covenant, far from being useful, as sacred law was to the Power States of the ancient world, became steadily more unequal and more dangerous to both parties. While principles may be eternal, interests are in all cases subject to change, and now this covenant, instead of being a covenant of principles, has become more and more a covenant of interests, and how far those interests will continue to march abreast is very doubtful. However conservative the behavior of the Church may be, in the long run the State sees in it, not a support, but an encumbrance.

In France, every time the State approximated to the ideas and the party of the French Revolution, it took over the Revolution's mortal hostility to the Catholic Church. The latter, however, had, in most disastrous fashion, been made a State institution by Napoleon's Concordat of 1801, in virtue of a general principle according to which the State must assume control of and organize every existing institution. The very beginning of the Revolution had brought about the *Constitution civile du clergé* of 1791, thus missing the one moment at which a successful separation could have been effected, and by 1795 the separation *de jure* came too late, because in the interim the Church was able to point to its martyrdom.

Now not only the Church, but religion itself, is to a certain extent essentially determined by these political conditions. At present, religion stands under the protec-

[1] The Revocation of the Edict of Nantes, which caused the French Protestants to emigrate.

tion of the State and in the pay of the State in a way which is unworthy of and shameful to it. Should that State fall into other hands, religion would be exposed, all unprepared, to the deepest enmity, and in any case it shares the general menace of the crisis in the European idea of the State which has already been discussed.

In the majority of Catholic countries, the prevailing situation is more or less the same. The State is on the point of abjuring the tottering covenant between the throne and the altar as unprofitable; the Catholic Church, on the other hand, relies far too little on inner strength and seeks far too much for external points of support.

As regards the State, however, it is ridiculous for it to wish to have "liberal-minded prelates," guaranteed not to give any trouble to its bureaucracy. It is a matter of utter indifference to the North American governments how "ultramontane" or "modernist" the Catholic bishops of the Union may be.

Additional Note, 1873. The association with the Catholic Church has long been a nuisance to the governments, Louis Napoleon alone having been able to make use of it to support his power. Prussia, on the other hand, has at least granted it every liberty and reaped the praise of Pius IX. The modern democratic and industrial spirit having grown increasingly hostile to it, the Church was faced with the necessity of systematizing its demands at the Vatican Council. The long-existing Syllabus became, in its main outlines, canon law; the doctrine of infallibility crowned the whole system.

All compromises were frustrated, the transitional stages, apparently so useful, of a liberal Catholicism totally disavowed, reasonable negotiations with States rendered difficult or impossible, and the whole position of Catholicism in the world enormously embarrassed.

What was the object? Above all, we must eliminate any prophetic connection with the war of 1870. Everyone saw the war coming, but even if Napoleon had won, the Church would hardly have been better off.

It was not mere theoretical pride. Some great practical intention must have been operative when the whole of superior Catholic culture was so rudely abandoned, and unconditional, uniform obedience demanded—and ultimately obtained.

A tightening of all the bonds of unity may have seemed necessary in view of the general development of the modern mind and the impending loss of the *dominio temporale*, for the Church could not look for active militancy anywhere. That factor it had to leave quite out of its reckoning.

And now the present differences in the attitude of the governments. Most of them regard the matter as a mere theoretical diversion of the Papacy, which may well be left to the Papacy. Germany and Switzerland, however, took up the struggle as a struggle. The great difficulty in those countries is to organize the seceders as a Church and to provide a new clergy for them.

The only real solution, the separation of Church and State, is in itself a matter of great difficulty, and several States no longer wish it because they would dread a religion and a Church genuinely independent of them. And for the most part, that is precisely what radicalism thinks too.

The Protestant State Church, arising of itself in the stress of the sixteenth century, felt its dependence on the

State from the outset, and often with bitterness. Without it, however, the Reformation would certainly have succumbed in most countries, because the mass of the irresolute would have turned back to the old Church, and because, even apart from that, the old Church would have led its States into the field against those of the new. The State Church was inevitable, if only for purposes of defence.

It was, however, also inevitable that the Church should become a branch of the State government. It was feared, and lent power to the State as long as the latter took the Church under its wing. Since the Age of Reason, the Church has become more and more embarrassing to the State, although for the time being the State remains the Church's protector in time of need.

The Church will have to venture on the change from a State Church to a people's church, or even the separation into a number of independent churches and sects, as soon as the crisis in the idea of the State has sufficiently matured.[1]

Given the statistically ascertainable number of unprivileged nonconformist churchgoers, the Anglican Church, with its constitutional privilege and pride, and its possessions, is most jeopardized of all.

At the present time, the European great powers grant an indirect security to all the religions they maintain or tolerate; their police and legislation make it extremely difficult for any new religion to rise (a thing which is impossible without legislation granting the right to form

[1] For the time being, even the Protestant great power may think it ought to drive a bargain over its protection of the churches. And it is by no means out of the question that this crisis may be arrested or postponed for a long time by the establishment of a pure dictatorship (January 1869).

associations and so on) even if any should make its appearance.

The country which has gone furthest in transforming its national church into a State institution at home, and at the same time in using it as an instrument of foreign policy, is Russia. The people are indolent and tolerant, but the State proselytizing and (as regards Polish Catholics and Baltic Protestants) persecuting.

The Byzantine Church continues its existence among the Greeks as a surrogate and support of Byzantine nationhood under the domination of the Turks, even without a State. But what would be the position of religion and culture in Russia without the compulsion of the State? Religion would most likely bifurcate into rationalism for the few and magic for the many.

RELIGION DETERMINED BY CULTURE

In considering religion as determined by culture, we are confronted by two related but diverse phenomena. Firstly, religion may arise through the worship of culture. Secondly, a given religion may also be changed in essence, or at any rate colored, by the action of the culture of various peoples and epochs. Indeed, in the course of time, there arises from the heart of culture a criticism of religion. In a special sense, the reaction of art on the religion which takes possession of it also comes under this heading.

In the classical religions, and indeed more or less in all polytheisms—for we find gods of war and agriculture nearly everywhere—there exists beside the worship of nature and the astral powers a quite naïve worship of certain branches of culture. The worship of nature comes first, and the worship of culture is then grafted on to it. But once the nature gods have become ethical and culture gods, the latter aspect ultimately predominates.

There is no original divergence between religion and culture. On the contrary, they are to a great extent identical. In time, religion comes to worship as many activities as people feel it should, installing individual gods as the patrons of those activities and giving those gods their names.[1] The ease with which gods are created, however, is a point which requires much thought, and we should like to confront the mythologist with the question: Are you really capable of entering into the spirit of such a time and people? Yet there is no happier exercise of the imagination than to plunge into that world, where every new idea at once found its poetic divinity and later its imperishable expression in art, where so much could remain inexpressible because it was expressed in art.

It is true that philosophy, the supreme branch of culture, found this religion an all too easy game. And after philosophy, with its critical Greek spirit, there came, first quietly, then with power, the thought of the other world which—though with the help of the Emperors—gave that religion its *coup de grâce*.

Germanic religion also had its culture gods. Several of them had, in addition to their elemental aspect, a cultural one; they were smiths, weavers, spinners, makers of runes, etc.

A medieval analogy is to be seen in the helpers in need and special saints such as St. George, Sts. Crispin and Crispinian, Sts. Cosmas and Damian, St. Eligius, etc. They are, however, mere belated echoes of the classical worship of culture.[2]

But what would the Olympus of the money-makers of today look like if they were to turn pagan?

[1] Cf. passages such as Pausanias, *Description of Greece*, I, 24, 3, where the "daimon of activity" appears side by side with "Athena the worker."

[2] In popular belief, the saints were also feared as the originators of diseases, and hence had to be propitiated. Cf. Rabelais, *Gargantua*, I, 45, where the pilgrims believe that *St. Antoine mettait le feu aux jambes, St. Eutrope faisait les hydropiques, St. Gildaz les folz, St. Genoû les gouttes* (obviously in part onomatopoeic). In II, 7, St. Adauras is effective against hanging.

Now, no religion has ever been quite independent of the culture of its people and its time. It is just when religion exercises sovereign sway through the agency of literally written scriptures, when all life seems to revolve round that centre, when it is "interwoven with life as a whole," that life will most infallibly react upon it. Later, these intimate connections with culture are no longer useful to it, but simply a source of danger; nevertheless, a religion will always act in this way as long as it is alive.

The early history of the Christian Church shows a series of modifications parallel to the successive entry of the peoples, the Greeks, Romans, Teutons, Celts. Above all, it is a totally different religion at different times, i.e. its fundamental feelings are diametrically opposed. For no man is so free that he can override the culture of his time and his social class in favor of a "revelation." And coercion means hypocrisy and a sense of guilt.[1]

Christianity was least in contact with culture in the apostolic age, for it was then dominated by the expectation of the Second Coming, and the community was in the main held together by that expectation. The end of the world and eternity were at the door, it was easy to turn away from the world and its delights, communism was a matter of course and, given the prevailing frugality and sobriety, involved no risks—which is not at all the case when it comes into conflict with the money-making spirit.

Under the pagan Emperors, the hope of the Second Coming had faded, giving place to that of the future life and last judgment, but Greek culture invaded religion at all points, together with a variegated Orientalism. Had it been left to itself, heresies and Gnostic sects might have

[1] The parallel of the history of Islam among its various peoples is far from being so instructive.

destroyed it altogether. It was probably only the persecutions which made the survival of *one* dominating central idea possible.

The epoch of the Christian Emperors brought about a radical change. The Church became the analogue of the Empire and its unity, and rose superior to it. The greatest power resided with the prelates, who held the enormous endowments and the benefices of the entire Empire. Internally, the Church fell victim on the one hand to Greek dialectics in the ratiocination on the doctrine of the Trinity, and to dogmatism in the Oriental sense on the other, which involved the extermination of dissenters. Such things were alien to the spirit of the classical world, for even the Christian persecutions of the pagan Emperors had not been directed against the Christian way of thinking. On the other hand, the effect of the great influx of the masses into the Church is recognizable in the fact that the cultus forcibly supplanted religion, i.e. that it saturated religion with ceremonies, images, the worship of the martyrs' tombs and relics sufficiently to satisfy the masses who, in their hearts, were still pagans.

Byzantine Christianity bears the marks of an oppressed people. While with all its might it helped to subdue the nation, it was devoid of any free influence on morality, for the interdict only applied to doctrine and external discipline. Orthodoxy and the keeping of fasts sufficed for life, and asceticism came easily to a temperate and avaricious people. It is true that, with the seventh century, the spirit of Syria, Egypt and Africa ceased to influence Byzantium, but only when its measure of evil was full. Later accretion was rather by way of Slav superstition, belief in vampires, etc., mingled here and there with resuscitated classical superstition. The Christianity of Abyssinia and other totally degenerate or mentally inferior peoples is actually compatible with entirely pagan ideas.

As regards Latin Christianity of the early Middle Ages, the Arian Teutons remained dumb, and we can only approach them by way of hypotheses. Orthodox bishops and other ecclesiastics were the only spokesmen of Religion.

Finally, after the overthrow of Germanic Arianism, with the rapid degeneration and secularization of the orthodox episcopacy, which issued from the conflict as the sole victor, we see writing confined to *one* corporation, a fact which colors all records. Here the influence of *non*-culture can be seen. The Benedictines were the only writers, and (though threatened themselves with secularization owing to their wealth) to a certain extent maintained Latin culture. The predominating outlook, once ecclesiastical, became monastic. Our one source of information is the monasteries, with a few secular details thrown in. Of the popular spirit of that age, we learn only as much as reached the walls of the monasteries and came into contact with the monks. Nevertheless, that was one of the most vital relationships of that time. Thus while two very different things—popular imagination and the monks—met at the monastery gate, there to exchange the little they had in common, history was superseded by local annals, legends and chronicles. The survey of the world and its history was threatened with extinction.

All that the people demanded of the clergy, however, was a vicarious asceticism and perpetual miracles. Unconsciously the Church fell in with these popular demands with an eye to their magic effect, and used such things to bolster up its secular and political power.

It is curious to see how miracles and asceticism fell into the background after the Empire was salvaged by the

Carolingians and during their period of power[1]—we hardly hear of them under Charlemagne—how they regained their ancient power in the ninth and tenth centuries because the Carolingian culture had once more yielded to the undisciplined spirit of the masses. In its mode of feeling, the tenth century almost coincided with the sixth and seventh.

The apparently most extreme subjection of culture to religion which ever happened is to be seen in the Christianity of the eleventh century. The highly praiseworthy endeavors of many Benedictine monasteries, which had been founded in the meantime, were submerged in the fanaticism of Cluny. With Gregory VII, Cluny ascended the Papal throne, and from that time on addressed its mandates to the world. Yet it is open to question whether the ruling Papacy did not itself represent the penetration of a peculiar form of worldliness into the Church, whether the militancy which, in the investiture dispute, appeared in the guise of the armed militia of St. Peter, was not perhaps a disguised force of the *world* and culture of the epoch. The Crusaders, in any case, were an ideal blend of clerical and secular elements.

The eleventh century realized that ideal, and did not merely sigh for it. The century closed with a huge act of the inflamed general will of the whole Western world.

In the twelfth century, a reaction quickly made itself felt in the West. Great secular interests, knighthood and the city, were activated by the general revival of strength and set up an unconscious rivalry to the Church. The Church, in its turn, again became less devout and more

[1] Chrodogang and Benedict of Anianus are no proof to the contrary, since they do not represent a personal, ecstatic asceticism, but only a new discipline, unwillingly undergone.

mundane; a distinct decline of asceticism becomes evident. In its place, ecclesiastical art and architecture come to the fore. Secular rationalism set in, there came into being the schools of Paris and the great heresies in the Netherlands, on the Rhine, in Italy and particularly in the south of France, with their partly pantheistic and partly dualistic doctrines. It is questionable how far these heresies represent the penetration of elements of alien culture, and how far they are a testimony to the religious *élan* of the preceding epoch. The latter holds good at any rate, for the representatives of the Primitive Church, the Waldensians.

Then followed the Christianity of the thirteenth to fifteenth centuries. As a reaction, the Church set itself up as the victor, or even as a police force. The Middle Ages were artificially resuscitated, the hierarchy, habituated to the most extreme methods, was crowded with noblemen and canonists, science was scholasticism, and as such, the abject tool of the Church, wielded by the mendicant orders.

Popular religion, however, then passed through a most remarkable transitional stage; it entered into the closest association with the popular culture of the epoch, and in this process it is impossible to say which dominated which. It allied itself with the whole of human life, outward and inward, with all its powers, mental and spiritual, instead of proclaiming its hostility to them.

The people, very religious, and seriously preoccupied with the saving of their souls by works, were now cut off from pantheistic and dualistic short-cuts. Even the mystics were orthodox and unpopular. The continuity of the cultus became a matter of grave concern, even under the interdict. The absorbing meditation on the Passion, the great intensification of the cult of the Virgin—all this was significant, if only as a protest against heresy in any form. In the naïvely polytheistic cult of the helpers in need, of patron saints of cities and trade saints, the real division of divine power is expressed. Nor must we forget the popular legends of the Virgin, the spiritual dramas, the wealth of customs which characterizes the calendar of the epoch, and the naïveté of its religious art.

In spite of all its abuses, the extortions, indulgences and so on, the religion of that epoch had one great advantage: it fully occupied *all* the higher faculties of men, especially the imagination. While the priesthood was at times deeply hated, religion itself was for that very reason really of the people. It was not only accessible to the masses; they lived in it. It *was* their culture.

Indeed, this would be the point to ask whether the real proof of the vitality of a religion does not, after all, lie in its power of venturing upon a close association with culture at any time. Christianity gave proof of growth as long as it put forth new dogmas, rites and forms of art, i.e. up to the Reformation. But the Reformation was immediately preceded by menacing portents on the horizon—the ruthless ambition of the princes, the terrible Popes, the rising power of the devil in the (half Dominican, half popular) witchcraft persecutions.

The Christianity of the Reformation re-established salvation as an inward process, namely, as justification and acquisition of grace by faith, while Calvinism promulgated the doctrine of election. The very antithesis of the Catholic justification by works became the main dogma of the new teaching. How mutable are all things carried to their logical conclusions!

Religion was "purified," i.e. it was deprived of any

external works and obligations which might seem to offer justification by works a cranny in which to lodge. Suddenly, it found itself divorced from a powerful faculty of man—the imagination—as from a purely sinful, mundane force, leading men astray, and had to "etherealize" itself in consequence. That process required leisure and education, and thus meant unpopularity in so far as popular consent was not obtained by force. Moreover, to prevent the imagination from taking unlawful excursions in its idleness cost much effort. It was for this reason that the Counter-Reformation, in art at any rate, restored by force the bond with popular imagination, and pomp became the predominating feature of the Baroque.

Further, the Primitive Christian conception of religion was restored as eternally valid, though in an age fundamentally alien to it, and among industrious, very energetic peoples. It was, moreover, a time of extreme ferment in the cultural world, which was, in its turn, forced into silent homage by two orthodoxies, the one Catholic, the other Protestant.

Culture, thus doubly subjected and rejected (i.e. *qua* imagination—art and manners, and *qua* education) fell back on concealed rebellion until, in the eighteenth century, the spiritual alienation broke out openly. In the Catholic Church it appeared as pure negation, in the Protestant as a degeneration into diffused rationalism, as reason and humanitarianism, or as personal religiosity, according to individual minds and imaginations. In the end, even official Protestantism, having arisen by a mental process, had perforce to make concessions.

And now the modern attitude of Christianity to culture. Firstly, culture, in the guise of learning, demonstrates to

Christianity that it is human in its origins and human in its limitations. It handles the scriptures in the same way as other documents. Christianity, born, like all religions, at a time ignorant of the critical spirit and among men afire with enthusiasm and incapable of criticism, could no longer maintain itself as *sensu proprio* and literally valid in face of a general intellectualization of life. It is impossible to exempt one portion of nature and history from the rational consideration of the whole. The more actively, however, the attempt is made, the more implacable the hostile camp is in its criticism and its disintegration of all myth. At the same time we must not forget that we, with our lop-sided culture, have great difficulty in *believing* and in entering into what and how others have believed, and in imagining the exclusiveness and obstinate readiness for martyrdom in distant peoples and ages which was an essential factor in the birth of religions.

Secondly, morality, as far as it can, tries to stand on its own feet apart from religion. In its later stages, religion is apt to lean upon morality as its own daughter. Yet this claim is opposed, on the theoretical side, by the doctrine of a morality independent of Christianity and directed solely by the inner voice, on the practical side by the fact that, on the whole, men do their duty today far more from a sense of honor and an actual sense of duty in the restricted sense of the word than from religious motives. This development can be distinctly traced back to the Renaissance.

The artificial assertion of Christianity in the interests of good behavior, however, has always been utterly useless. We may well wonder how long the sense of honor will hold as "the last mighty dam" against the general deluge.

A single proof of the separation of morality from Christianity can be seen, for instance, in the philanthropy of our time, which sets out from optimistic premisses. Inasmuch as it endeavors to help men on in life and to foster activity, it is far more a concomitant of the money-making spirit and mundane considerations than a fruit of Christianity, which, quite logically, is only concerned with the giving of all men have and with alms. Moreover, as liberal views of the future life gain ground, morality is increasingly ready to dispense with future retribution. The modern mind aims at a solution of the supreme enigma of life independent of Christianity.

Thirdly, mundane life and its interests, even quite apart from the optimism which hopes to establish the kingdom of heaven on this earth, now outweigh all other considerations. The vast movement in the life of this world and the work of every degree, including free intellectual activity, which gives no leisure for contemplation, are quite incompatible with the doctrine of the Reformation, which, whether we think of justification or predestination, is difficult in itself and has never been congenial to all minds. Primitive Christianity itself stands in complete contrast to the strictest Christianity of our time (with the possible exception of the Trappists). The humble surrender of self and the parable of the right and left cheek are no longer popular. People want to maintain the social sphere in which they were born; they must work and become rich, suffering, indeed, all kinds of interference from the world even when they hate beauty and enjoyment. In short: for all their religiosity, people are not disposed to forego the advantages and benefits of modern culture, testifying thereby to the change which is going on in the conception of a future life.

The Calvinist countries, which, from the Reformation

on, have been most outstanding in the money-making sense, have arrived at the Anglo-American compromise between Calvinistic pessimism in theory and ceaseless money-making in practice. They have exercised a great influence by it, but one has the feeling that they cannot have taken their "little band of the elect" very seriously.

Among the dangerous methods practised by present-day orthodoxies, we find them countenancing "the solidarity of conservative interests," the union with the State, which, for its part, no longer wishes that union, the affirmation of the myth at all costs, etc. In one way or another, however, Christianity will fall back on its fundamental idea of the world as a vale of tears. How, in the long run, the will to live and work in the world can be made compatible with that idea we cannot foresee.

Additional Note, 1871. Are we at the beginning of a great religious crisis? Who can tell? We shall be aware of ripples on the surface very soon, but it will be many years before we know whether a fundamental change has taken place.

In conclusion, the following considerations may supplement what has already been said of the peculiar influence of art and poetry on religion.

Both have at all times contributed very largely to the expression of religion. Yet every cause is in some way alienated and profaned by being expressed.

Even languages are traitors to causes: *ut ubi sensus vocabulum regere debeat, vocabulum imperet sensui,*[1] and matters are not improved by the host of men who are

[1] Bacon, *Sermones fideles,* 3, "whereas the meaning ought to govern the term, the term governs the meaning."

obliged to occupy their minds with causes for which they have no vocation, and are glad if they can come to terms, not with the spirit, but with the letter.

Art, however, is the most arrant traitor of all, firstly because it profanes the substance of religion, i.e. it robs men of their faculty for profounder worship, putting eyes and ears in its place, and substituting figures for feelings, which are only transiently deepened by them. Secondly, because it possesses a high and independent selfhood, in virtue of which its union with anything on earth is necessarily ephemeral and may be dissolved at any time. And those unions are very free, for all that art will accept from religion or any other themes is a stimulus. The real work of art is born of its own mysterious life.

It is true that, in the course of time, religion realizes how freely free art is behaving, moulding its material and so on. It then makes the always dangerous attempt to revive a past, unfree style in a hieratic sense, the function of which is to represent only the sacred aspect of things, i.e. it must abandon the totality of the living object. This style, therefore, is much inferior to the contemporary style which takes in the whole of life (whereby art has eaten of the tree of knowledge).

This process is exemplified in the morose decency and prudence of modern Catholic art and music. And Calvinism and Methodism know perfectly well why they rudely cast art out, just as Islam did. It may be, of course, that that casting-out is an unconscious after-effect of the pessimism of earlier Christianity, which had no feeling available for the representation of anything at all, even if the sinfulness of the creature had not envenomed any representation of it.

After all, everything depends on the temperament of

the various peoples and religions. We find the contrary of all this in the epochs in which art helped to mould the substance of religions: for instance, when Homer and Pheidias created gods for Greece; when, in the Middle Ages, the pictorial cycles, especially those of the Passion, prescribed step by step the whole of worship and its prayers; when the religious and festal Greek drama represented, on its own initiative, *coram populo,* the supreme questions; and when the Catholic dramas of the Middle Ages and the *autos sagramentales* crudely fed the popular imagination with the most sacred events and rites, heedless of profanation.[1]

Indeed, art is a strangely importunate ally of religion, and in the most surprising circumstances refuses to be driven from the temple. It represents religion even when the religious spirit (among the educated at any rate, and even among certain artists, such as Pietro and Perugino) is dead. In later Greece, in Italy at the Renaissance, religion (save perhaps in the form of superstition) was really alive only in the form of art.

Religions, however, are very much mistaken in imagining that art merely seeks its bread from them.

In its highest and primary representatives, art does not even seek its bread from contemporary secular culture, however much it may seem to do so when skilled and famous artists descend to illustrating the reading-matter of Philistia.

[1] The Protestantism of the sixteenth century, on the other hand, confined its drama, for very good reasons, to allegories, moralities, Old Testament scenes and some history.

IV

The Crises of History

So far, we have been concerned with the slow and lasting mutual influences and interactions of the great world forces. We can now pass on to consider the accelerations of the historical process.

These are extremely diverse, yet surprisingly akin in many isolated details which have their root in human nature as a whole.

For the present we must leave out of account the primitive crises, the course and consequences of which we do not know in detail, or must deduce from later conditions.

For instance, the earlier Völkerwanderungen and invasions. These were undertaken *either* under pressure of necessity, e.g. the migration of the Etruscans from Lydia to Italy, and the *ver sacrum* [1] of the ancient Italici, especially those of Middle Italy, *or* in a sudden ferment, as when the nomads rose to great conquests under a great individual; here the outstanding examples are the Mongols under Genghis Khan or even the Arabs under Mohammed.

Primitive peoples, in such circumstances, induce their native gods to present them with foreign countries and to

[1] The consecrated firstlings of spring; also the children vowed to the gods in critical circumstances, who must emigrate on reaching adult years. (Editor's note.)

charge them with the extermination of the previous inhabitants, e.g. the Israelites in Canaan.

We find in Lasaulx a somewhat facile optimism with regard to the fruits of such invasions. Proceeding exclusively from the Teutonic irruptions into the Roman Empire, he says: "At the moment at which a great people no longer possesses, as a community, a certain quantity of unused strength, a natural spring of refreshment and rejuvenation, it is near its decline, and there is no regeneration for it save by way of a barbarian influx."

Not every invasion is a rejuvenation, but only such as carry a youthful race capable of assuming culture into an older, already cultured race.

The action of the Mongols on Asiatic Mohammedanism —unless theirs is a case of *post hoc ergo propter hoc*—was purely destructive, so that its higher, creative spiritual power never recovered. Nor is this disproved by the fact that after Genghis Khan a few great Persian poets still appeared. Either they were already born and educated before his time, or, as sufis, no longer depended on any mundane environment. Crises bring out greatness, but it may be the last. Even if a few completely Mohammedanized Mongol dynasties later built splendid mosques and palaces, that does not prove much. On the whole, the Mongols (in so far as there were no Turks among them) were a different and mentally inferior race, as their supreme cultural product, China, proves.

Even superior Caucasian races have been doomed to permanent barbarism, i.e. to the incapacity to evolve into higher cultures, where a nomadic and warlike despotism was combined with a specific religion—for instance, the former Byzantine Empire under the rule of the Ottoman Turks.

While Islam of its very nature brings a certain barbarism in its train, the important point here is the contrast between a subjugating and a subjugated religion. Further, there was the ban on intermarriage, the slow habituation to permanent ill-treatment, indeed, the gradual extermination of the subjected people, creating a satanic pride in the victors, who came to display an utter contempt for human life, and made this kind of dominion over others the central spring of their emotional life.

The only salvation in such a case is intermarriage between the two peoples, and for intermarriage to bring salvation, the peoples in question must, it would seem, at least be of the same race, if the inferior race is not, in time, to rise again. Even when that happens, the movement at first looks like a decline. We have only to think of the terrible demoralization of the Germanic Empires on Roman territory.

That it was an absolutely horrible life becomes evident when we consider how often Teutons were false to their own nature. They seem to have sacrificed their innate racial qualities and assumed only the evil ones of the Romans. But in time the crisis subsided, and genuinely new nations appeared—though it was a long trial of patience. *Summa:* there is a healthy barbarism, in which superior faculties lie latent, but there is also a purely negative and destructive barbarism.

At this point we must already consider war as a crisis in the relations of the peoples and a necessary factor of higher development.

It is part of the wretchedness of life on earth that even the individual believes that he can only attain a full consciousness of his own value if he compares himself with others and, in certain circumstances, actually makes others feel it. The State, law, religion and morality are hard put to it to keep this bent within bounds, that is, to prevent its finding public expression. In the individual the open indulgence of it is regarded as ridiculous, intolerable, ill-mannered, dangerous, criminal.

On a big scale, however, nations from time to time assume that it is allowable and inevitable for them to fall upon each other on some pretext or other. The main pretext is that in international relations there is no other way of arriving at a decision, and: "If we don't, others will." We shall leave aside for the moment the highly diverse internal histories of the outbreaks of wars, which are often extremely complex.

A people actually feels its full strength as a people only in war, in the comparative contest with other peoples, because it only exists at that time. It must then endeavor to sustain its power at that level. Its whole standard has been enlarged.

In philosophic form, the dictum of Heraclitus, "war is the father of all things," is quoted in proof of the benefits of war. Lasaulx accordingly explains that antagonism is the cause of all growth, that harmony is born only of the conflict of forces, the "discordant harmony" (Horace, *Epist.*, I, 12, 19) or the "harmonious conflict" of things (Manilius, *Astron.*, I, 14). This means, however, that both sides are still in possession of some vital energy, and not that one triumphs while the other lies prostrate. Indeed, according to him, war is divine in character, a world law and present in all nature. Not without cause do the Indians worship Shiva, the god of destruction. The warrior, he says, is filled with the joy of destruction, wars clear the air like thunderstorms, they steel the nerves and restore the heroic virtues, upon which States were originally founded, in place of indolence, double-dealing and cowardice. We might here also recall H. Leo's reference to "fresh and cheerful war, which shall sweep away the scrofulous mob."

Our conclusion is—men are men in peace as in war, and the wretchedness of earthly things lies equally upon them both. In any case, we generally suffer from an optical illusion in favor of those parties and their members with whose interests our own are in any way connected.

Lasting peace not only leads to enervation; it permits the rise of a mass of precarious, fear-ridden, distressful lives which would not have survived without it and which nevertheless clamor for their "rights," cling somehow to existence, bar the way to genuine ability, thicken the air and as a whole degrade the nation's blood. War restores real ability to a place of honor. As for these precarious existences, war may at least reduce them to silence.

Further, war, which is simply the subjection of all life and property to *one* momentary aim, is morally vastly superior to the mere violent egoism of the individual; it develops power in the service of a supreme general idea and under a discipline which nevertheless permits supreme heroic virtue to unfold. Indeed, war alone grants to mankind the magnificent spectacle of a general submission to a general aim.

And since, further, only real power can guarantee a peace and security of any duration, while war reveals where real power lies, the peace of the future lies in such a war.

Yet it should, if possible, be a just and honorable war—perhaps a war of defence such as the Persian War, which developed the powers of the Hellenes gloriously in all ways, or such as the war of the Netherlands against Spain.

Further, it must be a genuine war, with existence at stake. A permanent smouldering of small feuds, for instance, may replace war but is without value as a crisis. The German feudal heroes of the fifteenth century were highly astonished when they were confronted with an elemental power like the Hussites.

Nor did the disciplined "sport of kings" of the eighteenth century lead to much more than misery.

In quite a special sense, however, the wars of today are certainly aspects of a great general crisis, but individually they lack the significance and effect of genuine crises. Civilian life remains in its rut in spite of them, and it is precisely the precarious existences referred to above which survive. But these wars leave behind them vast debts, i.e. they bequeath the main crisis to the future. Their brevity too deprives them of their value as crises. The full forces of despair do not come into play, and hence do not remain victorious on the field of battle, and yet it is they, and they alone, which could bring about a real regeneration of life, i.e. reconciliation in the abolition of an old order by a really vital new one.

Finally, it is quite unnecessary—as unnecessary as in the case of the barbarian invasions—to prophesy of all destruction that regeneration will come of it. It may be that this globe is already aged (nor does it matter how old it is in the absolute sense, i.e. how many times it has revolved round the sun—it may be very young for all that). We cannot imagine, in great tracts of denuded country, that new forests will ever arise to replace those which have been destroyed. And so peoples may be destroyed, and not even survive as component elements of other races.

And often it is the most righteous defence that has proved most futile, and we must be thankful that Rome went so far as to proclaim the glory of Numantia, that conquerors have a sense of the greatness of the conquered.

The thought of a higher world plan, etc., is cold comfort. Every successful act of violence is a scandal, i.e. a bad example. The only lesson to be drawn from an evil deed successfully perpetrated by the stronger party is not to set a higher value on earthly life than it deserves.

Let us first outline a general description of crises.

Even in remote antiquity, nations must often have been rent asunder by risings of classes and castes against a despotism or the oppression of a sacred law. Inevitably, religion must have played its part on both sides; indeed, new nations and religions may have arisen in this way. But the course of spiritual events is not sufficiently clear to us.

Then came many crises, of which we know more, in the Greek States, as they traversed the cycle of monarchy, aristocracy, democracy, despotism. Yet though these were genuine crises, they remained local, and can only be referred to incidentally for purposes of comparison. In Greece, the process was broken up into purely parochial and individual processes, and even the Peloponnesian War did not act as a great *national* crisis, the only possible result of which would have been the creation of a united State. That did not even come about under the Macedonians and only in a very restricted sense under the Roman Empire, which granted so much autonomy and freedom from tribute to devastated Greece that people could still believe in the continued existence of the polis.

In Rome, for all its revolutions, the real, great, fundamental crisis, i.e. the passage of history through the rule of the masses, was always avoided. Rome was already a world Empire before the revolution began. But while in Athens, where in the hegemony of the fifth century the masses of the ruling city aspired to the government of an Empire of some eighteen million souls, until Empire and city perished in the attempt, the State of Rome always passed from powerful hands into other powerful hands. Nor had Rome at that time any enemies at hand such as Athens had in Sparta and Persia. Carthage and the Diadochi were long since ruined. All that was left were the Cimbri and Teutons, who were menacing enough, and Mithridates.

The so-called civil wars after the time of the Gracchi present the following picture: an idle and increasingly degenerate aristocracy was attacked by a force of impoverished commoners—Latins, Italici, slaves. And that attack was actually led by members of the aristocracy, though in the guise of demagogues, and by men like Marius. The aristocracy, however, shackled by vast possessions already received or anticipated from the provinces, was, firstly, able to yield only on points of detail; and secondly, was held in a state of siege by its own ruined sons, such as Catiline.

Then Caesar, by his usurpation, rescued Rome from all Catalinarians, present and future. He aimed at no military despotism, yet actually determined the course of events by soldiers devoted to his cause. For that reason the last so-called civil war waged by his successors was also a soldiers' war.

The house of Julian then peaceably accomplished the extermination of the aristocracy begun by Marius and the civil wars. But the Empire was now really synonymous with peace, and was remarkably safe from revolution at home. The revolutions in the separate provinces have their own demonstrable causes in social conditions, e.g. the risings in Gaul against the burden of debt—the *aes alienum,* as instanced by that of Florus and Sacrovir [1] in the time of Tiberius. Or they were outbursts of religious fury such as the rising of the Jews under Hadrian led by Bar Kochba. All these movements were purely local.

The only menace lay in the proclivity of the Praetorian Guards and the frontier legions to proclaim Emperors. Yet even the so-called crises at the deaths of Nero and Pertinax were tempestuous episodes and not real crises. Nobody wished to transform the polity of the Empire, great Emperors occupied the army in great wars, and the usurpation of the third century was in essence entirely salutary. Every conceivable thing happened to preserve Rome *in statu quo.* The Roman sense of rule was always strong enough, even in frontier provincials such as the Illyrian Emperors, to sustain the whole.

Organic changes and other good intentions which modern historical science has tried to impute to the Emperors of that time came too late in any case. What had once been Rome could not change by any voluntary act, or at any rate not to its own profit. Rome remained Rome till the end.

Under Constantine and his successors, the Empire survived the gradual rise of an orthodox Christian society and Church which underpropped the tottering Empire. As long as the Empire survived, it had to lend the secular arm to the implacable persecution of Arians and pagans. And finally, after orthodoxy had been completely organized and had taken part of the tradition of the ancient world under its wing, the Empire was allowed to die.

[1] Cf. Tacitus, *Annales,* Book III, Chap. 40.

Genuine crises are rare. At various times, civil and religious disputes have filled the air with lasting and deafening clamor, yet without leading to vital transformations. The political and social foundations of the State were never shaken or even called in question. Hence they cannot be regarded as genuine crises. We find examples of this firstly in the Wars of the Roses in England, in which the people trooped after one of two factions of the nobility and the Court, and secondly the French Wars of Religion, where in actual fact the main issue lay between the followers of two noble houses, and the question was whether the King would maintain his position independently of either, or which he would join.

To return to Rome, however, the real crisis first supervened with the Völkerwanderung, which was pre-eminently a crisis in the true sense of the word—the fusion of a fresh physical force with an old one, which, however, survived in a spiritual metamorphosis, having changed from a State into a Church.

And that crisis is paralleled by no other we know of, but has remained unique of its kind.

If we confine ourselves to the crises in great civilized nations, while taking account of abortive crises, we find ourselves confronted with the following general phenomenon:

In that extraordinarily complex condition of life in which the State, religion and culture, in extremely derivative forms, are intimately associated, and in which most things, as they exist, have forfeited the link with their origin which justified their existence, one of the three will long since have attained an undue expansion or power, and, after the fashion of all earthly things, will abuse it, while the other powers must suffer undue restriction.

According to its nature, however, the suppressed power can either lose or enhance its resilience in the process. Indeed, the national spirit in the finest sense of the word may become aware of itself by having suffered oppression. In the latter case, something breaks out, subverting the public order. Either it is suppressed, whereupon the ruling power, if it is a wise one, will find some remedy, or, unexpectedly to most people, a crisis in the whole state of things is produced, involving whole epochs and all or many peoples of the same civilization, since invasions, undertaken and suffered, ensue of themselves. The historical process is suddenly accelerated in terrifying fashion. Developments which otherwise take centuries seem to flit by like phantoms in months or weeks, and are fulfilled.

The question now arises whether such crises could be arrested—and which—and why they are not.

The crisis in the Roman Empire could not be arrested because it was provoked by the impulse of young, very prolific peoples to take possession of southern, depopulated lands. It was a kind of physiological compensation which was to a certain extent carried out blindly.

The expansion of Islam is an analogous case. The Sassanids and Byzantines would have had to become totally different peoples if they were going to withstand the fanaticism which promised Paradise to the slain and the enjoyment of world dominion to the victor.

On the other hand, the Reformation could have been considerably checked and the French Revolution largely mitigated.

In the Reformation, a reform of the clergy and a moderate reduction of Church property carried out by the ruling classes, and by them alone, would have sufficed. Henry VIII and the Counter-Reformation after him show what could really have been done. There was in men's minds a profound discontent, but no general, clear ideal of a new Church.

It would have been much more difficult to avert an eruption in 1789, because the educated classes were inspired by a Utopia and the masses by an accumulated store of hatred and revenge.

Castes, however, such as the priesthood and the old French nobility, are absolutely incorrigible even when a large number of their members clearly see the abyss. For the moment, it is more unpleasant to join forces with men of like mind and be doomed to *certain* destruction than to have the feeling that a cataclysm *may* come. And quite apart from any such calculation of probability, conditions may already be so far gone that castes can no longer hope to reform themselves. There may already be an overwhelming likelihood that other elements from outside will make themselves masters of the movement once it has been set going.

Whether the spirit of an age which paves the way for crises is the mere sum of many individuals of like mind, or, as Lasaulx thinks, the higher cause of the ferment, is a question which may be left open, like that of liberty or bondage as a whole.

In the last resort, the impulse to great periodical changes is rooted in human nature, and whatever degree of average bliss were granted to man, he would one day (indeed, then more than ever) exclaim with Lamartine: *La France s'ennuie.*

An essential preliminary condition would seem to be a

high development of traffic and a widespread similarity of thought on other questions.

Yet when the hour and the real cause has come, the infection flashes like an electric spark over hundreds of miles and the most diverse peoples, who, for the rest, hardly know of each other's existence. The message goes through the air, and, in the one thing that counts all men are suddenly of one mind, even if only in a blind conviction: *Things must change.*

In the First Crusade, it was the great masses who set out, a few months or even weeks after the beginning of the preaching, bound either for a new, unknown home or certain death.

It was the same thing in the Peasants' War. In hundreds of petty States, the peasants were at one and the same time of *one* mind.

As regards our own time, on the contrary, with its unprecedented system of communications, we might say that it is less prone to crises—that so much discussion, reading and travel has a stupefying effect. If crises do nevertheless occur the railways will of course play a part in them. We shall return to that double-edged instrument later.

Urban populations are more moved to crises by argument and are within easier reach of demagogues, but rural populations may be more terrible.

As regards the physiognomy of nascent crises, they appear first in their negative, accusing aspect, as the accumulated protest against the past, mingled with dark forebodings of still greater, unknown oppression. While Bacon [1] overrates the latter, they may none the less contribute to

[1] *Sermones Fideles,* 15: *De seditionibus et turbis* (*Of Seditions and Troubles*).

the actual outbreak, i.e. to the subversion of public order in its existing form. And that subversion is infallibly precipitated by fanatics who, once the first excesses have been committed, howl the others on.

The crisis which has one specific cause is borne along on the storm-wind of many other things, yet not a man involved in it but is absolutely blind as to the force which will finally win the day. Individuals and masses attribute everything that irks them, without exception, to the existing dispensation, while for the most part what they are suffering under is inherent in human frailty. A glance at the inadequacy of everything on earth, at the thrift of nature in her household outside of human life, should suffice to prove it. But men generally imagine that history behaves differently from nature.

In the end, the movement is swelled by anyone who simply wants a change, whatever it may be.

The entire blame for the whole previous state of things is cast on its present representatives, if only because men no longer want change, but revenge, and cannot reach the dead.

The facile display of heroism against those representatives, more especially when they can be reached and persecuted individually, is reinforced by a horrible injustice towards all that has been. It looks as if one half of things had decayed and the other had long been under the strain of waiting for a general change.

It is, of course, only this blind coalition between all malcontents that can disrupt a long-existing dispensation. Without it, the old institutions, good and bad, would continue to exist forever, i.e. until the downfall of the nation as a whole.

Surprising allies may now join forces with a nascent

crisis, and it cannot disavow them, even if there is a premonition that it will be pushed aside in its turn and that other forces than those which set the revolution going aim at carrying it on.

In order to attain relatively modest results—and it is open to question whether such results were desired or even desirable—history requires vast preparations and a quite disproportionate clamor. It is the same thing in the life of the individual. In a climax of dramatic excitement, decisions are taken which are to work wonders, and the result is an ordinary, but inevitable fate.

But now the *positive,* ideal side of the initial stage. This is given by the fact that it is not the most wretched, but the energetic spirits which make the real start. It is they who cast an ideal light on the nascent crisis, whether by their oratory or by other personal gifts.

And now the curtain rises on the brilliant farce of hope, this time for vast classes of people on a gigantic scale. Even in the masses, the protest against the past is blended with a radiant vision of the future which frustrates any cool consideration. Sometimes that vision may reveal the imprint of the people which conceived it. Promises of rejuvenation may illuminate it, to deaden the rheumatic twinges of age. On Medea's advice, the sons of Peleas boiled their own father; but he remained dead.

At such times, common crime declines. Even the wicked are moved by the great moment.[1]

And even a Chamfort, double-dyed pessimist as he was in his *Maximes* and *Caractères,* where he was dealing with the common run of earthly life, became an accusing optimist at the outbreak of revolution.

[1] Cf. Guibert, *Novigent. ap. Bongars,* for the First Crusade.

Thucydides (VI, 24) describes a similar riot of enthusiasm on the occasion of the negotiations preceding the Sicilian expedition. The atmosphere of Athens was charged with hope—of the possession of the country, of the treasures revealed by Segesta and of permanent military pay. The younger men, however, joined in "because they wished to see and know a distant country and were confident that they would save their lives." Everywhere in the hemicycles groups of men could be seen tracing the outline of the island on the ground,[1] and, to increase the tension, there came the excitement aroused by the trials of those accused of mutilating the Hermae, which was fanned to flame by the secret opponents of the expedition.

In the First Crusade, which is of such supreme importance because its real, lasting historical results were achieved not in its actual goal, Palestine, but in a totally different sphere, a strange vision must, according to Guibert, have helped to inspire the masses.

We might think, too, of the visions preceding Charles VIII's expedition to Italy, which, with quite unwarranted importance, set forth under all the aspects of a world crisis, but merely ushered in an age of intervention.

In the Peasants' War, on the other hand, the beginnings were in no way visionary, and the Chiliasts only a subsidiary element.[2]

In the Civil War in England, quite particularly, we find nothing of the kind. It has no place in the present discussion because it did not for one moment attack the principles of civic life, never stirred up the supreme powers of the nation, spent its early years as a slow legal process,

[1] Cf. Plutarch, *Alcibiades,* 17.

[2] For the ideas of the Chiliasts, cf. Ranke, *Deutsche Geschichte im Zeitalter der Reformation,* Vol. II, pp. 185, 207 ff. Trans. *History of the Reformation in Germany,* Book III, Chap. VI.

and by 1644 had passed into the hands of the Parliamentary army and its Napoleon, thus sparing the nation the years 1792–1794. Moreover, all true Calvinism and Puritanism is of its very nature too pessimistic to indulge in brilliant visions. Hence the wild preachings of the Independents were powerless to convulse life.

The power of the original vision, on the other hand, is beautifully demonstrated in the *Cahiers* of 1789; its guiding principle was Rousseau's doctrine of the goodness of human nature and the value of feeling as a warrant of virtue. It was the time of flags and festivals, which saw its last brilliant moment in 1790 on the Champ de Mars. It is as though human nature, at such moments, had to give full rein to its power of hope.

We are too prone to take the vision for the specific spirit of a crisis. The vision is merely its wedding finery, which must be laid aside for the bitter workaday life which follows.

It will always be impossible to assess the force and value of a crisis, and more especially its power of expansion, at its outset. At that moment, the decisive factor is less its programme than the quantity of explosive material at hand, i.e. the number and state of mind not only of the sufferers pure and simple, but of those who have long been ready for a general change. Only one thing is certain—genuine crises first show their true force under opposition. Counterfeit or inadequate ones are paralysed by opposition, however great the preceding clamor may have been.

If, at the beginning, at an apparently decisive moment, the crisis is postponed and does not come to a head, the party of renewal tends to imagine itself at an advantage, since the opposing party, had it lain in their power, could not but have wished to annihilate them. We might here recall the crisis in the market-place at Münster in 1534, which gave the victory to the Anabaptists without a struggle. A great deal, however, depends on which side captivates the imagination. If the crisis is not to subside, it must remain the guide of that imagination, and tries to do so by means of demonstrations, for mere demonstrations may of themselves be a proof of power, and *should,* as a rule, be one. People ought to see how much the powers that be will stand.

The official arenas of crises are the great national assemblies. But they often fall very rapidly into obsolescence, and are incompatible with the presence of a really strong man (as Napoleon emphasized in 1815).[1] The real barometer of power is rather to be sought in clubs and *hetairia,* which can be reconstituted at any moment and are mainly characterized by their frivolity.

In the first stage of the crisis, when old oppressions have to be swept away and their representatives persecuted, we already find the phenomenon which causes so much foolish amazement, namely that the initiators of the movement are ousted and replaced.

Either they had been the agents of very diverse forces, while from now on *one* force stands revealed as the real leader, annihilating the others or carrying them with it; this, for instance, was the case in the Civil War in England, which was set in motion by the Cavaliers but carried through by the Roundheads alone, a proof that the essential impulse was not the defence of the constitution but the Independent movement.

Or else those initiators were carried away by imagination (their own or others'), with their minds in a state of

[1] Cf. Fleury de Chaboulon, *Mémoires,* Vol. II, p. 111.

confusion, and thus found themselves at the head of affairs without any right to be there, perhaps by the mere effect of their oratory.

The bright and bellying sail conceives itself to be the cause of the ship's motion, but it only catches the wind, which may change or drop at any moment.

Any man who flags for an instant, or can no longer keep pace with the increasing momentum of the movement, is replaced with astonishing rapidity. In the shortest space of time, a second generation of leaders has found time to mature, and is already representative of the crisis alone, and of its essential, specific spirit. They feel their bond with the former state of things far less strongly than the men who came first. It is at such times that power can least suffer suspension. Whenever a man—or a party—wearies, another is waiting to take his place, and though he may, in his turn, be extremely inadequate to his moment, the whole movement may crystallize round him just for that moment. Men take for granted that every power must ultimately behave rationally, i.e. in the long run recognize and restore to honor the general conditions of existence. Even so-called anarchy is, as quickly as possible, shaped into separate fragments of power, i.e. into representatives of a whole, however crude they may be. Both in the north of France and later in Italy, the Normans began as pirates but soon founded firmly established States.

In all crises, turbulence very quickly turns into obedience and vice versa. But unity and obedience immobilize the sense of responsibility and the vertigo which it causes.

In its further progress, a great crisis brings into play that "social" phenomenon which makes the hair of its idealistic originators stand on end, namely distress and greed, due partly to the stoppage of ordinary traffic, partly to the spoils which have become available and partly to impunity.

According to the circumstances, Religion will soon take sides for or against it, or else the principle of the crisis will be a rift through religion, a religious split, so that all its battles also partake of the character of a war of religion.

Indeed, all the rest of the world's life is involved in the ferment, is implicated in the crisis in a thousand ways, friendly or hostile. It would even seem as if the crisis absorbed into itself the whole mobility of an epoch, just as other diseases decline in an epidemic, the movement hastening, slowing down, relapsing and re-starting according to the main impulses operative at the moment.

When two crises intersect, the stronger temporarily carves its way through the weaker. Twice the opposition between Hapsburg and France was overshadowed and shouted down by the conflict between the Reformation and the Counter-Reformation, the first time before 1589 and the second between the death of Henry IV and the rise of Richelieu.

The struggle between the Hussites and the Catholics was actually supplanted by a struggle between Bohemians and Germans, leading to an extreme accentuation of the Slav element on the Bohemian side.

And now the opposing forces. These include all antecedent institutions which have long since become vested rights, or even law, to whose existence morals and culture have become linked up in all kinds of ways; further, the individuals who incorporate those institutions at the time of the crisis and are chained to them by duty or interest. (For this there are phrases but no remedy.)

Hence the fierceness of these struggles, the unleashing of passion on both sides. Each side defends "what it holds most sacred"—on the one hand, an abstract loyalty and a religion; on the other, a new "world order."

And hence also the indifference as to methods, which may go as far as an exchange of weapons, so that the secret reactionary may play the democrat and the "man of liberty" turn his hand to every kind of arbitrary violence.

In illustration, we might recall the decay of Greek political life in the Peloponnesian War, as described by Thucydides (III, 81–83), which was actually a reaction against the terrorism practised by the demos and the sycophants on any man of standing. After the atrocities of Corcyra, we read how all Hellas was shaken to its foundations. War, which of its very nature teaches the use of force, permitted the parties to appeal for outside help; belated vengeance was taken in belated outbreak. Even in language, the meaning of every expression changed. A general rivalry in cruelty set in. Men assembled in *hetairia* to uphold their cause in the teeth of the law, and the bond between them was the breaking of the law. Vows of reconciliation were void, malice the favorite method of action, and men preferred to be wicked and astute rather than benevolent and clumsy. Everywhere tyranny, self-seeking and ambition prevailed. Those without a party, because they held their ground, were *a fortiori* doomed to destruction. Every kind of iniquity had its representatives, simple honesty was derided and vanished, and the prevailing tone was one of crude physical violence.

At such times the necessity of reaping success at all costs soon leads to an utter unscrupulousness in methods and a complete oblivion of the principles originally appealed to; thus men bring upon themselves a terrorism which frustrates any really fruitful, constructive activity and compromises the whole crisis. In its initial stage, that terrorism is wont to put forward the time-worn plea of threats from outside, while it is actually born of a fury keyed up to the highest pitch against elusive enemies at home, and further, of the necessity of finding an easy method of government and the growing awareness of being in the minority. In its progress, this terrorism comes to be taken for granted, for should it flag, retribution for what has already been committed would immediately descend. Of course, should a menace from outside present itself, it must rage all the more fiercely, as at Münster in 1535.

The extermination of the adversary then appears to the demented eye the only salvation. Nor shall sons and heirs remain behind: "the venom dies with the serpent." Under the lash of a genuine and general hallucination, extermination is carried out by categories selected on principle, in comparison with which the most indiscriminate general massacres, occurring anonymously and at random, produce only a slight effect, for they are occasional, while the other executions are periodical and endless. This was frequently carried to extreme lengths in the Greek and Italian republics, and the proscriptions of Marius in his dotage against the nobility as a caste (87–86 B.C.) come under this head. Men find a sop for their consciences in the realization that the adversary would do the same if he could.

It is against the émigrés that the fury rages most fiercely. Those at home immensely overrate, or pretend to overrate, their power. To have eluded maltreatment and murder is considered high treason. When princes such as the Grand Duke Cosimo and Francesco Medici pursued their distant émigrés with poison, the whole world was indignant, but if republics imprison or execute such relatives of émigrés as have remained at home, it is regarded as a "political measure."

Now and then, however, the aftermath of terrorism falls upon the crisis itself. *La révolution dévore ses enfants.* Every stage of the crisis, moreover, devours the representatives of the preceding stage as "moderates."

Now, while the crisis is affecting a number of countries belonging to the same civilization (it is particularly prone to carry small countries along with it), combining there with repressed forces and passions, and producing its own peculiar reflection in the minds of their inhabitants, it may, in the country of its origin, be already weakening and waning. In this process its original tendency may be reversed, i.e. what is called a reaction sets in. The causes of that reaction are the following:

(1) The very excesses committed must, by any normal human reckoning, lead to fatigue.

(2) The masses, whose irritability is great only at the beginning, either fall away or are overcome by apathy. They may already have conveyed their spoils to safety, or perhaps have never had their hearts in the matter at all. It has merely been blindly assumed that they had. Indeed, the vast majority of the rural population has never been really consulted.[1]

[1] For instance, the Roman colonials of the fourth century were not asked whether they wanted to be Christians, nor the Polish peasants of the sixteenth century whether they wanted to be Catholics. Their feudal lord decided for them.

(3) Violence having been once unchained, a host of latent forces have been aroused and now take up their stand, suddenly demand their spoils from the chaos and devour the movement without a thought for its quondam ideals. The majority of both the Guelfs and the Ghibellines were so minded.

(4) Since the scaffold has already despatched those who were the most obvious representatives of the successive climaxes of the crisis, the most powerful men have already disappeared. The so-called second generation already have a look of epigoni about them.

(5) The surviving representatives of the movement have passed through an inward change. Some want to enjoy, some to save their lives if nothing else.

And even if the *causa* survives, *it falls into other hands,* losing its irresistible momentum. The German Reformation was, till 1524, a popular movement, and there seemed every likelihood that it would overcome the old Church before long. Then the Peasants' War seemed to hoist the Reformation on to its shoulders in order to rush it through to safety. The disastrous end of the war did permanent harm to the Reformation because, firstly, where the Reformation triumphed, it was taken over by the government and subjected to dogmatic systematization, and secondly, as a result of the strengthening of the Catholic governments, it was kept out of north-west Germany. The Anabaptist sequel at Münster merely made matters worse.

When disillusionment sets in, quite apart from any material distress, it is devastating. With the utmost patience, men will then tolerate the most inept governments and will silently endure the very abuses which would, but a short time before, have provoked a general paroxysm. In England under Charles II, for instance, those Presbyterians to whom he owed his crown were ruthlessly sacrificed.[1]

This disillusionment may, as the French Revolution shows, go hand in hand with brilliant success abroad and a quite tolerable economic situation at home. It is vastly different from the bitterness following defeat, and has demonstrably different causes.

Some element of the original movement probably triumphs for good. Thus in France, for instance, equality, though the Revolution naïvely imagined that it had educated men for liberty as well. It even called itself liberty, though in reality it had as much liberty as the elements or a forest fire. The permanent result, however, remains astonishingly meagre in comparison with the great efforts and passions which rise to the surface during the crisis. It is true that, after a great crisis, the genuine (i.e. the relatively genuine) results as a totality (the so-called good and evil, i.e. what each observer regards as desirable or undesirable, for beyond that we cannot get) can only be surveyed after a lapse of time proportionate to the severity of the crisis; it is open to question in what forms it will assert its specific principles on its second and third reappearances.

It may be accounted a blessing if a crisis does not provoke foreign intervention, or even make its arch-enemy its master. In this respect the Hussite movement stands alone; side by side with the terrorist party in the towns,

[1] For the disappointment following the German Reformation, see Sebastian Franck, preamble to Book III of *Chronica, Zeitbuch und Geschichtsbibel.* Cf. also the survival of Catholicism in the Netherlands in 1566 and 1567.

the moderate party (later called Calixtine) steadily held its ground and joined the terrorists in meeting the attack from the outside, but later, when the terrorists were a little exhausted, finished them off, closed the gulf of revolution with a high hand and in all essentials had its own way for a century.

The Peloponnesian War was originally a dispute between the two hegemonies, both of which were out to lead a united Greece against Persia, and even to be the educators of Hellas. In the beginning, the contrast between them was stressed to the utmost, Pericles and the orators representing it as that of two conflicting philosophies, a fact which did not prevent Sparta, untrue to herself, from dominating the scene for a few decades with Persian money.

France had to suffer the three invasions of 1814, 1815 and 1870–1871. Even the last aimed at a weakening of the revolutionary nation *par excellence*.

The next point is the effect of the redistribution of wealth. Here we must first note the physiological fact that in every crisis a certain number of able, resolute and flint-hearted men swim with the tide, determined simply to make a fortune out of the crisis and ready to make it with any party. This type of Holdfast, Steal-quick and Speed-booty keeps his head above water at any cost,[1] and is the more secure in that no higher aim clouds his vision. One or another of the type may be caught and succumb,[2] but

[1] Cf. the devils in *Faust,* II., Act IV, and in Dante's Malebolge, *Inferno,* XXI. (Editor's note.)

[2] We have only to think of the moral indignation, in part affected, of the French Revolution against such a man as Fabre d'Eglantine. In 1794 people were not so squeamish, although the outcry against *les vendus,* the men who had sold themselves, continued.

the type itself is immortal, while the born leaders of any movement are few in number and are engulfed by successive climaxes of the crisis. Turpitude is immortal on earth. It is this type, however, which sets the tone among the new possessing class.

Now, property of any kind, though its tenure be immemorial, can turn traitor to its cause. Even Pericles prophesied of the treasury of Delphi that it would one day be spent in a recruiting campaign, and Jason of Pherae and the elder Dionysius having first cast their eyes upon it, that is what actually happened in the Holy War. The main impulse of the Reformation also came from the property of the Church.

New wealth, however, regards itself and its preservation —not the crisis by which it came into being—as the be-all and end-all of existence. Whatever happens, the crisis must not be arrested, but must come to a halt at the precise point at which wealth was secured. Thus the new property-owners in France after 1794–1795 were horrified at what had gone before, but equally anxious for a despotic government to safeguard property. As for liberty, that could look after itself.

A similar state of things prevailed after the Albigensian War. It was in the interests of the four hundred and thirty feudal nobles in the south of France that the French crown should prevent the Count of Toulouse from rallying; while the dispute over the heresy never came up again, i.e. in their own minds they were quite indifferent whether their serfs were Albigensians or Catholics.

In the Greek cities, the grip on the property of the parties exterminated by exile or massacre, which had been seized in the name of some principle or other—demos or aristocracy—was apt to turn into a tyranny to which both democracy and aristocracy succumbed.

And now wars and militarism have their part to play. Infallibly, wars and armies come into existence. They may be necessary to quell recalcitrant provinces; for instance, Cromwell had to fight the Irish, and the French generals the Fédéralistes and the Vendée. Or they may be used for purposes of offence or defence against other countries, threatened or threatening, as in the case of the resistance of the House of Orange to the Spaniards,[1] and of the French to the Coalitions after 1792. Moreover, the movement itself requires some manifest power if all the currents which have been released are to be conducted into one channel. As a rule, however, what it fears is their effect on its principle.[2] The first symptom of that fear is terrorism directed against its own military leaders. In a certain way we can see this as early as the impeachments of the generals after the battle of Arginusae, and very distinctly in the behavior of the French in 1793 and 1794.

But the one man who is never caught is the right man, because he is still unknown.

And then, as soon as the crisis has gathered too much momentum, and fatigue sets in, the former instruments of power of the antecedent dispensation, namely the police and the army, reorganize themselves spontaneously in their old discipline. The mortally weary, however, inevitably fall into the arms of the strongest element that happens to be at hand—and this does not consist of newly elected, moderate assemblies, but of soldiers.

[1] In this case a real military party came into being under Maurice, who used it for his own political purposes.
[2] St. Just said to Barrère: "You praise our victories too much."

Now come the *coups d'état.* One form is the abolition by military force of political representation regarded as constitutional, and surviving the crisis, while the nation applauds or looks on indifferent. This was ventured by Caesar in 49 B.C., by Cromwell in 1653 and by the two Napoleons. At such moments the constitutional aspect of public life is *pro forma* retained and re-constituted, or even expanded; Caesar enlarged the Senate, and Napoleon introduced universal suffrage, which had been restricted by the decree of May 31, 1850.

The spirit of the military, however, will, after some transitional stages, tend towards a monarchy, and a despotic one. It re-forms the State in its own image.

Not every army vanishes as quietly as Cromwell's, which, of course, was only called into being during the Civil War and therefore had no monarchist or militarist institutions to fall back on. It had *not* given the crown even to Cromwell, but had been and remained the army of a republican despotism. And since Monk deceived it, it was not responsible for the Restoration. In the end, in 1661, it melted into private life, not unlike the American Army after the last war. In both cases, of course, the respective nations were by temperament utterly non-militaristic.

When the crisis has affected other nations in such a way that the converse movement (provoked, perhaps, by attempts at imitation) has been established,[1] while in the country of its origin it has also gone into reverse, it comes to an end in purely national wars waged by despot against despot.

[1] For example, after the death of Joseph II the French Revolution provoked stricter police surveillance in Austria.

Despotism following crises is primarily a restoration of purposeful command and willing obedience, in which the loosened bonds of State are reknotted, and more firmly. It is born not so much of the openly confessed realization that the people is incapable of government as of the horror men feel of what they have just experienced, namely the rule of anyone ruthless and terrible enough to take the reins into his hands. The abdication men desire is less their own than that of a gang of ruffians.

Even aristocracies abdicate voluntarily from time to time, as the Roman Republic did in nominating a dictator, for *creato dictatore magnus plebem metus incessit.*[1] With the Council of Ten, the Venetian aristocracy hung a permanent sword of Damocles over its own and the people's head, as though it had no confidence in itself.

Democracies, however, abdicate from time to time with the greatest willingness. In Hellas, they made the man who had broken or evicted their aristocracy their tyrant and assumed that such a man would for ever fulfil their unchanging will. When this turned out to be not quite the case, Hybreas the demagogue said to the tyrant Euthydemos at Mylasa: "Euthydemos, you are a necessary evil, for we can live neither with you nor without you."[2]

The despot can do infinite good. The one thing he cannot do is to establish lawful liberty. Even Cromwell set up generals to rule England by districts. Were the despot to give his country a free constitution, not only would he himself be speedily set aside; he would be replaced, not by liberty, but by another and smaller despot. For the moment, men do not want liberty, because the hands they

[1] Livy, II, 18: "When the dictator was named great fear fell on the people."

[2] Strabo, XIV, 2, 24. The anecdote comes, of course, rather late, at the time of the Second Triumvirate.

have seen it in were too evil. We might recall how the France of our day dreads its own shadow.

The next phenomenon to appear under a despotism may be great prosperity, by which the memory of the crisis is wiped out. Despotism, however, bears within itself its own consequences. It is by nature irresponsible and personal, and, having fallen heir to a great, derelict power, prone to acts of aggression against other countries, if only because it recognizes in them a metastasis of the preceding unrest at home.

Then come the restorations. These must be distinguished from those already discussed, for there it was a question of the re-establishment of a people or a State, but here of the re-establishment of a defeated party within the same nation, i.e. of those partial political restorations which are carried out by émigrés returning home after crises.

In themselves, they may be a restoration of justice, or even a closing of the breach in the nation. In practice, they are dangerous in exact proportion to the severity of the crisis.

Thus even in Greece we can see a large number of exiled bodies of citizens returning to their cities. But since, for the most part, they had to share those cities with their new owners, their return was not always a blessing for the cities and themselves.

For while the homecomers are striving to restore some of the relics and principles of the past, they are confronted with the new generation which has grown up since the crisis and has on its side the privilege of youth. And this absolutely new form of life is founded on the destruction of what has gone before, is largely guiltless of that destruction, and hence regards the restitution demanded of it as an infringement of an acquired right. And at the same time it has a transfigured and alluring awareness of how easy revolution was, and in that feeling the memory of suffering fades.

It would be better for émigrés never to return, or at any rate not to return with claims for compensation. It would be better for them to accept their sufferings as their share of the common lot, recognizing a law of superannuation which would pronounce judgment not merely according to the lapse of time but also according to the greatness of the breach.[1]

The new generation, which is expected, for its part, to be repentant, does nothing of the sort, but schemes for new revolutions to blot out the shame that has been put upon it. And so the spirit of change rises again, and the more often, the more inexorably an institution has triumphed over it, the more inevitable becomes that institution's ultimate overthrow by the secondary and tertiary creations of the crisis. "Institutions are destroyed by their triumphs" (Renan).

From time to time a philosopher appears with a Utopia to demonstrate in what way and how far a people should be or should have been organized in order to avoid all the frauds of democracy, a Peloponnesian War, or another Persian intervention. Plato's *Republic* contains a theory of the avoidance of crises. What bondage is the price of that avoidance! And even then, we might ask how soon, even in Utopias, a revolution would break out. In Plato's Re-

[1] On émigrés of political freedom and the advisability of their return, cf. Quinet, *La Révolution,* Vol. II, p. 545.

public the matter would present no difficulty. As soon as his philosophers began to fall foul of each other, the remaining, suppressed classes would rise of themselves.

At other times, however, the Utopian has been there first, and has helped to light the fire, as Rousseau did with his *Contrat Social.*

In praise of crises, we might first say that passion is the mother of great things, real passion, that is, bent on the new and not merely on the overthrow of the old. Unsuspected forces awake in individuals and even heaven takes on a different hue. Whoever *is* anybody can make himself felt because barriers have been or are being trampled down.

Crises and even their accompanying fanaticisms are (though always according to the age of the people passing through them) to be regarded as genuine signs of vitality. The crisis itself is an expedient of nature, like a fever, and the fanaticisms are signs that there still exist for men things they prize more than life and property. Yet men must not merely be fanatics in opposition to others and quivering egoists for themselves.

All spiritual growth takes place by leaps and bounds, both in the individual and, as here, in the community. The crisis is to be regarded as a new nexus of growth.

Crises clear the ground, firstly of a host of institutions from which life has long since departed, and which, given their historical privilege, could not have been swept away in any other fashion. Further, of those pseudo-organisms which ought never to have existed, but which had nevertheless, in the course of time, gained a firm foothold in the rest of life, and were, indeed, mainly to blame for the preference for mediocrity and the hatred of excellence. Crises also abolish the cumulative dread of "disturbance" and clear the way for strong personalities.

Crises stand in quite a peculiar relationship to art and literature, when they do not merely destroy or cause a partial and permanent suppression of individual spiritual forces, as happened when Islam put an end to painting, sculpture and the epic.

The mere disturbance does little or no harm to art and literature. In the general insecurity, great spiritual forces, hitherto latent, arise, and quite dumbfound the mere exploiters of the crisis. Mere ranters, however, are in any case powerless in times of terror.[1]

At such times it can be seen that vigorous thinkers, poets and artists love an atmosphere of danger because they are vigorous human beings, and feel at ease in the more bracing currents of air. Great and tragic experience may mature the mind and give it a new standard, a more independent judgment of life on earth. If it had not been for the collapse of the Roman Empire in the West, St. Augustine's *City of God* would not have become such a great and independent book, while Dante wrote the *Divina Commedia* in exile.[2]

It is unnecessary for artists and poets to describe the actual *content* of the crisis they live through, or even to glorify it, as David and Monti did, if only a new meaning has come into men's lives, if they only know again what they love and what they hate, what is trivial and what is fundamental in life.

Quant à la pensée philosophique, elle n'est jamais plus

[1] *An amplification:* Unfortunately, fools are not.

[2] Even the great Persian poets of Mongol times come under this heading, though they were the last of their race. Saadi says: "The world was crinkled like a negro's hair."

libre qu'aux grands jours de l'histoire, says Renan. Philosophy flourished in Athens in spite of all that was reckless and unbalanced in Athenian life, which actually moved in a continuous crisis with continuous terrorism, in spite of the wars, the political and religious trials, the sycophantism and the perils of journeys on which men risked being sold into slavery.

In times of complete calm, on the other hand, private life with its interests and comforts weaves its web round the naturally creative mind and robs it of its greatness. But then mere talents push their way into the front rank, betraying themselves for what they are by the fact that art and literature are for them a kind of speculation, and that they can turn their dexterity to account without suffering for it, since there is no upwelling genius to waylay it. And very often not even talent.

Great originality, shouted down at such times, has to wait for times of tempest, when publishers' agreements and copyright laws lapse spontaneously. In such a tempest, the reading public changes, and the patrons who have hitherto supported and provided occupation for *sui generis* vanish of themselves.

As to the specific nature of crises in our own times, we might refer in particular to certain earlier passages in which we tried to show how culture dictates its programmes to the State.

Crises in our day are predominantly due to the influence of the press and of commerce, things which are not exceptional, but our daily bread, and may therefore either stimulate or stupefy. They have at all times an oecumenical character.

Hence the many counterfeit crises, based on artificial agitation, on reading, on unjustified imitation of the wrong things, on artificial inoculation. Such crises, when they come to grief, produce a totally different result from what was intended or imagined, bringing to light something that had long since underlain them, and that might have been seen long since, but could only be finally brought to light by a shift of power.

A striking instance of this is to be seen in France in 1848. The Republic, suddenly imposed, had to yield to a sense of property and money-making, the intensity of which had till then been unsuspected.

Further, much energy is frittered away in talk before it can develop into a factor in a crisis.

What is new is the weakness of the legal principles opposing the crisis. Former crises found themselves confronted by divine law, which, when it came off victor, was justified in exacting the utmost rigor of punishment. Now, on the contrary, the ruling principles are universal suffrage, which can, from the elections, be extended to all and sundry, absolute civic equality, and so on. This is the focus from which one day the main crisis will rise against the money-making genius of our age.

Railways have their own relationship to revolution, reaction and war. Anyone controlling them, or even only their rolling stock,[1] can immobilize whole nations.

And menacing rises a vision of the intertwinement of the present crisis with tremendous national wars.

[1] Nowadays one would have to add: "and the supplies of oil." (Editor's note.)

SUPPLEMENTARY NOTES ON THE ORIGIN AND NATURE OF THE PRESENT CRISIS

The long peace dating from 1815 had created an optical illusion, namely that a permanent balance of power had been established. In any case, from the very outset too little account was taken of the mutability of national temperaments.

The Restoration and its ostensible principle of Legitimacy, which was in effect a reaction against the spirit of the French Revolution, restored in most unequal fashion a number of former modes of life and law and a series of national frontiers; on the other hand, it was impossible to banish from the world the continuing after-effects of the French Revolution, namely, the actual and far-reaching equality before the law (in taxation, qualification for office, the division of inheritances), the transferability of landed property, the placing of all property at the disposal of industry, and religious parity in a number of countries whose populations were now very mixed.

The State itself, moreover, was determined not to relinquish one of the results of the Revolution, namely the great expansion in the idea of its power which had come about in the interim and was due, among other things, to the Napoleonic Caesarism which had been imitated everywhere. The Power State of its very nature postulated equality, even where it abandoned places at Court and in the army as spoils to its aristocracy.

Opposing this, there stood the spirit of those peoples who had waged the wars of 1812–1815 in a state of extreme national fervor. A spirit of criticism had awakened which, however much men needed rest, could no longer lie still, and henceforth applied a new standard to life as a whole.

When the July Revolution broke out in 1830, its general significance as a European crisis far outweighed its specific political significance. Austria, Prussia and Russia remained to all appearances where they were. Everywhere else the constitution was hailed as a panacea, where any serious efforts were made in that direction.

Constitutions, however, were as powerless as anything else on earth to satisfy the greed that had been aroused. Firstly, the French constitution itself was a very unsatisfactory structure. The suffrage was so restricted that the Chamber was later powerless to come to the help of the government in its impasse, because it was itself representative only of a small minority. At the same time, the government's programme, *la paix à tout prix,* was artificially charged with hatred. Louis Philippe would have been able to bequeath his peace programme to the Chamber had it been on a much broader basis, namely that of universal suffrage.

In Western Europe, during the Thirties, politics developed into a general radicalism, namely that way of thinking which attributed all evils to existing political conditions and their representatives, and thought to find salvation in demolishing and rebuilding the whole structure from the foundations with the help of abstract principles which already revealed a much closer kinship with North America.

With the Forties there set in a development of Socialistic and Communistic theories, in part the product of conditions in the great English and French industrial towns; they embraced the whole social edifice, an inevitable result of untrammelled traffic. The freedom actually existing was ample for such ideas to spread unchecked, so that, according to Renan, after 1840 a deterioration of their quality was distinctly perceptible. At the same time, nobody had any idea of what and how strong the opposing forces might be. How far the right of defence was misunderstood became evident in February 1848.

This state of affairs was reflected in the literature and poetry of the time. Derision, loud snarling and *Weltschmerz* characterized its new, post-Byronic attitude.

Then came the February Revolution of 1848. In the midst of the general upheaval, it caused a sudden clearing of the horizon. By far its most important, though only ephemeral, result was the proclamation of union in Germany and Italy. Socialism proved far less powerful than people had imagined, for the June days in Paris almost at once restored the monarchist and constitutional party to power, and the sense of property and money-making was more intense than ever.

The climax of the movement in the first battle of Custozza was followed, it is true, for the time being by a general reaction, the forms and frontiers previously existing being for the most part restored. The reaction, however, was in most countries far from complete, and cross-currents set in everywhere.

With dynasties, bureaucracies and militarisms continuing to exist, the *inward* crisis in men's minds had to be left almost entirely out of account. Public opinion, the press, the swiftly rising tide of traffic, won the day everywhere and were already so intrinsic a part of money-making that any check on the one meant damage to the other. Everywhere industry was striving for a place in world industry.

At the same time, the events of 1848 had given the ruling classes a deeper insight into the people. Louis Napoleon had risked universal suffrage for the elections, and others followed his lead. The conservative strain in the rural populations had been recognized, though no attempt had been made to assess precisely how far it might be extended from the elections to everything and everybody (institutions, taxes, etc.).

With all business swelling into big business, the views of the business man took the following line: on the one hand, the State should be no more than the protective guarantor of his interests and of his type of intelligence, henceforth assumed to be the main purpose of the world. Indeed, it was his desire that his type of intelligence should obtain possession of the State by means of constitutional adjustments. On the other hand, there prevailed a profound distrust of constitutional liberty in practice, since it was more likely to be used by destructive forces.

For at the same time the ideas of the French Revolution and the reform principles of modern times were both finding active expression in democracy, so-called, a doctrine nourished by a thousand springs, and varying greatly with the social status of its adherents. Only in one respect was it consistent, namely, in the insatiability of its demand for State control of the individual. Thus it effaces the boundaries between State and Society, and looks to the State for the things that Society will most likely refuse to do, while maintaining a permanent condition of argument and change and ultimately vindicating the right to work and subsistence for certain castes.

Meanwhile, the general menace of the political situation was deepening. All positions had been radically changed, and many profoundly unsettled, by the events of 1848. The governments of the greatest powers could not but welcome some foreign diversion.

Only complete unanimity among all the governments could have preserved existing frontiers and the so-called balance of power.

March 1873. The first great phenomenon to follow the war of 1870–1871 was a further extraordinary intensification of money-making, which went far beyond the mere making good of gaps and losses, and was combined with the exploitation and activation of an infinite number of sources of wealth and the inevitable fraudulent schemes connected with them (big business).

The spiritual results, however, of which some are already visible, and some about to become so, are that the so-called "best minds" are going into business or are actually being educated to that end by their parents. Bureaucracy, like the army in France and other countries, is no longer a career. In Prussia the most strenuous efforts are necessary in order to keep it as such.

Art and science have the greatest difficulty in preventing themselves from sinking into a mere branch of urban money-making and from being carried away on the stream of general unrest. The utmost effort and self-denial will be necessary if they are to remain creatively independent in view of the relation in which they stand to the daily press, to cosmopolitan traffic, to world exhibitions. A further menace is the decay of local patriotism, with its advantages and disadvantages, and a great decrease even in national patriotism.

What classes and strata of society will now become the real representatives of culture, will give us our scholars, artists and poets, our creative personalities?

Or is everything to turn into big business, as in America?

Now for the political results. Two great nations, Germany and Italy, have been founded, partly with the help of public opinion, long since in a state of extreme agitation, partly by means of great wars. A further factor is the spectacle of rapid demolition and reconstruction in countries whose established polity had long been regarded as immutable. Hence political adventure has become a matter of daily occurrence among the nations, and the opposing convictions, which tended to defend any existing institutions, grow steadily weaker. Statesmen no longer seek to combat "democracy," but in some way or other to reckon with it, to eliminate risks as far as possible from the transition to what is now regarded as inevitable. The form of a State is to all intents and purposes no longer defended, but only its area and power, democracy for the time being lending a helping hand. The sense of power and democratic feeling are for the most part indistinguishable. The Socialist systems have been the first to abandon the quest for power and to place their specific aims before anything else.

The republics of France and Spain may very well subsist as republics by sheer force of habit and from fear of the terrible moment of change, and if, from time to time, they take on some other form, it will tend to be a Caesarian rather than a dynastic monarchy.

One wonders how soon the other countries will follow suit.

These ferments, however, conflict with the money-making current, and ultimately the latter proves the stronger. The masses want their peace and their pay. If they get them from a republic or a monarchy, they will cling to either. If not, without much ado they will support the first constitution to promise them what they want. A decision of the kind, of course, is never taken directly, but is always influenced by passion, personalities and the lingering effects of former situations.

The most complete programme is contained in Grant's last speech, which postulates one State and one language as the necessary goal of a purely money-making world.

And finally, the question of the Church. In the whole of Western Europe the philosophy issuing from the French Revolution is in conflict with the Church, particularly the Catholic Church, a conflict ultimately springing from the optimism of the former and the pessimism of the latter.

Of late, that pessimism has been deepened by the Syllabus, the *Concilium* and the doctrine of infallibility, the Church, for obscure reasons, having decided to offer a conscious opposition to modern ideas on a wide front.

Italy profited by the occasion to take Rome. Otherwise Italy, France and Spain, etc., have left theoretical questions alone, while Germany and Switzerland are attempting to force Catholicism into perfect obedience to the State, not only depriving it of any exemption from the common law, but reducing it to permanent impotence.

The great decision can only come from the mind of men.

Will optimism, under the guise of power and money, continue to survive, and how long? Or, as the pessimist philosophy of today might seem to suggest, will there be a general change in thought such as took place in the third and fourth centuries?

V

The Great Men of History

Nor is fame in itself enough. The general education of our time knows a vast army of more or less famous men of all nations and times, yet with each single one of them we must ask whether he is to be called great, and few stand the test.

Yet what is the standard? It is uncertain, fluctuating, illogical. Sometimes the predicate is bestowed more on intellectual, sometimes more on moral grounds, sometimes more by the conviction that comes from written records, sometimes (and, as we have said, oftener) by mere feeling. Sometimes the personality counts more, sometimes the persisting influence. Often judgment finds its place usurped by prejudice.

Finally it begins to dawn upon us that the whole of the personality which seems great to us is producing upon us, across the peoples and the centuries, a *magical* after-effect, far beyond the limits of mere tradition.

From this point, a further definition, though not an explanation, of greatness is given by the words—unique, irreplaceable. The great man is a man of that kind, a man without whom the world would seem to us incomplete because certain great achievements only became possible through him in his time and place and are otherwise unimaginable. He is an essential strand in the great web of causes and effects. "No man is irreplaceable," says the proverb. But the few that are, are great.

The strict proof that a man was unique and irreplaceable is certainly not always possible, if only because we have no knowledge of the presumable store from which nature and history have taken one great individual instead of another to put on to the scene. But we have reason to believe that that store is not very great.

The only unique and irreplaceable human being, however, is the man of exceptional intellectual or moral power whose activity is directed to a general aim, i.e. a whole nation, a whole civilization, humanity itself. It might be said here in parenthesis that there is something like greatness even among nations, and further, that there is a partial or momentary greatness in which an individual entirely forgets himself and his own existence for the sake of a general aim. Such a man at such a moment seems sublime.

We must grant the nineteenth century a special faculty for appreciating greatness of all times and kinds. For by the exchange and interconnection of all our literatures, by the increase of traffic, by the spread of European humanity over all the oceans, by the expansion and deepening of all our studies, our culture has attained a high degree of general receptivity, which is its essential characteristic. We have a standpoint for everything and strive to do justice even to the things that seem to us most strange and terrible.

Former times had *one* or few standpoints; in particular, only a national or a religious one. Islam had regard to itself alone. For a thousand years, the Middle Ages looked upon classical antiquity as the devil's own. Now, on the other hand, our historical judgment is carrying out a great general revision of all famous men and things of the past. We are the first to judge the individual from his own premisses, in his own time. False greatnesses have fallen and real ones been proclaimed anew. And here our right to pass judgment springs not from indifference but rather from enthusiasm for all past greatness, so that, for instance, we acknowledge greatness in hostile religions.

In art and poetry also the past lives for us as it did not

for our forebears. Since Winckelmann and the humanists of the late eighteenth century, we have seen the whole of antiquity through other eyes than the greatest scholars of former times, and it is only since the revival of Shakespeare in the eighteenth century that we have really known Dante and the *Nibelungen*, and have acquired a true and universal standard of poetic greatness.

It may be that some future epoch will revise our judgments in its turn. And in any case, let us be content here to cast light, not on the idea but on the actual use of the phrase "the great men of history." In doing so, we may encounter great inconsistencies.

We are now faced with the following mysterious turn of fate. Peoples, cultures, religions, things, whose significance seemed to reside only in their totality, which seemed to be only the products and manifestations of that totality, are suddenly given a new content or a commanding expression by great individuals.

Time and the man enter into a great, mysterious covenant.

But nature here proceeds with her familiar thrift, and life besets the great man, from youth up, with quite peculiar dangers, in particular, false aims, such as conflict with his true destiny. These need only to be a shade too strong in order to become insuperable.

And when life itself provides no occasion for greatness to reveal itself, it perishes unborn, unknown, or in an inadequate arena, admired by a few.

Thus greatness has probably always been rare, and will remain so, or even become rarer.

The common activity which culminates in great men or is transformed by them is very diverse in kind.

Firstly, scholars, discoverers, artists, poets, in short the representatives of mind, must be considered apart. It is generally admitted that without the great men there would be no progress, that art, poetry and philosophy and all the great things of the mind undeniably live by virtue of their great representatives, and owe the rare raising of their standard to them alone. The rest of history, on the other hand, according to the observer, arraigns great men and declares them to be harmful or unnecessary, since nations would have got on better without them.

For artists, poets, philosophers, scholars and discoverers do not come into collision with the "opinions" from which the masses derive their philosophy; their work does not act upon "life," i.e. the profit and loss of the mass. People are under no necessity to know anything about them, and hence can let them go their way.

(It is true that our age is driving the most competent artists and poets into money-making. We can see this by the fact that they meet the "culture" of our time half-way and illustrate it, submit to any kind of material patronage, and lose their power of listening to the inner voice. For the moment, therefore, they have their reward, they have served "opinions.")

Artists, poets and philosophers have a dual function—to give ideal form to the inner content of time and the world and to transmit it to posterity as an imperishable heritage.

Why inventors and discoverers are not great men, even though a hundred statues have been set up to their memory and the actual results of their discoveries have changed the face of whole countries, may be answered by pointing out that they were not concerned with the world as a whole, like the three other types. We have the feeling that they could have been replaced and that others would have arrived at the same results later, while every single great artist, poet and philosopher is irreplaceable in the absolute sense, the universe having entered into a union with his personality, which has existed only once, yet has universal authority.

The man who merely improves the revenues of a region is not, in the full sense of the word, a benefactor of humanity.

Of the discoverers of distant lands, Columbus alone was great, but he was very great because he staked his life and expended a vast power of will upon a hypothesis which gives him a rank among the greatest philosophers. The confirmation of the spherical shape of the earth was a premise of all subsequent thought, and all subsequent thought, in so far as it was liberated by that one premise, flashes back to Columbus.

And yet it might be possible to argue that the world could have done without Columbus. "America would soon have been discovered, even if Columbus had died in his cradle"—a thing that could not be said of Aeschylus, Pheidias and Plato. If Raphael had died in his cradle, the *Transfiguration* would assuredly never have been painted.

All other discoverers of distant countries, on the other hand, are of the second rank. They lived exclusively on the hypothesis put forward and proved by Columbus. It is true that Cortez, Pizarro and others had, over and above that, peculiar greatness as conquistadores and organizers of great, new, uncivilized lands, but their very motives were infinitely meaner than those of Columbus. The work of Alexander the Great bears a nobler stamp, because in him it was really the discoverer who spurred on the conqueror. The most famous travellers of our day, after all, merely traverse countries such as Africa and Australia, the outlines of which are already known.

In the case of important discoveries in distant countries, however, the *first* discoverer (e.g. a Layard in Nineveh) reaps a disproportionate share of fame even though we realise that the greatness lies in the object and not in the man. It is a feeling of gratitude awakened by the great desirability of the discovery, though it remains open to question how long posterity will feel gratitude for what was, after all, a single service.

Among scientists, the history of each branch of research has a number of relatively great men to show. Its starting-point, however, is the particular interest of that branch of research and not mankind as a whole. It enquires who did most to promote that branch.

Side by side with this, there exists a totally different, independent standard of judgment which, in the scientific sphere, grants or refuses the surname "great" in its own peculiar way. It rewards neither ability *qua* ability nor moral merit and devotion to the cause—for that confers worth but not greatness—but great discoverers in definite directions, namely the discoverers of the primary laws of life.

It appears, meanwhile, that the representatives of the historical sciences have no place in this category. They fall under a purely literary valuation because, however superb their knowledge and their power of communicating it, they are only concerned with the knowledge of parts of the world and not with the formulation of laws, for "historical laws" are indefinite and contested. Whether economics, with its laws of life, has already produced representatives of unquestionable greatness is doubtful.

In mathematics and science, on the other hand, there have been universally acknowledged great men.

All thought was first liberated when Copernicus dismissed the earth from the centre of the universe and assigned it to its place in a subordinate orbit of a single solar system. In the seventeenth century, beyond a few astronomers and scientists—Galileo, Kepler and some others—there is no single scientist who might be called great, yet their conclusions were the foundation of all later consideration of the universe, indeed, of all thought. Hence they rank with the philosophers.

It is with the great philosophers that we first enter the domain of greatness properly speaking, the domain, that is, of uniqueness and irreplaceability, of more than ordinary powers and of reference to the world as a whole.

Each in his own way brings humanity nearer to the solution of the great riddle of life. Their matter is the universe in all its aspects, man included; they alone survey and dominate the relation of the individual to the whole and can hence impart to the various branches of science their proper aims and perspectives. And they are obeyed, though often unconsciously and unwillingly. The individual sciences are often unaware of the threads by which they depend on the thought of the great philosophers.

With the philosophers we might class those who seem to stand above life, so objective has their outlook become and so versatile their comments on it—a Montaigne, a Labruyère. They are the link between the philosophers and the poets.

And now, in its high station between philosophy and

the visual arts, we find poetry. The philosopher's only equipment is truth, therefore his fame lives only after his death, though then it is all the more intense. To poets and artists, on the other hand, is given beauty, inviting and serene, wherewith "to overcome the resistance of the brutish world." Through beauty, they speak in symbols.[1] Poetry, however, shares with science the word and a wide community of fact, with philosophy the interpretation of the world, with the visual arts the form and imagery of its whole mode of expression and its status as a creator and a power.

Let us here consider in a general way why poets and artists are called great.

Unsatisfied with mere knowledge, the domain of the specialized sciences, and even with insight, the domain of philosophy, aware of its multiform, enigmatic nature, the human mind feels that there are still other powers which respond to its own obscure impulses. It comes to realize that great worlds surround it which speak only in images to the images it bears within it—the worlds of art. To the representatives of those worlds it will infallibly attribute greatness, since it owes to them the increase of its own most inward essence and power. For they are able to embrace nearly the whole of man's existence wherever it rises above the daily round, to express his state of mind in a much higher sense that he could himself, to grant him a transfigured image of the world which, cleared of the debris of the contingent, gathers into itself only what is

[1] As regards the relation of the poet to the philosopher, cf. Schiller's letter to Goethe (Jan. 17, 1795): "One thing is certain, that the poet is the only true *man,* and the best of philosophers is a mere caricature in comparison with him."

great, significant and beautiful. Even tragedy is then consoling.

The arts are a faculty of man, a power and a creation. Imagination, their vital, central impulse, has at all times been regarded as divine.

To give tangible form to that which is inward, to represent it in such a way that we see it as the outward image of inward things, as a revelation—that is a most rare power. To re-create the external in external form—that is within the power of many. But the other awakens in the beholder or listener the conviction that only the creator of this work could do this, and so is indispensable.

Further, from the beginning of time, we find the artists and poets in solemn and great relationship with religion and culture. The mightiest purposes and feelings of past times speak through them, have chosen them for their interpreters.

They alone can interpret and give imperishable form to the mystery of beauty. Everything that passes by us in life, so swift, rare and unequal, is here gathered together in a world of poems, in pictures and great picture-cycles, in color, stone and sound, to form a second, sublimer world on earth. Indeed, in architecture and music we can only experience beauty through art; without art we should not know that it exists.

Among the poets and artists, however, the truly great reveal themselves by the authority they exercise, even in their lifetime, over their art, for here, as everywhere, men know, or dimly feel, that a great gift is always a very rare thing. Men become aware that *this* master is absolutely irreplaceable, that the world would be incomplete, could not be imagined without him.

For our consolation, there is, beside the supreme rarity

of men of the first rank, a second rank in art and poetry. What the great masters have given to the world in free creation can, by virtue of the way tradition is propagated in these fields, be retained by excellent minor masters as style. It is, of course, as a rule, recognizably minor art, unless the endowment of the particular master was of the first rank and the first place happened to be indisputably occupied.

The masters of the third stage, that of commercialization, give, at any rate, fresh proof of how great the great men must have been; they also show, in very instructive fashion, which of his aspects seemed specially *worth* appropriating, and secondly, which could be most easily appropriated.

But we are ever and again thrown back on the masters of the first rank; they alone seem to possess true originality in every word, line or tone, even when they repeat themselves (although we may not always see quite clearly in this point, and it is, of course, one of the saddest of sights when a first-class endowment descends to mass-production for money).

They are, moreover, characterized by a plenitude which has nothing whatever in common with the hasty mass-production of mediocrity, and which is sometimes so remarkable that we might imagine it to be born of the premonition of early death. Such is the case with Mozart, and even Schiller with his ruined health. The man who, having once produced his great work, becomes a mass-producer, more especially for the sake of gain, has never been a great man.

The springs of that plenitude are, firstly, exceptional strength, and secondly, the power and the desire to make manifold use of any step forward. With Raphael, for instance, every new stage is represented by a group of Madonnas or Holy Families; another example is Schiller's ballad year, 1797. Finally, the great master may also be indebted to a style already established and to a great demand among his people. Such was the case with Calderon and Rubens.

We have now to ask in how far the great poets and artists may dispense with personal greatness. In any case, they must have singleness of purpose, for without that no greatness can be imagined, and it is the feeling of that singleness of purpose in the work of art which holds us in its spell. Here poets and artists must be great whether they will or no, and he who is not great in this sense may soon sink into obscurity in spite of exceptional gifts. Indeed, without this degree of force of character, the man of the most brilliant "talent" is either a fool or a knave. All great masters have, first and foremost, learned, and never ceased to learn, and to learn requires very great resolution when a man has once reached heights of greatness and can create easily and brilliantly. Further, every later stage is achieved only by a terrible struggle with the fresh tasks they set themselves. At the age of sixty, and in spite of his world fame, Michelangelo had to discover and enter into possession of a new domain before he could create the *Last Judgment*. We might also think of the strength of will Mozart displayed in the last months of his life, and yet there are people who imagine that he remained a child till the end.

On the other hand, we are tempted to ascribe to the great masters a fuller, happier life and personality, and in particular a more felicitous relationship between spirit and sense. A good deal of this is pure supposition; we overlook, moreover, very great dangers which beset their life and work. The present-day description of the lives of poets and artists is vitiated at its source. It would be better for us to abide by their works; Gluck, for instance, gives us the feeling of majesty and quiet pride, and Haydn the feeling of gaiety and goodness. Nor have men at all times judged these things by the same standards. The whole of pre-Roman Greek culture has notably little to say of its very greatest artists and sculptors, while giving a very high place to poets and philosophers.

The next question is the *recognition* which is given to greatness in the various arts.

Poetry has its supreme moments: It may, in the idyll, play for a while in the stream of life, in the contingent and the mediocre, but soon the time comes when it seeks the supreme expressions of humanity and embodies them in the ideal figures which incorporate human passion struggling against superhuman fate—not obstructed by the accidental, but pure and mighty. Then it reveals to man the secrets which lie within him and which, without poetry, would never find a voice. It speaks to him a wonderful language which, he feels, must once have been his in a better life. It transmutes the joys and sorrows of the individual of all times and peoples into an imperishable work of art, so that it may be said *spirat adhuc amor,* from the savage grief of Dido to the wistful ballad of the forsaken mistress. The sufferings of later generations who listen to these songs are transfigured and uplifted into a higher whole: the sufferings of mankind. All this poetry can achieve because in the poet himself suffering, and suffering alone, calls forth supreme power. At its sublimest, poetry evokes those emotions which transcend sorrow and joy: when it enters that domain of religious feeling which is the innermost spring of every religion and all wisdom, the conquest of things earthly—as such it finds its supreme dramatic expression in the prison scene between Cyprian and Justina in Calderon, but also echoes sublimely through Goethe's *Der Du von dem Himmel bist*—and when, borne on the wings of a mighty tempest, it speaks to whole nations as the prophets did, rising to that incomparable outburst of inspiration, the sixtieth chapter of Isaiah.

The great poets would seem great to us if only as the most important witnesses to the spirit of all the ages which their poems have handed down to us, secure in writing; but in their totality they form the greatest coherent revelation of the mind and soul of man.

The "greatness" of the individual poet, however, is to be distinguished from the extent to which he is known or the use to which he is put, which is to a certain extent dependent on different factors.

We might, of course, imagine that greatness alone was the test of poets of past times, but a poet may have a value as an element of culture and a witness to his age which far surpasses his merit as a poet. This is the case with many a poet of antiquity, every document of that time being of inestimable value in itself.

We could, for instance, enquire whether Euripides can be called "great" in comparison with Aeschylus or Sophocles. And yet he is by far our most important evidence for a turning-point in Athenian thought. Yet here we have a striking example of the distinction. Euripides embodies an ephemeral stage in the history of the human mind, Aeschylus and Sophocles the eternal.

On the other hand, creations that are unquestionably great and splendid—epics, folk-songs and folk-music—seem to stand in no need of the instrumentality of great individuals; their work is done by a whole people which we imagine *ad hoc* to have been in a particularly happy, unspoilt state of culture.

Yet this substitution is actually due to the defects of historical records. The epic bard whose name we no longer know or know only in a collective sense was very great at the moment at which he gave imperishable form to one offshoot of the saga of his people. At that moment he was the magic embodiment of the spirit of that people, a thing that is only possible to very finely constituted men. And thus folk-song and folk-music can only be created by very exceptional individuals and only at great moments when the concentrated spirit of a people speaks through them. Otherwise the song would not endure.

If confronted with an anonymous tragedy, we immediately think of an author, yet we conceive we have no right to do so in the case of so-called national epics, that is mere modern opinion and habit. There are dramas which are at least as "popular" in their origins as the epics etc.

Then come the painters and sculptors.

Originally, artists worked anonymously in the service of religion. There, in the sanctuary, they took their first steps toward the sublime. They learned to eliminate the contingent from form. Types came into being; ultimately, the first ideals.

Then individual names and their fame began to emerge, in that beautiful half-way house of art, where its sacred, monumental origin was still a living force, yet freedom in methods and joy in that freedom had been won. The ideal was discovered in all directions, and the real invested with compelling magic. From time to time, art plunged deep into the bondage of the real, but only to rise again gloriously as a higher parable of life. Its contact with the universe is essentially different from that of poetry. Akin almost exclusively to the sunny side of things, it creates its world of beauty, power, inwardness and happiness, and even in mute nature, sees and represents the spirit.

The masters who took the decisive steps in this direction were extraordinary men. It is true that in the Greek world of art, where we know their names, we can only rarely attach those names with certainty to definite works of art. In the heyday of the Northern Middle Ages, names are also lacking. Who carved the statues on the portals of Chartres and Rheims? It is a pure assumption that even the most excellent of these things were simply the stock-in-trade of the workshops, and the merit of the individual master only moderate. We have here exactly the same state of things as in folk-poetry. The first man to give supreme expression to the Christ type which we see in the north portal of Rheims was a very great artist, and certainly created many a splendid thing for the first time.

In fully historical times, when definite names of artists are firmly attached to certain works, the predicate "great" is awarded with absolute certainty and almost universal agreement to a certain pleiad of masters in whom every instructed eye becomes aware of a primordial element, of the immediacy of genius.

However abundant the works they created, only a small number of them are scattered over the earth, and we may well tremble for their continued existence.

Among the architects, there is perhaps not one whose greatness is so clearly admitted as that of certain poets, painters, etc. From the outset they have to share recognition with those who have commissioned them: much of the admiration they evoke falls to the share of their people, priesthood or rulers, and it is accompanied by the more or less conscious feeling that greatness in architecture is altogether the product of its people and epoch rather than of a great master. Size, moreover, confounds judgment, and the gigantic, or the merely splendid, will have special claims to admiration.

Architecture is, in any case, regarded as more incomprehensible than painting or sculpture, because it does not represent human life. As art, however, it is just as easy or as difficult to grasp as they.

Further, we are faced here with the same or a similar phenomenon as in the other arts; the creators of styles, to whom we should like to attribute greatness, are as a rule unknown, and we know only those who have perfected or refined styles. Thus, among the Greeks, we do not know the master who created the type of the temple, while we do know Ictinus and Mnesikles. In the Middle Ages we do not know who built Notre-Dame, and so took the last momentous steps to Gothic, but we do know a fair number of master-builders of famous cathedrals from the thirteenth to the fifteenth century.

With the Renaissance the case is different. Here we have exact knowledge of a number of famous architects, not only because they are nearer to us in time, and documents are much more numerous and reliable, but because they do not merely repeat a prevailing type; they always conceive fresh combinations, so that each could create independent work within a system of forms which, though general, was extremely flexible. Further, we still feel how great was the faith in these architects, to whom were given space, material and unprecedented liberty.

Greatness in the true sense of the word, however, is

only attributed to Erwin von Steinbach and Michelangelo. Immediately after them, we might name Brunelleschi and Bramante. Both Erwin von Steinbach and Michelangelo were, of course, obliged to fulfil the primary condition of massive size, and it fell to Michelangelo's lot to build the chief temple of a whole religion. To Erwin's account there stands the tallest spire yet built in the world; it was not built after his plans, but without it his façade, with its lovely, transparent Gothic, would never have attained its exceptional, yet fully merited fame. Michelangelo, however, created the most beautiful outline and the most splendid interior on earth in the dome of St. Peter's. Here popular and instructed opinion coincide.

At the extreme frontier of art, and most often in fleeting relationship to architecture, we find music, which, if we wish to penetrate the essence of its being, must be taken as instrumental music, detached from words and, above all, apart from dramatic representation.

Its position is wonderful and strange. While poetry, sculpture and painting can still lay claim to be the representation of a higher aspect of human life, music is only a parable of it. It is a comet, circling round life in a vastly high and remote orbit, yet suddenly sweeping down closer to it than any other art, and revealing to man his inmost heart. Sometimes it is a kind of mathematics of the imagination—then again pure soul, infinitely far, yet close and dear.

Its effect (where such effect is genuine) is so great and so immediate that the feeling of gratitude at once seeks for its creator and spontaneously proclaims him great. The great composers are among the most undisputed great men. The question of their immortality, however, is more doubtful. It depends, firstly, on the sustained efforts of posterity, that is, on the performances which have to compete with the performances of all subsequent and contemporary works, while the other arts can set up their works once for all. Secondly, it depends on the survival of our tonal system and rhythm, which are not eternal. Mozart and Beethoven may become as incomprehensible to future humanity as Greek music, so highly praised by its contemporaries, would be to us. They will then remain great on faith, by virtue of the expressions of delight we have uttered, not unlike the painters of antiquity whose works have been lost.

And now one concluding remark. When the man of culture sits down to the banquet of the art and poetry of past times, he will not be able, or wish, to resist the lovely illusion that these men were *happy* when they created their great works. Yet all they did was to rescue the ideals of their time at the cost of great sacrifice, and wage in their daily life the battle we all fight. It is only to us that their creations look like youth rescued and perpetuated.

The next step from art and poetry is to those great figures which mainly owe their existence to art and poetry, namely the figures of myth. Hence we can now pass on to those who either never existed, or whose existence was quite different from that described to us, the men, ideal or idealized, who either stand as the founders or leaders of the various peoples, or, as the most beloved figures of popular imagination, have been given a place in the heroic age of their people. We cannot leave them out of account, if only because this whole question of the non-existent figure is the strongest proof that a nation has need of great men to represent it.

They include those mythological heroes who are half-forgotten gods, sons of gods, geographical and political abstractions, etc., and primarily the eponymous heroes and fathers of a people as the mythical representatives of its unity.

They are (more especially the eponymous heroes) almost without predicates, or, like Noah, Ishmael, Hellen, Tuisko and Mannus, barely outlined as the founders of their peoples. The songs which may have told about them (such as those concerning Tuisko and Mannus in the *Germania* of Tacitus) have been lost.

Or, on the other hand, their biography contains in symbolic form a part of the history of their people, and especially of its more important institutions. Thus Abraham, Jamshid, Theseus,[1] Romulus and his complement Numa.

Others are less founders than pure ideals, in which the people personifies directly, not the history of a City State, but the noblest thing it knows: Achilles, who dies early *because* the ideal is too splendid for this world, or Odysseus, who battles for years against the hatred of certain gods and wins victory through ordeal. He is the representative of the *real* qualities of the primitive Greeks—cunning and endurance.

Later peoples even exalt and idealize historical figures into popular ideals with the utmost freedom, as the Spaniards did the Cid and the Serbs Marco, both having been transfigured into prototypes of the people.

On the other hand, we find purely imaginary popular caricatures, showing life from some seamy side. They may be quoted here in proof of the facility of poetic personifi-

[1] In Plutarch's *Theseus* the significance of a "founder" is emphasized.

cation. Thus an Eulenspiegel; or the masks of the popular Italian stage—Meneking, Stentorello, Pulcinella, etc.; or the personification of cities with the help of dialect; while drawing comes in to create figures which even personify nations, like John Bull.

Finally, we may find forecasts of the future, for instance the future hero in Simplicissimus,[1] and the strangest figure of this category—Antichrist.

On the threshold of historical greatness in the strict sense of the word we find the founders of religions occupying a very peculiar place. They rank with the greatest of men in the highest sense because in them there lives that metaphysical element by which, for thousands of years after their death, not only their own but many other peoples are dominated, that is, morally and religiously united. In them, what existed unconsciously becomes conscious, and obscure desires are revealed as laws. They discover their religion by no calculation of averages based on cold-blooded observation of the men about them. The community lives in their personality with irresistible force. Even the most dubious example, Mohammed, has a tinge of this greatness.

This is the place of the specific greatness of the Reformers. A Luther gives an aim to the moral striving, indeed to the whole outlook of his followers. Calvin, on the other hand, was impossible precisely in his own homeland, France. He only won over the majority in Holland and England.

Finally, the great men of the rest of the world movement in history.

[1] An English translation, *Simplicissimus the Vagabond,* of Grimmelshausen's picaresque novel was published in 1912 by A. T. S. Goodrick.

History tends at times to become suddenly concentrated in one man, who is then obeyed by the world.

These great individuals represent the coincidence of the general and the particular, of the static and the dynamic, in *one* personality. They subsume States, religions, cultures and crises.

A most amazing spectacle is presented by the men through whom a whole people suddenly passes from one stage of culture to another, for instance, from nomadism to world conquest, like the Mongols under Genghis Khan. Even the Russians under Peter the Great come under this heading, for under him they were transformed from Orientals into Europeans. Yet full greatness seems to us to be attained by those who have led *civilized* peoples from a more primitive condition into a more advanced one. Those who merely destroy by violence, on the other hand, are not great. Timur did not lead the Mongols forward; things were worse after him than before. He was as little as Genghis Khan was great.

In crises, the old and the new (the revolution) culminate together in the great men, whose nature is one of the true mysteries of world history. Their relationship to their time is a "sacred marriage." Such a union can only be consummated in times of terror, which provide the one supreme standard of greatness and are also unique in their need of great men.

It is true that, at the onset of a crisis, there is always a superfluity of men regarded as great, since those who happen to be party-leaders—often men of genuine talent and initiative—are indulgently regarded as such. A judgment of this kind is based on the naïve assumption that a movement must find from the outset the man who will permanently and completely represent it. In actual fact, it is soon involved in transformations of which there was no inkling in its initial stage.

These initiators, therefore, are never the accomplishers, but are devoured because they represented the movement in its first phase and hence could not keep pace with it, while the next phase already has its men ready waiting. In the French Revolution, where the shifts changed with striking precision, really great men (Mirabeau) could no longer cope with the second stage. By far the largest number of the early celebrities of revolution are cast aside as soon as another comes to satisfy the ruling passion, a matter of no great difficulty. Yet why are Robespierre and St. Just and even Marius not great, in spite of all their vehemence and unquestionable historical importance? Such men never stand for a general aim, but only for the programme and fury of a party. Their adherents may try to give them a place among the founders of religions.

Meanwhile, the man born to bring the culminating movement to its close, to calm its separate waves and stand astride the abyss, is slowly growing to maturity, menaced by huge dangers and recognized by few.

The dangers threatening his first steps are characteristically represented by Herod's search for the Child Jesus. Caesar went in danger of his life for his defiance of Sulla, who suspected many Mariuses in him. Cromwell was persecuted by the law and prevented from leaving the country. For something of the exceptional quality of the man generally seems to appear early.

How many richly endowed men have perished before one fought his way through from stage to stage appears, in the guise of a reaction, in the fatalism of great men. Yet the feeling is not untinged by the sense of glory, for they openly regard themselves as important enough for fate to take seriously.

The hereditary prince of a great Empire is, of course, beyond the reach of early dangers, and at once assumes in its entirety the power within which he can develop greatness. Between him and the achievement of greatness, on the other hand, there stands the early opportunity for self-will and enjoyment. Nor is he spurred from the outset to develop *all* his inner powers. By far the most impressive example is Alexander the Great. After him we might name Charlemagne, Peter the Great, Frederick the Great.

Before we proceed to characterize greatness, we might take the opportunity of discussing "relative greatness," which consists mainly in the folly or abjectness of others and is actually born only of the difference. Without some outstanding qualities, however, we cannot imagine even this form of greatness. It appears more especially in hereditary dynasties, and is in essence the greatness of Oriental potentates, which can very rarely be assessed since their characters are not formed in conflict with their world. Hence they have no inward history, no development, no growth. Even the greatness of Justinian, for instance, was of this kind, though he was—in error—regarded for a thousand years as a great, good and holy man. There are, moreover, empty centuries, in which people are more ready to be satisfied with greatness such as his than at other times. Between the death of Theodoric and the rise of Mohammed is precisely the place for an official figure of his kind. But the only really great man of that epoch was Gregory I.

And now we may contemplate the great man advancing upon mankind. How and when is he first recognized by his contemporaries? Men as a whole are unsure of themselves, confused in mind and glad to run with the herd, or else they are envious or totally indifferent. What then will be the qualities or deeds which turn the admiration of a man's immediate entourage, which has long existed in a latent state, into open and general admiration?

If the point at issue here is the nature of greatness, we must, first and foremost, be on our guard against the idea that what we have to describe is a moral ideal, for in history the great individual is not set up as an example, but as an exception. For our present purpose, we may sketch the following outline of greatness:

The great man's faculties unfold naturally and completely, keeping pace with the growth of his self-confidence and the tasks before him. It is not only that he appears complete in every situation, but every situation at once seems to cramp him. He does not merely fill it. He may shatter it.

It is doubtful how long he will be able to keep himself in hand and be pardoned for the greatness of his nature.

Further, he has the natural faculty of concentrating at will on *one* issue, and then passing on to concentrate on another. Hence things appear to him simple, while to us they seem highly complicated, perpetually throwing each other out of gear. Where we grow confused, he begins to see really clearly.[1]

The great individual sees every connection as a whole and masters every detail according to cause and effect.

[1] According to Napoleon himself, his various concerns were laid away in his head as though in a chest of drawers. "When I want to discontinue one business I close its drawer and open that of another. . . . If I want to sleep, I shut all the drawers, and behold, I am asleep."

That is an inevitable function of his brain. He sees even small connections for the simple reason that by multiplication they become great, while he can dispense with the knowledge of small individuals.

Two main things he beholds with perfect clarity: first and foremost, the true situation and the means at his command, and he will neither allow appearances to blind him nor any momentary clamor to deafen him. From the very outset he knows what can be the foundations of his future power. Confronted with parliaments, senates, assemblies, press, public opinion, he knows at any moment how far they are real or only imaginary, and makes frank use of them accordingly. Afterwards they may wonder at having been mere means even while they conceived themselves to be ends.

Secondly, he knows in advance the moment when to act, while we first read about events afterwards in the papers. With that moment in view, he will curb his impatience and know no flinching (like Napoleon in 1797). He looks at everything from the standpoint of its utilizable strength, and there no study is too toilsome for him.

Mere contemplation is incompatible with such a nature. It is moved primarily by a genuine will to master the situation and at the same time by an exceptional *strength* of will, which creates an atmosphere of fascination, attracts to itself every element of power and rule, and subjects them to its own ends. Yet the great man is not confused by the breadth of his view and his memory, but manipulates the elements of power in their due co-ordination and subordination, as though they had always been his.

Common obedience to those who have risen to power in common ways is soon obtained. But in the case of great men, thinking contemporaries begin to feel that he has come to fulfil much that is necessary, but only possible to him. Contradiction at close quarters becomes utterly impossible. Anyone desiring to oppose him must live outside of the reach of the man, with his enemies, and can only meet him on the battlefield.

"I am a fragment of rock hurled into space," said Napoleon. Thus equipped, a man can achieve in a few years "the work of centuries."

Finally, as the most characteristic and necessary complement to all these things, comes the strength of soul which is alone able, and therefore alone loves, to ride the storm. This is not merely the passive aspect of strength of will. It is a different thing.

The fate of peoples and States, the trends of whole civilizations, may depend on the power of one exceptional individual to endure certain acute stresses at certain times.

The fact that Frederick the Great possessed that power in a supreme degree from 1759 to 1763 has determined the course of all subsequent European history.

No sum of ordinary minds and hearts can replace that power.

In the endurance of great and perpetual menaces, such as the constant threat of assassination, even while his mind is strained to the utmost, the great man obviously fulfils a purpose going far beyond his earthly existence. That was the greatness of William the Silent and Cardinal Richelieu. Richelieu was no angel, and his constitutional policy was not sound, but it was the only possible one for his time. And both William the Silent (to whom Philip perpetually made secret offers) and Richelieu might have made their peace with their adversaries.

Louis Philippe and Victoria, on the other hand, may

claim our sympathy for the many attempts on their lives, but have no claim to greatness, because the danger was inherent in their position.

The rarest thing of all in men who have made history is greatness of soul. It resides in the power to forgo benefits in the name of morality, in voluntary self-denial, not merely from motives of prudence but from goodness of heart, while the political great man *must* be an egoist, out to exploit every advantage. Greatness of soul cannot be demanded *a priori* because, as we have already seen, the great individual is set up as an exception, and not as an example. The great man of history, however, regards it as his prime duty to stand his ground and increase his power, and power never yet improved a man.

We wish, for instance, that we could, like Prévost-Paradol in *La France Nouvelle,* expect greatness of soul from Napoleon after Brumaire, when he was faced with a tottering France which could be restored by a free constitution. Yet Napoleon said (February 1800) to Matthieu Dumas: "I soon learned, on seating myself here (on the throne of Louis XVI) that I must beware of attempting to do all the good one might do; opinion would outrun me." And he proceeded to treat France not as a protégé or a patient, but as a prey.

One of the clearest proofs of greatness in the past makes its appearance when we (posterity) ardently desire to know more about the personality behind it, i.e. to complete the picture as far as it lies in our power.

In the case of great figures of primitive times, popular imagination, with its bias to personification, comes to our help; indeed it most likely first creates the picture.

In the case of figures nearer to us in time, only documentary evidence can be of use, and that is often lacking. The dreamers of history, however, fill up the picture as it pleases them best, and historical novels exalt or debase great figures in their own way.

There are very great individuals who have suffered peculiar misfortune. Charles Martel, whose historical influence was of the highest importance, and whose personal power was unquestionably great, has neither a transfiguration in legend nor even a single line of personal description to show. Whatever may have lived on in oral tradition has probably fused with the figure of his grandson.

But when knowledge flows more freely, it is supremely desirable that the great man should be shown in conscious relationship to the spirit, to the culture of his time; that an Alexander should have had an Aristotle as his tutor. Only in such a man can we imagine a supreme quality of genius, a genuine enjoyment of his historical position during his lifetime. That is how we imagine Caesar.

And all things are fulfilled when to all these qualities there are added personal grace, an hourly contempt of death, and, as in Caesar too, the wish to win and reconcile, a grain of goodness! At the very least, a passionate soul, like Alexander's!

The outstanding portrait of a man of the first rank with a defective equipment is that of Napoleon in Prévost-Paradol's *La France Nouvelle*. Napoleon was self-will incorporate, inasmuch as he took unto himself alone the forces of half a world, which were concentrated in his hands. The most striking contrast to him is William III of Orange, whose whole political and military genius and magnificent fortitude coincided perfectly and always with the real, enduring interests of Holland and England. The general result of his work has always outweighed whatever there might be to say about his personal ambition, and his really great fame only set in after his death. William III possessed and used the very gifts which were supremely desirable in *his* position.

It is often difficult to distinguish greatness from mere power, which is extraordinarily dazzling when it is newly acquired or increased. As for our tendency to regard those as great on whose work our own existence is founded, we may refer to the beginning of the present discussion. The source of this tendency is our need to excuse our dependence by the greatness of another's power.

It is better to pass over in silence the further error which consists in assuming that power is happiness, and that happiness is something due and proper to man. Nations have definite qualities to bring to light without which the world would be incomplete, and they must do so without any respect to the happiness of the individual or the greatest possible sum of happiness.

Warlike exploits in particular are disproportionately dazzling, for they directly affect the fate of countless peoples, and again indirectly by establishing new conditions of life, which may be very durable.

In this case the new kind of life is the criterion of greatness. Military glory pure and simple withers in time into mere recognition by specialists and military historians.

These new conditions of life, however, must not merely consist in shifts of power. They must produce a great regeneration of national life. When this happens, posterity will ascribe to its originator, infallibly and rightly, a more or less conscious intention in his enterprises, and hence greatness.

The revolutionary general is in a class apart. When a profound upheaval is going on in the life of the State—the nation may still be fresh, mentally and physically, or even in a period of reviving strength, though politically exhausted—men are sometimes overcome by moods in which the craving for the powers they once possessed and possess no longer, or can no longer exercise, becomes irresistible. Then they imagine or expect that some fortunate military leader will be the source of fresh experiences. They will even attribute to him the gift of political leadership, since the life of the State can, for the time being, consist at best in command and obedience. Military exploits are then accepted as perfectly satisfactory guarantees of resolution and energy, and indeed they are *one*—at times when men have had to endure, or must fear, unprecedented evils, not from one visionary or criminal, but from many. The one man of action profits by past fear, the impatience of those who declare that they want their peace ("If only he would put an end to it once for all"), and the fear both of him and of the others. This fear, in order to save its own face, is very prone to turn into admiration. Imagination, in any case, always busies itself about a figure of this kind. And the critical moment at which greatness becomes possible is precisely the moment at which the imagination of many is preoccupied with one.

Yet such a one may die all the same, like Hoche, or prove politically inadequate, like Moreau. Napoleon only came after these two. For Cromwell, however, matters were much more difficult. Although from 1644 onward he had actually mastered the country by means of the army, it was he who saved it from the profoundest upheaval and terror. But by that very fact he stood in his own light.

In the ancient world, or at any rate in the Greek States, where a whole caste of free men wished to be great and strong and excellent, it was not possible to come to the fore as a man of war only. Nor did any tyrant become historically great, though there were plenty of interesting and important minds among the tyrants. There simply was not enough room, so that none subjected even a considerable part of the Greek nation. Hence none in any way embodied the whole. Nevertheless there were in Hellas men to whom we attribute true greatness, even though it was exercised in the most restricted space. Their contemporaries and posterity were faced in them with men in whose hands there lay the fate of at most a few hundreds of thousands of men, but who had the strength of mind to confront their homeland with detachment, in the good and the bad sense.

Let us take as an outstanding example Themistocles. He was a doubtful character from boyhood up. His father is said to have repudiated him, his mother to have hanged herself on his account, and yet he later became "the common pledge, whether of hope or despair, of Europe and Asia." (Valerius Maximus, VI, 11.) He and Athens were perpetually at loggerheads. The way he saved the city in the Persian War is absolutely unique, yet he was able to preserve intact his detachment, his inner freedom from her.

Those who rose in Greece succeeded in doing so by virtue of a complex of great qualities and only amid constant dangers. The whole of life was a spur to the keenest personal ambition, yet could hardly suffer ambition in a position of command, combated it in Athens by ostracism and drove it in Sparta to crime, open and secret.

That is the famous ingratitude of republics. Even Pericles nearly succumbed to it, because he stood above the Athenians and united their supreme qualities in himself. It is not recorded that he called the gods to witness that ingratitude as an unheard-of injustice. He could not but know that Athens could hardly support him.

Alcibiades, on the other hand, incorporated Athens both in the good and bad sense. Here there is a kind of greatness in the complete coincidence between a city and an individual. In spite of the shocking events that had occurred, the city threw herself into his arms like a passionate woman, only to abandon him again.

In him we find the early and lasting intention to focus his fellow-citizens' imagination upon himself, and himself alone. The imagination of the Romans was in actual fact focussed upon Caesar in his youth, but his natural distinction was such that he seemed to have no hand in it. It is true that, when the time came for seeking office, he bribed the Romans more insolently than all his rivals, though only the mass of the voters, and only *ad hoc*. In other ways, too, the greatness of the Romans was of a different quality from that of the Greeks.

The greatness of the hierarchs—Gregory VII, St. Bernard, Innocent III, and it may be even later ones—has always been very doubtful.

First and foremost, the falseness of their aim—to make their kingdom a kingdom of this world—is avenged on their memories. But even if we leave that out of account, the men are not great. They are certainly remarkable by virtue of the overweening insolence with which they confronted the secular world, expecting it to submit to their dominion, but they lacked the opportunity of developing greatness as rulers, since they did not rule directly but in part through the intermediary of secular powers which they had previously ill-treated and degraded. Hence they were actually identified with no national feeling and only influenced culture by prohibitions and as a police force.

St. Bernard did not even wish to be consecrated bishop, let alone Pope, but imposed his will from the outside in Church and State all the more fearlessly. He was an oracle and helped to crush the spirit of the twelfth century. When his chief enterprise, the Second Crusade, came to grief, he had a tidy responsibility to bear on his shoulders.

These hierarchs did not even need to develop into true, complete human beings, since every personal defect, every bias and shortcoming, was cloaked by their consecration.

They were shielded, too, in their conflict with the secular powers and privileged by the weapons of spiritual coercion.

Posterity and history, however, in appraising such personalities, takes account of their unjustified privileges.

One advantage they had—they could appear great in suffering, and in defeat were not *eo ipso* in the wrong, like great laymen. But they had to exploit that advantage, for if they ran into danger and tried to escape without martyrdom, the effect was disastrous.

Real greatness and saintliness, however, is to be found in Gregory the Great. He really cared deeply for the salvation of Rome and Italy from the savagery of the Lombards. His kingdom was not yet of this world in the true sense of the word. He was in active touch with many bishops and laymen of the Western world, without the power or the wish to use coercion upon them. He made no serious use of excommunication and interdict, and was ingenuously convinced of the sanctity of the Roman soil and the tombs of its saints.

If time permitted, we should find many other categories of great men. We must, however, confine ourselves to these so that we may turn our attention to the fate and vocation of the great man.

When he makes use of his power, he will appear alternately as the supreme embodiment of the corporate life or the deadly enemy of existing conditions, until one or the other succumbs.

If the great man succumbs in this conflict—for instance, a William the Silent and in a certain sense Caesar too—the feeling of posterity takes vengeance and atonement upon itself and repeats the whole drama by proving how deeply the man embodied the community, how entirely it was represented in his personality—though we must not forget how often this is done from reasons of personal vanity and in order to annoy certain contemporaries.

The vocation of greatness seems to be to fulfil a will that is greater than the individual will, and is denoted, according to its point of departure, as the will of God, the will of a nation or a community, the will of an epoch. Thus the will of a certain epoch seems to have been supremely fulfilled in the work of Alexander, namely the opening up and Hellenization of Asia, for durable conditions of life and long-lived civilizations were to be founded on that work. A whole nation, a whole age, seems to have looked to him for life and security. But achievements of such a magnitude require a man in whom the strength and ability of infinitely many are united.

Now the common purpose which the individual serves

may be a conscious one; he carries out those enterprises, wars and acts of retribution which the nation or the time demands. Alexander took Persia, and Bismarck united Germany. It may, on the other hand, be an unconscious one. The individual knows what the purpose of the nation ought to be, and fulfils that. The nation, however, later realizes that what was fulfilled was right and great. Caesar subjected Gaul, Charlemagne Saxony.

There would seem to be a mysterious coincidence between the egoism of the individual and the thing we call the common weal, or the greatness, the glory of the community.

Here we become aware of the great man's strange exemption from the ordinary moral code. Since that exemption is allowed by convention to nations and other great communities, it is, by an inevitable logic, also granted to those individuals who act for the community. Now, in actual fact, no power has ever yet been founded without crime, yet the most vital spiritual and material possessions of the nations can only grow when existence is safeguarded by power. The "man after God's heart" then appears—a David, a Constantine, a Clovis; his utter ruthlessness is generally condoned for the sake of some service rendered to religion, but also where there has been none. Richard III, it is true, met with no such indulgence, for all his crimes were mere simplifications of his personal situation.

The crimes of the man, therefore, who bestows on a community greatness, power and glory, are condoned, in particular the breach of forced political treaties, since the advantage of the whole, the State or the people, is absolutely inalienable and may not be permanently prejudiced by anything whatever; but he must then continue to be great and realize that he will bequeath to his successors a fateful legacy, the necessity of genius, if what has been won by force is to be preserved until the world regards it as a right.

Here everything depends on success. The same man, endowed with the same personality, would find no such condonation for crimes which entailed no such results. Only because he has achieved great things does he find indulgence even for his private crimes.

As regards the latter, he is not condemned for yielding to his passions, because men feel that life works more violently, more greatly in him than in ordinary natures. Great temptation and impunity may also in part excuse him. Nor must we forget the indubitable kinship of genius with madness. Alexander may have shown the first signs of madness when, in his sorrow for Hephaestion, he tried to give it visible expression by ordering all the horses' tails to be docked and all the city battlements to be demolished.

There would be no objection to that exemption if nations were really absolute entities, entitled *a priori* to permanent and powerful existence. But they are not, and the condonation of a great criminal has its shady side for them too, in that his misdeeds are not confined to acts which make the community great, that the delimitation of praiseworthy or necessary crime after the fashion of the *Principe* is a fallacy,[1] and that the methods a man uses recoil on his own head and, in the long run, may destroy his taste for greatness.

[1] Napoleon on St. Helena simply took necessity as his standard: "My chief maxim has always been, in politics as in war, that all evil—even if within the law—is excusable only in so far as it is necessary; anything beyond this is a crime."

A secondary justification for the crimes of great men seems to lie in the fact that by them an end is put to the crimes of countless others. When crime is thus monopolized by a communal criminal in the seat of government, the security of the community may prosper greatly. Before he came on to the scene, the powers of a brilliantly gifted nation may have been employed in a permanent and internecine war of destruction, which prevented the rise of everything which can flourish only in peace and security. The great individual, however, destroys, domesticates or employs unbridled individual egoisms. They suddenly gather into a power which continues to serve his purpose. In such cases—we might think of Ferdinand and Isabella—we are sometimes astonished by the rapid and brilliant bloom of culture till then retarded. Later it bears the name of the great man—the age of so-and-so.

Finally, political crime profits by the familiar doctrine: "If we do not do it, others will." People would think themselves at a disadvantage if they acted morally. Indeed, some dreadful deed may be on the way, in the air; whoever performs it will secure, or obtain, dominion or an increase of power, and the existing government, for fear of being set aside, perpetrates the crime. Thus Catherine de' Medici usurped the massacre of St. Bartholomew from the Guises. If, in the sequel, she had given proof of greatness and genuine political capacity, the French nation would have entirely overlooked the horror. But she was later drawn completely into the Guises' wake, and a profitless condemnation was her portion. The *coup d'état* of 1851 might also be mentioned here.

As for the inner spur of the great man, we generally place first the sense of glory, or its common form, ambition, that is, the desire of fame in the contemporary world, a fame which actually consists more in a feeling of dependence than in admiration of an ideal.[1] Ambition, however, is not a primary motive, and the thought of posterity still less so, however crass its expression may look at times, as when Napoleon said on Elba: "My name will live as long as God's." (Fleury de Chaboulon, *Mémoires,* Vol. I, p. 116.) There must have been a very great thirst for that glory in Alexander, but there have been other great men whose minds have not demonstrably dwelt on the thought of posterity. They may have been satisfied if their action contributed to settling the fate of posterity. Powerful men, moreover, may prefer flattery to fame, since the latter only pays homage to their genius while the former confirms their power.

The decisive impulse which matures and disciplines the great man is far more than the sense of power. It is that which irresistibly urges him into the light. As a rule it is combined with so low an estimate of mankind that he no longer aims at that consensus of their opinion which is fame, but at their subjection and exploitation.

But fame, which flees the man that seeks it, overtakes the man who is heedless of it.

And it overtakes him with little regard to detached or expert opinion. For in tradition, in popular judgment, the notion of greatness is not based exclusively on services rendered to the greater prosperity of the community, nor even on a nice appraisal of ability, nor yet on historical importance. In the last resort, the deciding factor is "personality," whose image is propagated by a sort of magic. This process is well illustrated by the Hohenstaufens. Henry VI Hohenstaufen, who was extremely important, is

[1] Nor is fame among posterity quite free from it. We honor men long since dead who have influenced our lives.

quite forgotten, not even the names of Conrad III and Conrad IV are remembered (the pathos of Conradin is of very recent growth), while Frederick I, on the other hand, is merged in Frederick II, who has faded into the distance. And now men look for the return of the man whose chief purpose in life, the subjection of Italy, had come to grief, and whose system of government in the Empire was of very doubtful value. His personality must have far outweighed his achievements, but the real object of men's expectations was indubitably Frederick I.

A peculiar phenomenon is the transformation and coloring undergone by those once acknowledged great. *On ne prête qu'aux riches.* Men lend of their own free will to the great, and thus great men are invested by their nations and partisans not only with certain qualities, but also with legend and anecdote, in which some aspect of the national type is expressed. An example illumined by the full light of history is Henry IV. Even the later historian cannot always remain impartial here. His very sources may be unconsciously contaminated, and a general truth is nevertheless hidden in these fictitious ingredients.

Posterity, on the other hand, tends to be rather severe with men who were once merely powerful, such as Louis XIV, and imagines them worse than they really were.

Apart from the symbolization of the national temperament or the development of the personality into a type, an idealization also sets in. For in time great men are liberated from all doubt of their value, from every effect of the hatred of those who suffered under them, and their idealization can then proceed in many senses at once—for instance, that of Charlemagne as hero, king and saint.

Between the pines of the high Jura we see in the distance a famous peak shrouded in eternal snow. It can be seen in other ways from many other places at the same time, from vine arbors, or across a great lake, enframed in church windows or along the narrow arcaded streets of Upper Italy. Yet it is for ever the same Mont Blanc.

The great men who survive as ideals are of great value for the world, and more especially for their own countries. They are for the latter a source of emotion, an object of enthusiasm, and stimulate the minds even of the lowest classes by a vague sense of greatness. They maintain a high standard of things: they help to restore self-respect. All the evils that Napoleon brought down upon France are outweighed by his incalculable value to her as a national possession.

In our own day, we must first eliminate a class of men who declare themselves and the age emancipated from the need of great men. They declare that the present wants to look after its own affairs, and imagine that with no great men to commit great crimes the reign of virtue will set in. As if little men did not turn evil at the slightest opposition, not to speak of their greed and mutual envy!

Others actually achieve that emancipation (*N.B.* as a rule in the intellectual sphere only) by a general guarantee of mediocrity, the insurance of second-rate talents and false reputations, recognizable as such by the speed and noise of their rise. Such reputations, however, are very quickly exploded.[1] The rest is done by the official suppression of all splendid spontaneity. Powerful governments have a repugnance to genius. In the State, it is hardly of use except by supreme compromise, for in the life of the State everything is judged by its "utility." Even in the

[1] Of course, according to the domain, there is genuine fame which may be very quickly acquired by a sudden revelation of genius.

other walks of life, men prefer great talents, i.e. the capacity for making the most of what is to hand, to the great, i.e. the new.

From time to time, however, there is an outcry for great men, and that mainly in the State, because in all countries matters have taken such a turn that ordinary dynasts and higher officials no longer suffice. Great men should be there. (Prussia, for instance, to maintain her position and increase her power, could do with a whole series of Frederick the Greats.)

Yet even though the great man should come and survive his beginnings, the question still remains whether he would not be talked out of existence or overcome by contempt. Our age has a great power of attrition.

On the other hand, our age is very apt to be imposed upon now and again by adventurers and visionaries.

We can still remember how, in 1848, Europe sighed for a great man, and who was later accepted as such.

Not every age finds its great man, and not every great endowment finds its time. There may now exist great men for things that do not exist. In any case, the dominating feeling of our age, the desire of the masses for a higher standard of living, cannot possibly become concentrated in one great figure. What we see before us is a general levelling down, and we might declare the rise of great individuals an impossibility if our prophetic souls did not warn us that the crisis may suddenly pass from the contemptible field of "property and gain" on to quite another and that then the "right man" may appear overnight—and all the world will follow in his train.

For great men are necessary to our life in order that the movement of history may periodically wrest itself free from antiquated forms of life and empty argument.

And for the thinking man, reviewing the whole course of history hitherto, one of the few certain premisses of a higher spiritual happiness is an open mind for all greatness.

VI

On Fortune and Misfortune in History

In our private lives, we are wont to regard our personal fate under the two categories "fortunate" and "unfortunate," and we transfer these categories without hesitation to history.

Yet from the outset we should feel misgivings, since, in our own affairs, our judgment may change radically with age and experience. Not until the last hour of our lives can we pronounce a final judgment on the men and things we have known, and that judgment may be totally different according to whether we die in our fortieth or our eightieth year. It has, moreover, no objective validity but only a subjective validity for ourselves. This is the common experience of any man whose youthful desires appear to him folly in later life.

Nevertheless, historical judgments of good and evil fortune in the past have been pronounced both on isolated events and on whole epochs and conditions of life, and it is mainly modern times that are prone to pronounce them.

There are, of course, older expressions of opinion. The well-being of a class with slaves at its command is apparent here and there, for instance in the *Skolion* of Hybreas. Machiavelli [1] praises the year 1298, though only

[1] *Stor. Fior.*, Vol. II. There are several English translations.

as a contrast to the revolution which immediately followed, and Justinger gives a similar picture of old Berne about 1350. All these judgments are, of course, much too local, and the happiness they praise was in part based on the sufferings of others; nevertheless, they are at least ingenuous, and were not devised to throw light on world history.

We, however, judge as follows:

It was fortunate that the Greeks conquered Persia, and Rome Carthage;
unfortunate that Athens was defeated by Sparta in the Peloponnesian War;
unfortunate that Caesar was murdered before he had time to consolidate the Roman Empire in an adequate political form;
unfortunate that in the migrations of the Germanic tribes so many of the highest creations of the human spirit perished, but fortunate that they refreshed the world with new and healthy stock;
fortunate that Europe, in the eighth century, on the whole held Islam at bay;
unfortunate that the German Emperors were defeated in their struggle with the Papacy and that the Church was able to develop its terrible tyranny;
unfortunate that the Reformation triumphed in only half of Europe and that Protestantism was divided into two sects;
fortunate that first Spain, then Louis XIV were eventually defeated in their plans for world dominion, etc.

The nearer we come to the present, of course, the more opinions diverge. We might, however, reply that this does not invalidate our right to form an opinion which, as soon as a wider survey in time enables us to assess at their true value causes and effects, events and their consequences, finds its justification.

By an optical illusion, we see happiness at certain times, in certain countries, and we deck it out with analogies from the youth of man, spring, sunrise and other metaphors. Indeed, we imagine it dwelling in a beautiful part of the country, a certain house, just as the smoke rising from a distant cottage in the evening gives us the impression of intimacy among those living there.

Whole epochs, too, are regarded as happy or unhappy. The happy ones are the so-called high epochs of man. For instance, the claim to such happiness is seriously put forward for the Periclean Age, in which it is recognized that the life of the ancient world reached its zenith in the State, society, art and poetry. Other epochs of the same kind, e.g. the age of the good Emperors, have been abandoned as having been selected from too one-sided a standpoint. Yet even Renan [1] says of the thirty years from 1815 to 1848 that they were the best that France, and perhaps humanity, had ever experienced.

All times of great destruction naturally count as eminently unhappy, since the happiness of the victor is (quite rightly) left out of account.

Judgments of this kind are characteristic of modern times and only imaginable with modern historical methods. The ancient world believed in an original golden age, with respect to which the world had steadily deteriorated. Hesiod paints the "present" age of iron in sinister tints of night. In our day, we may note a theory of perfection (so-

[1] *Questions Contemporaines*, p. 44.

called progress) in favor of the present and the future. Discoveries in pre-history reveal at least this much—that the pre-historical epochs of the human race were probably spent in profound torpor, half-animal fear, cannibalism, etc. In any case, those epochs which have hitherto been regarded as the youth of the individual peoples, namely those in which they can first be recognized, were actually very derivative and late epochs.

But who is, as a rule, responsible for such judgments?

They arise from a kind of literary consensus which has gradually taken shape out of the desires and arguments of the Age of Reason and the real or imagined conclusions of a number of widely read historians.

Nor do they spread haphazard. They are turned to journalistic uses as arguments for or against certain trends of the time. They form part of the fussy baggage of public opinion and, in part, bear very clearly in the very violence, not to say crudity, of their appearance, the impress of the time from which they issue. They are the deadly enemies of true historical insight.

And now we may enquire into some of their separate sources.

The most important of these is *impatience*, and it is the writer and the reader of history who are most subject to it. It supervenes when we have had to spend too long a time on a period, and the evidence—or perhaps our own effort—is inadequate to enable us to form an opinion. We wish things had moved more quickly, and would, for instance, willingly sacrifice one or two of the twenty-six dynasties of Egypt if only King Amasis and his liberal reform would at last carry the day. The Kings of Media, though only four in number, make us impatient because we know so little about them, while that great mover of the imagination, Cyrus, seems to be already waiting at the door.

In short, we take sides for what our ignorance finds interesting against the tedious, as if for happiness against unhappiness. We confuse what was desirable to remote epochs (if anything was) with the pleasures of our imagination.

From time to time we try to delude ourselves with an apparently nobler explanation, but our only motive is one of retrospective impatience.

We pity for their unhappiness past ages, peoples, parties, creeds and so on which passed through long struggles for a higher good. Today we should like to see the aims with which we sympathize triumph without a struggle, and pluck victory without effort; and we transfer the same wish to the past. We pity, for instance, the Roman plebeians and the pre-Solonian Athenians in their century-long struggle with the hard-hearted patricians and Eupatridae and the pitiless debtors' law.

Yet it was only the long struggle which made victory possible and proved the vitality and great worth of the cause.

But how short-lived was the triumph, and how ready we are to side with one decadence against another! Through the victory of democracy, Athens declined into political impotence; Rome conquered Italy, and ultimately the world, at the cost of infinite suffering to the nations and great degeneration at home.

The state of mind which would like to spare the past its troubles, however, comes out most strongly in connection with the wars of religion. We are indignant that any truth (or what we regard as such) should have only been able to make headway by material force, and that it should be suppressed if that force proved inadequate. And it is true that truth infallibly sacrifices something of its purity and sanctity during prolonged struggles, owing to the worldly intentions of its representatives and devotees. Thus it seems to us a misfortune that the Reformation had to contend with a terrible material opposition and hence had to be represented by governments whose heart was in the property of the Church rather than in religion.

Yet in struggle, and in struggle alone, and not in printed polemics, does the full, complete life develop that must come of religious warfare. Only struggle makes both sides fully conscious. Only through struggle, at all times and in all questions of world history, does mankind realize what it really wants and what it can really achieve.

Firstly, Catholicism again became a religion, which it had almost ceased to be. Then men's minds were opened in a thousand directions, political life and culture were brought into all kinds of contact and contrast with the religious conflict, and ultimately the world was transformed and spiritually vastly enriched. None of these things could have come about in mere smooth obedience to the new creed.

Then comes the judgment according to *Culture.* It consists in appraising the felicity and morality of a people or a state of life in the past by the diffusion of education, of general culture and comfort in the modern sense. Here nothing stands the test and all past ages are disposed of with more or less commiseration. For a time, the "present" was literally synonymous with progress, and the result was the most ridiculous vanity, as if the world were marching towards a perfection of mind or even morality. Imperceptibly, the criterion of security, which will be discussed later, creeps in, and without security, and without the culture just described, *we,* at any rate, could not live. But a simple, strong mode of life, with the physical nobility of the race still intact, and the people perpetually on its guard against enemies and oppressors, is also culture, and possibly productive of a superior quality of feeling. Man's mind was complete early in time. And the enquiry as to "moral progress" we may justifiably leave to Buckle, who was so naïvely astonished that there is none to be found, forgetting that it is relevant to the life of the individual and not to whole epochs. If, even in bygone times, men gave their lives for each other, we have not progressed since.

Now follows the judgment by *personal taste,* under which we may group a number of factors. It regards such times and peoples as happy in and among whom precisely that element was predominant which lies nearest the heart of whoever is passing judgment. According as feeling, imagination or reason is the central value of life, the palm will go to those times and peoples in which the largest possible number of men were seriously occupied with spiritual things, or in which art and poetry were the reigning powers, and the greatest possible amount of time was free for intellectual work and contemplation, or in which the greatest number of people could earn a good livelihood and there was unimpeded activity in trade and traffic.

It would be easy to make the representatives of all these three categories realize how one-sided is their judgment, how inadequately it comprehends the whole life of the age concerned, and how intolerable, for many reasons, they themselves would have found life in that age.

Judgment by *political sympathy* is also common. To one, only republics were happy; to another, only monarchies. To one, only times of great and incessant unrest; to another, only times of calm. We might here quote Gibbon's view of the age of the good Emperors as the happiest the human race had ever lived through.

Even in the cases already mentioned, and more especially in the case of judgment by *culture,* the criterion of *security* creeps in. According to this judgment, the prime condition of any happiness is the subordination of private purposes to a police-protected law, the treatment of all questions of property by an impartial legal code and the most far-reaching safeguarding of profits and commerce. The whole morality of our day is to a large extent oriented towards this security, that is, the individual is relieved of the most vital decisions in the defence of house and home, in the majority of cases at any rate. And what goes beyond the power of the State is taken over by insurance, i.e. the forestalling of definite kinds of misfortune by a corresponding annual sacrifice. As soon as a livelihood or its revenues has become sufficiently valuable, the neglect to insure it is considered culpable.

Now this security was grievously lacking at many times which otherwise shine with an immortal radiance and till the end of time will hold a high place in the history of man.

Piracy was of everyday occurrence, not only in the age which Homer describes, but obviously in that in which he lived, and strangers were quite courteously and ingenuously questioned on the subject. The world was swarming with murderers, voluntary and involuntary, who sat at kings' tables, and even Odysseus, in one of his fictitious stories of his life, lays claim to a murder. And yet what simplicity and nobility of manners those people knew! And an age in which the epic lay was the common property of many singers, and moved from place to place, the common delight of nations, is for ever enviable for its achievements, its emotions, its strength and its simplicity. We have only to think of the figure of Nausicaa.

The Periclean Age in Athens was in every sense of the word an age in which any peaceful and prudent citizen of our time would refuse to live, in which he could not but be mortally unhappy, even if he was neither a member of the slave-majority nor a citizen of a city under the Attic hegemony, but a free man and a full citizen of Athens itself. Huge contributions levied by the State, and perpetual inquisitions into the fulfilment of duties towards the State by demagogues and sycophants, were the order of the day. Yet the Athenians of that age must have felt a plenitude of life which far outweighed any security in the world.

A very popular judgment in our day is the judgment by *greatness*. Those who pass such judgment cannot, of course, deny that great political power rapidly acquired, whether by the State or by the individual, can only be bought at the cost of untold sufferings to others. But they ennoble the character of the ruler and those about him to the utmost limit, and attribute to him the prophetic vision of all the great and good results which later came of his work. Finally, they assume that the spectacle of genius must have transfigured and made happy the people he had to deal with.

They dismiss the sufferings of the multitude with the utmost coolness as a "temporary misfortune"; they point to the undeniable fact that settled conditions, i.e. subsequent "happiness," have only been established when terrible struggles have bestowed power on one side or the other. As a rule, the origin and life of the man who applies this standard is based on conditions established in that fashion, hence his indulgence.

And now at last the common source trickling through all these judgments, and long since perceptible in them, the judgment by *egoism*. "We" judge thus and thus. It is true that somebody else, who is of the contrary opinion—perhaps out of egoism too—also says "we," while in the absolute sense as much is achieved by both as by the prayers of the individual farmer for sun or rain.

Our profound and utterly ridiculous self-seeking first regards those times as happy which are in some way akin to our nature. Further, it considers such past forces and individuals as praiseworthy on whose work our present existence and relative welfare are based.

Just as if the world and its history had existed merely for our sakes! For everyone regards all times as fulfilled in his own, and cannot see his own as one of many passing waves. If he has reason to believe that he has achieved pretty nearly everything that lay in his power, we can understand his standpoint. If he looks for change, he hopes that he will soon see it come, and may help to bring it about.

But every individual—we too—exists not for his own sake, but for the sake of all the past and all the future.

In face of this great, grave whole, the claims of peoples, times and individuals to happiness and well-being, lasting or fleeting, is of very subordinate importance, for since the life of humanity is one whole, it is only to our frail powers of perception that its fluctuations in time or place are a rise and fall, fortune and misfortune. The truth is that they are governed by a higher necessity.

We should try to rid the life of nations entirely of the word "happiness" and replace it by some other, while, as we shall see later, we cannot do without the word "unhappiness." Natural history shows us a fearful struggle for life, and that same struggle encroaches far upon the historical life of nations.

"Happiness" is a desecrated word, exhausted by common use. Supposing that there was a world plebiscite to decide on the definition of the word. How far should we get?

And above all, only the fairy-tale equates changelessness with happiness. From its childish standpoint it may strive to hold fast to the image of a permanent, joyous well-being (about half-way between Olympus and the Land of Cockayne). But even the fairy-tale does not take it really seriously. When the wicked magician at last lies dead and the wicked fairies are punished, Abdullah and Fatima live happily ever after into a ripe old age, but imagination, their trials over, forthwith dismisses them, to claim our interest for Hassan and Zuleika or Leila, or some other couple. The end of the *Odyssey* is so much nearer the truth. The trials of him who has suffered so much are to continue, and he must at once set out on a grievous pilgrimage.

The conception of a happiness which consists in the permanence of certain conditions is of its very nature false. The moment we set aside a primitive state, or state of nature, in which every day is like every other day, and every century like every other century, until, by some rupture, historical life begins, we must admit that permanence means paralysis and death. Only in movement, with all its pain, is life. And above all, the idea of happiness as a positive feeling is false in itself. Happiness is mere absence of pain, at best associated with a faint sense of growth.

There have been, of course, arrested peoples who present the same general picture for centuries and hence give the impression of tolerable contentment with their fate. As a rule, however, that is the product of despotism, which inevitably appears when a form of State and society has been achieved (presumably at great cost) and has to be defended against the rise of opposing forces, and with all available measures, even the most extreme. The first generation must, as a rule, have been very unhappy, but succeeding ones grow up in that order of ideas, and ultimately they pronounce sacred everything that they cannot and do not wish to change, praising it perhaps as supreme happiness. When Spain was on the point of material extinction, she was still capable of deep feeling as soon as the splendor of the Castilian name came into question. The oppression of the government and the Inquisition seems to have been powerless to humiliate her soul. Her greatest artists and poets belong to that age.

These stationary peoples and national epochs may exist in order to preserve definite spiritual, intellectual and material values from earlier times and to pass them on uncontaminated as a leaven to the future. And their calm is not absolute and deathly; it is rather of the nature of a refreshing sleep.

There are other ages, peoples, men, on the other hand, which at times spend their strength, indeed their whole strength, in rapid movement. Their importance resides in the destruction of the old and the clearing of the way for the new. But they were not made for any lasting happiness, or indeed for any passing joy, save for the short-lived rejoicing of victory. For their power of regeneration is born of perpetual discontent, which finds any halt tedious and demands to advance.

Now this striving, however important its consequences, however great its political consequences may be, actually appears in time in the garb of the most unfathomable human egoism, which must of necessity subdue others to its will and find its satisfaction in their obedience, yet which is insatiable in its thirst for obedience and admiration and claims the right to use force in all great issues.

Now evil on earth is assuredly a part of the great economy of world history. It is force, the right of the stronger over the weaker, prefigured in that struggle for life which fills all nature, the animal and the vegetable worlds, and is carried on in the early stages of humanity by murder and robbery, by the eviction, extermination or enslavement of weaker races, or of weaker peoples within the same race, of weaker States, of weaker social classes within the same State and people.[1]

Yet the stronger, as such, is far from being the better. Even in the vegetable kingdom, we can see baser and bolder species making headway here and there. In history, however, the defeat of the noble simply because it is in the minority is a grave danger, especially in times ruled by a very general culture which arrogates to itself the rights of the majority. The forces which have succumbed

[1] Cf. Hartmann's prophecy. *Philosophie des Unbewussten,* pp. 341-3: English transl. *The Philosophy of the Unconscious,* Vol. II, Ch. X, pp. 11-13.

were perhaps nobler and better, but the victorious, though their only motive was ambition, inaugurate a future of which they themselves have no inkling. Only in the exemption of States from the general moral law, which continues to be binding on the individual, can something like a premonition of it be divined.

The greatest example is offered by the Roman Empire, inaugurated by the most frightful methods soon after the end of the struggle between the patricians and plebeians in the guise of the Samnite War, and completed by the subjection of East and West in rivers of blood.

Here, on the grand scale, we can discern a historical purpose which is, to us at any rate, plainly apparent, namely the creation of a common world culture, which also made possible the spread of a world religion, both capable of being transmitted to the Teutonic barbarians of the Völkerwanderung as the future bond of a new Europe.

Yet from the fact that good came of evil, and relative happiness of misery, we cannot in any way deduce that evil and misery were not, at the outset, what they were. Every successful act of violence is evil, and at the very least a dangerous example. But when that act was the foundation of power, it was followed by the indefatigable efforts of men to turn mere power into law and order. With their healthy strength, they set to work to cure the State of violence.

And, at times, evil reigns long as evil on earth, and not only among Fatimids and Assassins. According to Christian doctrine, the prince of this world is Satan. There is nothing more un-christian than to promise virtue a lasting reign, a material divine reward here below, as the early Church writers did to the Christian Emperors. Yet evil, as ruler, is of supreme importance; it is the one condition of selfless good. It would be a horrible sight if, as a result of the consistent reward of good and punishment of evil on this earth, all men were to behave well with an ulterior motive, for they would continue to be evil men and to nourish evil in their hearts. The time might come when men would pray Heaven for a little impunity for evildoers, simply in order that they might show their real nature once more. There is enough hypocrisy in the world as it is.

Let us now try to see whether the consolation we have divined will stand the test of a few of the most justified indictments of history.

Firstly, by no means every destruction entails regeneration. Just as the destruction of a finer vegetation may turn a land into an arid waste for ever, a people which has been too brutally handled will never recover. There are (or at any rate there seem to be) absolutely destructive forces under whose hoofs no grass grows. The essential strength of Asia seems to have been permanently and for ever broken by the two periods of Mongol rule. Timur in particular was horribly devastating with his pyramids of skulls and walls of lime, stone and living men. Confronted with the picture of the destroyer, as he parades his own and his people's self-seeking through the world, it is good to realize the irresistible might with which evil may at times spread over the world. In such countries, men will never again believe in right and human kindness. Yet he may have saved Europe from the Osmanlis. Imagine history without him, and Bajazet and the Hussites hurling themselves simultaneously on Germany and Italy. The later Osmanlis, people and sultans, whatever terror they may have meant for Europe, never again approached the climax of power represented by Bajazet I before the battle of Angora.

Even ancient times present a picture of horror when we imagine the sum of despair and misery which went to establish the old world Empires, for instance. Our deepest compassion, perhaps, would go out to those individual peoples who must have succumbed to the Kings of Persia, or even to the Kings of Assyria and Media, in their desperate struggle for independence. All the lonely royal fortresses of individual peoples (Hyrcanians, Bactrians, Sogdanians, Gedrosians) which Alexander encountered marked the scenes of ghastly last struggles, of which all knowledge has been lost. Did they fight in vain?

We feel quite differently about the peoples whose last struggle and end are known to us; that of the Lydian cities against Harpagus, Carthage, Numantia, Jerusalem against Titus. They seem to us to have taken their place in the ranks of those who have been the teachers and examples of mankind in the one great cause—that all must be staked on the cause of the whole and that individual life is not the supreme value. And thus, of their despair, a happiness, harsh but sublime, is born for all the world.

And if Persian tablets should be discovered bringing us greater knowledge of the end of those peoples in the Eastern provinces, were they only conceived in the bombastic Ormuzd style of the mindless victor, they would go to swell the number of those great memories.

We may here leave out of account the consolation we derive from the thought that without such temporary destroyers as Assyria and Persia, Alexander could not have borne the elements of Greek culture so far into Asia. Beyond Mesopotamia it had little influence. We must always be on our guard against taking our historical perspectives for the decrees of history.

One thing, however, must be said of all great destructions: since we cannot fathom the economy of world history, we never know what would have happened if some event, however terrible, had not occurred. Instead of one wave of history which we know, another, which we do not know, would have risen; instead of one evil oppressor, perhaps one still more evil.

Yet no man of power should imagine that he can put forward for his exculpation the plea: "If we do not do it, others will." For then every crime would be justified. (Such men in any case feel no need of exculpation, but say: "What *we* do turns out well because *we* do it.")

It may be, too, that if those who succumbed had lived longer, they would no longer have seemed worthy of our compassion. A people, for instance, that succumbed early in the glorious struggle might later not have been very happy, not very civilized, early corrupted by its own iniquity and deadly to its neighbors. But, having perished in the flower of its strength, we feel towards it as we feel towards exceptional men who have died young; we imagine that, had they lived, they could not but have progressed in good fortune and greatness, while perhaps their meridian already lay behind them.

Consolation comes from another direction in the mysterious law of compensation, which becomes apparent in one point at least, namely in the increase of populations after great plagues and wars. There seems to be a total life of humanity which makes losses good.[1]

[1] Cf. especially the constants in statistics, theory of population, etc. Schopenhauer, *Die Welt als Wille und Vorstellung,* Vol. II, p. 575. Transl. *The World as Will and Idea,* end of Chapter XLI, Supplements to Book IV.

Thus it is not certain, yet it appears to us probable, that the retreat of culture from the eastern half of the Mediterranean in the fifteenth century was made good, spiritually and materially, by the expansion overseas of the peoples of Western Europe. The accent of the world shifted.

Thus as, in the one case, another manner of death would have come instead of the one we know, in this case the vital power of the world replaces a vanished life by a new one.

The compensation, however, must not be taken as a substitute for suffering, to which its originator might point, but only as a continuance of the life of wounded humanity with its centre of gravity shifted. Nor must we hold it out to the sufferers and their dependents. The Völkerwanderung was a great rejuvenation for the moribund Roman Empire, but if we had asked the Byzantine, living under the Comneni in the twelfth century in the Eastern remnant of it, he would have spoken with all the pride in the world of the continued life of Rome on the Bosphorus, and with an equal contempt of the "renewed and refreshed" Occident. Even the Greco-Slav of our day under the Turks does not consider himself inferior to, and probably not more unhappy than, the man of the West. Indeed, if people were consulted, they could not pay for the greatest regeneration in the world, if the price were their own end and the influx of savage hordes.

The theory of compensation is, after all, generally the theory of desirability in disguise, and it is and remains advisable to be exceedingly chary in the use of such consolation as is to be gained from it, since we cannot finally assess these losses and gains. Bloom and decay are certainly the common lot, but every really personal life that is cut off by violence, and (in our opinion) prematurely, must be regarded as absolutely irreplaceable, indeed as irreplaceable even by one of equal excellence.

Another variant of compensation is the postponement of an event which seemed imminent. From time to time a great event, ardently desired, does not take place because some future time will fulfil it in greater perfection. In the Thirty Years' War, Germany was twice on the point of union, in 1629 by Wallenstein, in 1631 by Gustavus Adolphus. In both cases a terrible, unbridgeable breach would have remained in the nation. The birth of the nation was postponed for 240 years, and came at a moment when that breach had ceased to be a menace. In the realm of art we may say that Pope Nicholas V's new St. Peter's would have been immeasurably inferior to the St. Peter's of Bramante and Michelangelo.

Another variant is the substitution of one branch of culture for another. In the first half of the eighteenth century, when poetry was almost completely negligible and painting half dead, music reached its sublimest heights. Yet here too there are imponderabilia which we must not play off against each other too glibly. The one thing certain is that *one* time, *one* people cannot possess everything at the same time, and that a great many talents, of themselves indeterminate, are attracted by the art that has already reached its zenith.

The most justified indictments which we seem to have the right to bring against fate are those which concern the destruction of great works of art and literature. We might possibly be ready to forgo the learning of the ancient world, the libraries of Alexandria and Pergamum; we have enough to do to cope with the learning of modern times, but we mourn for the supreme poets whose works have been lost, and the historians too represent an irreparable loss because the continuity of intellectual tradition has become fragmentary over long and important periods. But that continuity is a prime concern of man's earthly life, and a metaphysical proof of the significance of its duration, for whether a spiritual continuity existed without our knowledge, in an organ unknown to us, we cannot tell, and in any case cannot imagine it, hence we most urgently desire that the awareness of that continuity should remain living in our minds.

Yet our unfulfilled longing for the lost is worth something too. We owe to it, and to it alone, the fact that so many fragments have been rescued and pieced together by incessant study. Indeed, the worship of relics of art and the indefatigable combination of the relics of history form part of the religion of our day.

Our capacity for worship is as important as the object we worship.

It may be, too, that those great works of art had to perish in order that later art might create in freedom. For instance, if, in the fifteenth century, vast numbers of well-preserved Greek sculptures and paintings had been discovered, Leonardo, Raphael, Titian and Correggio would not have done their work, while they could, in their own way, sustain the comparison with what had been inherited from Rome. And if, after the middle of the eighteenth century, in the enthusiastic revival of philological and antiquarian studies, the lost Greek lyric poets had suddenly been rediscovered, they might well have blighted the full flowering of German poetry. It is true that, after some decades, the mass of rediscovered ancient poetry would have become assimilated with it, but the decisive moment of bloom, which never returns in its full prime, would have been irretrievably past. But enough had survived in the fifteenth century for art, and in the eighteenth for poetry, to be stimulated and not stifled.

Having reached this point, we must stop. Imperceptibly we have passed from the question of good and evil fortune to that of the survival of the human spirit, which in the end presents itself to us as the life of *one* human being. That life, as it becomes self-conscious *in* and *through* history, cannot fail in time so to fascinate the gaze of the thinking man, and the study of it so to engage his power, that the ideas of fortune and misfortune inevitably fade. "Ripeness is all." Instead of happiness, the able mind will, *nolens volens,* take knowledge as its goal. Nor does that happen from indifference to a wretchedness that may befall us too—whereby we are guarded against all pretence of cool detachment—but because we realize the blindness of our desires, since the desires of peoples and of individuals neutralize each other.

If we could shake off our individuality and contemplate the history of the immediate future with exactly the same detachment and agitation as we bring to a spectacle of nature—for instance, a storm at sea seen from land—we should perhaps experience in full consciousness one of the greatest chapters in the history of the human mind.

At a time when the illusory peace of thirty years in which we grew up has long since utterly vanished, and a series of fresh wars seems to be imminent;

when the established political forms of the greatest civilized peoples are tottering or changing;

when, with the spread of education and communications, the realization and impatience of suffering is visibly and rapidly growing;

when social institutions are being shaken to their foundations by world movements, not to speak of all the accumulated crises which have not yet found their issues;

it would be a marvelous spectacle—though not for contemporary earthly beings—to follow with enlightened perception the spirit of man as it builds its new dwelling, soaring above, yet closely bound up with all these manifestations. Any man with such a vision in mind would completely forget about fortune and misfortune, and would spend his life in the quest of that knowledge.

Editor's Note

The present volume consists of notes for the following lectures delivered by Jacob Burckhardt at Basle:

(1) A course entitled *Introduction to the Study of History* covering Chapters I-IV, held at the University in the winter semester of 1868–1869, and again in 1870–1871;

(2) A cycle of three lectures entitled *The Great Men of History* held at the Museum of Basle in 1870;

(3) A single lecture *On Fortune and Misfortune in History* also held at the Museum in 1871.

The notes were prepared for publication after Burckhardt's death by his nephew, Jacob Oeri of Basle, who made them into a coherent whole with a minimum of necessary expansion and gave the book the title by which it has gone since, *Weltgeschichtliche Betrachtungen.*

In 1941, Professor Werner Kägi, Burckhardt's successor in the Chair of History at Basle University, published a revised and slightly expanded edition of the book, which has been used for the present translation.

Certain minor modifications have been made in the American edition. In the *Supplementary Notes on the Origin and Nature of the Present Crisis* about seven pages of detailed political narrative referring to current events of that time have been deleted. Citations of superseded or inaccessible literature have also been suppressed, while other citations have been rephrased to make them more useful to the English-speaking readers. A minimum of explanatory notes has been added by the editor.

Index

F

G

H

I

J

K

L

T

U

V

W

X

Z